Mountford John Byrde Baddeley

The Peak District of Derbyshire and Neighbouring Counties

With maps, general and sectional, adapted from the Ordnance survey. Fourth Edition

Mountford John Byrde Baddeley

The Peak District of Derbyshire and Neighbouring Counties

With maps, general and sectional, adapted from the Ordnance survey. Fourth Edition

ISBN/EAN: 9783337254155

Printed in Europe, USA, Canada, Australia, Japan

Cover: Foto ©Andreas Hilbeck / pixelio.de

More available books at **www.hansebooks.com**

Thorough Guide Series.

THE
PEAK DISTRICT OF DERBYSHIRE
AND NEIGHBOURING COUNTIES

BY

M. J. B. BADDELEY, B.A.,

AUTHOR OF THE "THOROUGH GUIDES TO THE ENGLISH LAKE DISTRICT,"
"SCOTLAND," "WALES," "DEVON AND CORNWALL," ETC.

WITH MAPS, GENERAL AND SECTIONAL
(*Adapted from the Ordnance Survey*)
By BARTHOLOMEW.

FOURTH EDITION, REVISED.

"By Dove's fair waters let me stray;
Where Derwent cleaves its rocky way;
Where Haddon's glades half-hidden lie,
Beside the bright, meandering Wye."

LONDON:
DULAU & CO., 37, SOHO SQUARE, W.
1887.

J. S. LEVIN,
ENGLISH AND FOREIGN STEAM PRINTING WORKS,
75, LEADENHALL STREET, LONDON, E.C.

MAP INDEX.

———o———

N.B.—All the country public-houses on these maps are marked as "Inns," but the tourist should consult the body of the book before jumping at the conclusion that anything more than roadside refreshment can be obtained at them.

General Map . . . Opposite Title Page.

SECTIONS.
- I. Castleton, Baslow, Sheffield, &c.   84
- II. Ashbourne, Dovedale, Alton, &c.   47
-     Plan of Buxton 60
- III. Buxton, Castleton, Kinder Scout, &c.   62
- IV. Matlock, Chatsworth, Haddon, &c.   99

CONTENTS.

	Route.	Page.
Introduction		viii
Skeleton Tours		xx
Hints to Cyclists		xxii
Approaches		
Derby to Alton, Ashbourne, &c.	1	3
,, Matlock and Buxton	2	8
Leek to Buxton	3	12
Macclesfield to Buxton	4	17
Manchester to Castleton and Buxton (L. & N. W. R.)	5	19
,, ,, ,, (Midland)	6	21
,, Hayfield and Castleton	7	23
,, Glossop and Ashopton	8	27
Penistone to Ashopton	9	28
Sheffield to Baslow (direct)	10	33
,, ,, (by Froggatt Edge)	11	35
,, Hathersage and Castleton	12	37
,, Ashopton and Glossop	13	41
Ashbourne and Dovedale Section		46
Ashbourne to Dovedale, Buxton, &c.	14	47
Dovedale to Bakewell or Rowsley		56
,, Matlock		58
Buxton Section		60
Short Excursions from Buxton		
Axe Edge		63
"Cat and Fiddle"		63
Chee Tor and Dale		64
Corbar Wood Walks		65
Diamond Hill and Solomon's Temple		65
The Duke' Drive		65
The Goyt Valley		66
Lud's Church		66
Poole's Hole		68
Buxton to Chatsworth, Haddon, Matlock, &c.	16	69
,, Castleton	17	73
,, Dovedale, &c.	18	76
,, Eyam, Baslow, &c.	19	80

CONTENTS.

	Route	Page
Castleton Section		84
The Caverns, Mam Tor, &c.		85
Castleton to Ashopton	20	90
,, Eyam and Hathersage	21	91
,, Bakewell	22	92
,, Buxton	23	95
,, Chapel-en-le-Frith	24	95
,, Hayfield	25	96
,, Rowsley and Matlock	26	96
Matlock Section		98
Walks from Matlock		
Bonsall		103
Black Rocks		103
Crich Stand		104
Matlock to Chesterfield and back		105
Chatsworth House		110
Chatsworth to Haddon Hall		116
Haddon Hall		117
Haddon Hall to Chatsworth		120
Matlock to Dovedale, or Ashbourne	27	122
,, Winster, Rowsley, &c.	28	123
,, Bakewell and Buxton	29	127
,, Hathersage and Castleton	30	131
Hardwick Hall and Bolsover		134
Wirksworth		139
Index		141
Advertisements		

Introduction.

Definition of the Peak District. "Can you tell me which is the Peak?" asked a gentleman whom we once found surveying with an unsatisfied expression of countenance the prospect from the Ordnance cairn on Axe Edge. "With pleasure...." we began. A man who was writing a guide book to the Peak district could surely have no difficulty in pointing out which was the Peak, especially from a viewpoint commanding the greater part of it. A difficulty there is, however, and it is two-fold—natural and artificial. Natural, because except the little pimple which forms the summit of Win Hill and the two or three abrupt little limestone crags rising from the upper valley of the Dove, there is nothing whatever in the whole panorama from Axe Edge to correspond with the Johnsonian definition of a peak as a "sharply-pointed hill." There is scarcely a hill-country in Britain which has fewer peaks than the Peak itself. A more appropriate name would be the "Cop"—a word signifying a rounded hill as opposed to a peak, and actually occurring in one or two instances in or near the district: *e.g.*—Mow Cop, Wardlow Hay Cop.—It seems to be of the same origin as the Dutch "Kop" and the Latin "Caput." Then, artificially or politically—whichever it be—the geography of the district has got strangely mixed up. The area described in this book includes the whole of the hill-country of North Derbyshire and such parts of the adjacent counties as physically belong to it:—the basins, to wit, of the Derwent, the Wye, the Dove, the Dane, and the Goyt. This definition, however, is purely arbitrary. Neither the Ordnance surveyors nor the local authorities support it. The former, being apparently in as great a difficulty as ourselves, and not finding any peak of sufficient importance to stand godfather to the district, pounced upon the highest ground in it, and printed the "Peak" in capital letters on the plateau of Kinder Scout, utterly ignoring the claims of the limestone country between Buxton, Bakewell and Hartington, which, in the old division of the county into hundreds, forms part of the High Peak district, and is traversed by the High Peak railway.

The High Peak hundred is itself sub-divided into the Districts of High Peak and Bakewell, the former comprising the wild, thinly-populated region of hill and valley which occupies the most northerly portion of the county, and is bordered by Cheshire and Yorkshire, and the latter extending southwards to the Wirksworth Hundred, a great part of which is itself physically included in the Peak District. These facts must be our excuse for ignoring all artificial limitations of the Peak District, and adopting the natural ones laid down on the previous page. The word peak, we may add, is not the only instance of an apparent misnomer in the county. Many of the mound-shaped eminences which form the highest parts of a particular plateau are called "Lows"—a word which seems to be essentially the same as "Law" in the lowlands of Scotland—Berwick and Haddington Law, to wit.

Mr. Ruskin, again, can hardly have had in mind the valleys of Derbyshire when he gave as the proper distinctive meaning of the word *dale*, " a tract of level land on the borders of a stream, continued for so great a distance as to make it a district of importance." If this be more than a local distinction the nomenclators of Dovedale, Cheedale, and a host of other Derbyshire valleys must have been very poor scholars.

The above remarks will, we hope, prevent tourists from sharing the perplexity of the gentleman whom we met on Axe Edge.

*Characteristics of the Scenery. Next to Cumberland and Westmorland, and that part of Lancashire which

---

* In offering these remarks on the scenery of the Peak district we wish to disclaim all intention of being dictatorial—our aim is merely to be suggestive—rather to draw out the opinions of others than to insist upon our own. *Quot homines, tot sententiae* is a motto which would well apply to the various opinions we have heard expressed on particular scenes in the district. Mr. Jennings, to wit, an author of whom, in one instance, the "Spectator" declared that he had only just escaped writing a classic, and who is a heart-and-soul lover of Nature, writes in his book about Derbyshire, that Beresford Dale is "on the whole better worth visiting than Dovedale," which he declares is a "thing to be seen once and not often, unless a person should take a particular fancy to it." "In parts" he admits that it " makes very pretty pictures," and that the scenery is striking, but not extraordinarily beautiful, "the first mile is very like all the rest," and "the Twelve Apostles are so many ninepins."

is included in the Lake District, there can be little question that the two English counties most remarkable for beauty and diversity of scenery are Derbyshire and Devonshire. The introduction of the latter county into a book whose subject matter is solely the former may appear irrelevant, but in writing about scenery, as about other matters, we can by the use of comparison, or rather, perhaps, contrast, convey a much closer and clearer idea of what we mean than by abstract description. Taken separately, Borrowdale may be described as beautiful, and the Vale of Evesham may be described as beautiful, but no sane person who had to describe the two in the same letter would dream of applying the same epithet to both. Comparison necessitates careful discrimination to a far greater extent than abstract description.

The points of difference between Derbyshire and Devonshire scenery are many and obvious:—the soil of Devonshire is generally rich, that of Derbyshire comparatively poor; Devonshire owes a large portion of its attractiveness to its sea-coast; Derbyshire has no sea-coast: the colour of the surface-rock in most parts of Devonshire is bright and glowing; in Derbyshire it is dull and sombre: Devonshire is but little spoilt by works of commercial industry; Derbyshire is very much so; but taking all these and many more differences into consideration, there is still much left in which the two counties resemble one another. The primal cause of their beauty is the gathering of waters on their uncultivated, unenclosed moorlands. The perennial fountains of Dartmoor and Exmoor have helped to form the valleys of the southern county, just as those of the Peak uplands have helped to form the basins of the Wye, the Derwent, and the Dove; and it is to the valley

In fact, altogether, it fails to impress him with anything but weariness of spirit, and from a picturesque point of view, is far inferior to that paradise of peat and stunted heather—the plateau of Kinder Scout. What our own opinion of Dovedale is, readers of this book will very soon find out. As to Beresford Dale it is merely a little handmaiden to Dovedale, very pretty in itself, but of utterly different rank and character. Mr. Jennings again seems to rate the beauty of what to most people would seem dull, wearisome limestone uplands, with their interminable stone walls and poverty-stricken clumps of fir trees, higher than that of the deep leafy valleys which radiate from their centres. Mr. Rhodes' highly coloured descriptions of Matlock and its surroundings, make hearty sport for Mr. Jennings' pen, but whether Mr. Jennings is not more wanting in discrimination than Mr. Rhodes in moderation, is quite an open question.

Rambles among the Hills, p.p. 69-83.

scenery so formed that both shires owe the main part of their beauty. But it is rather in what they have not than in what they have that there is affinity between the two. Two important elements in the formation of scenery are wanting in both—mountains, as distinguished from uplands, and lakes. For the absence of these Devonshire offers in compensation a sea-coast nearly always beautiful, if not grand; Derbyshire, a diversity of valley scenery which is hardly surpassed by any district in the kingdom. In the latter point, and in the more interesting character of its uplands, Derbyshire atones for its inferiority to Devonshire in the features we have already mentioned.

To begin with the most elevated portions of the two counties, we may admit at once that the hills and moorlands of neither present those striking outlines and broken, rugged slopes which make the fells of the Lake District and the mountains of Scotland and Wales in themselves the chief contributors to the scenery of the regions to which they respectively belong. Strong as are the praises which have been lavished on Dartmoor, most tourists will agree with us that a more uninteresting upland area of equal extent does not exist in the country. Its summit-level is a "dreary, dreary moorland," so monotonous in character that you are almost bound to lose your way for want of those distinctive landmarks which in ordinary mountain scenery are your chief aids in finding it. The same remark applies almost equally to Kinder Scout, the highest upland of the Peak district, and to the long line of limestone hills culminating in Axe Edge. Taken as a whole, however, the Derbyshire uplands afford finer outlines than those of Devonshire.

And now let us descend a little from our mountain heights:—first to the water-sheds and cup-shaped hollows wherein are born the streams, which as they grow from their merry, prattling infancy into the full strength and vigour of maturity, give to the widening valleys their beauty and fertility. The water-sheds, or rather swamps, both in Derbyshire and Devonshire are as dull as dull can be, but the moment the water escapes from its comparative stagnation and commences its downward course in real earnest, the spell of monotony is broken: beauty and brightness begin. On Dartmoor, especially, is the transition noticeable, because the rock formation is entirely granite, and on no other bed does running water appear so beautiful. On a sunny day the waters threading the hollows of Dartmoor glisten and sparkle down their winding channels with the lustre of a chain of brilliants, relieving the dull moorland around them "like a rich jewel in an Ethiop's ear." In Derbyshire the river-fountains do not affect the scenery with equal suddenness—partly from natural and partly from artificial causes. The Derwent illustrates the one cause, the Wye the other. The former river having its main source in the wild and pathless hill-country between Sheffield and Manchester, suffers as little from human interference as the remotest of the Dartmoor streams, but the dark colour and friable nature of its bed—consisting entirely of millstone grit—give the channel a more sombre appearance, except perhaps for the first few miles of its course, in which its tiny russet-tinted pools are broken by the spray and foam of repeated cataracts. With the Wye it is very different. Flowing almost entirely over a bed of limestone, its waters when left to themselves are beautifully clear and transparent, though not so rich in colour as those of the granite-bedded Dartmoor streams. Friends and foes alike, however, have mal-treated the poor Wye almost throughout. Even before it sees the light of day, it is made use of to petrify pots and pans in Poole's Hole. The moment it emerges from its underground course it is taken in hand by the Buxton Improvements Company, and made to execute fluvial gymnastics in the form of ornamental pools and cascades. So far, however, the purity and clearness of the water is very little affected—but Buxton is indifferent to such things. It makes a ditch of the stream, which receives its last and "unkindest cut" from the Gas Company, about a mile below the town, beyond which the water is for some distance so discoloured that the marvel is how it ever recovers itself at all, and becomes the pure limpid stream which meanders through the meadows of Bakewell and Haddon.

In speaking of the upland valleys of Derbyshire, we must not forget a very remarkable peculiarity which has a great effect on the general character of the scenery. In what we may perhaps call the limestone half of the district it may often be said of these valleys, as of the coal mines in Iceland, "there are none." The main river gathers its rivulets and travels with them underground until it has formed a considerable stream, which bubbles up from an unseen opening, and changes the character of the surrounding country almost at once. In several instances, too, notably in that of the Manifold, between Thor's Cave and Ilam, these streams after running for a greater or less distance above ground, suddenly disappear again, leaving a dry channel and bobbing up and down like a black-diver on a northern sea. These eccentricities affect the tourist as well as the farmer. The latter is deprived, as it were, at a moment's notice, of his principal sources of irrigation; the former, after a couple of hours' eye-weariness, caused by gazing on a network of stone walls, bare fields, and little isolated clumps of beech and fir hugging one another for dear life, and for want of proper sustenance from without, finds himself all in a moment looking down into a beautiful valley, with all the accessories of wood, rock, and verdure, which ordinary streams require ten or a dozen miles to form. The explanation is simple. The preliminary work has all been done underground. You travel, say, from Buxton to Castleton, wondering as you go along what has become of the water. Here and there you see marked on the map the mysterious word "swallow." This means that at one time or other there was running water about, and that it was there swallowed by the ground. Now there is little visible water to swallow. The tendency is, we believe, to run more and more underground. On the Ordnance Survey, published 40 years ago, there is scarcely any indication of the river Manifold following a subterranean course at all. Now, as we have above stated, it does so for about three miles, and, the writer is informed, is from time to time increasing the distance. But, continuing on our way to Castleton, we reach the top of the Winnats. Around us all is dull, dreary, and unprofitable. Suddenly a downward peep in front—what have we? the wide dale and green meadows of Castleton—no scene of Devonian richness to be sure—but a wonderful contrast to the previous part of our journey. Through them flows a well-fed brooklet, an important contributor to the Derwent. Then we descend through the Winnats, which should contain the chief feeder of this brook, but there is not a drop of water in the whole pass. As we near the village the sound of water salutes our ears, and we cross a clear and goodly stream. Whence comes it? Walk a few hundred yards to the right, and you will see it issuing from the rock close to the mouth of the Peak Cavern. It is the "Styx" of that famous cavern, and the producer of that "loud roar of waters," which tourists hear issuing from the "unfathomable abyss" of the Speedwell Mine, but until it breaks forth into the valley of Castleton, it has never been gladdened by the light of the sun or fleckered by a passing cloud.

Still following the course of our streams, we come to the

spacious dales and sylvan glens which constitute the scenery of their lowest parts. Here both counties afford very striking **contrasts not** only with each other **but** also with themselves. The wide-spread luxuriance of the valleys of **South Devon is as** different from the concentrated **beauty of the narrow V** shaped ravines of North **Devon, as it is from the** strongly-marked individualities of **the limestone and gritstone** dales of Derbyshire. **We** need only speak particularly of the latter.

No two kinds of scenery are **more distinct in their characteristics than limestone** and gritstone. A convenient illustration may be found in the valley of one river—the Derwent. From its source in the wild hills **near Penistone to within a mile of Matlock** Bath, this stream, **as well as** its tributaries,*runs through a gritstone country. On both sides of the water is **a strip** of meadow **and** pasture **land, dark green in colour and in parts** diversified with abundant **wood, climbing to a greater or** less height the **adjacent hills.** The name "Woodlands," by which an extensive district **in the upper part of** the valley **is known,** was at one time, we **believe, peculiarly** appropriate, and though a good deal **of the timber** has disappeared there is still **a sufficient quantity left on** both sides of **the valley to** suggest **to us its condition centuries ago. Above the meadows and woods the hill-slopes, green as either, rise steeply, often strewn with boulders and clothed with bracken, to** the **long broken line of crags, locally called "edges," which are a special characteristic of this** geological **formation, and which form** rock-platforms, **from which the spectator commands the** country below **and around as completely as the** occupant of the loftiest "three-decked" **pulpit commands his** congregation. The rock of **which these edges consist, is** broken, split, and worn into **all manner of** extraordinary shapes. **In places, huge rectangular blocks rise** from the **top** of **the** platform, **entirely isolated from their** fellows—such are the Andle **Stone on Stanton Moor, and** the Eagle Stone over Baslow: **in other places they lie** layer over layer, in **a way** which **has given them such names as the** "Cakes of Bread," the **"Salt Cellar."** But, perhaps, the most peculiar shape **which they assume is one** which may be likened to the **appearance of a toad about to** jump, **or still more to that of** a field-**gun on the** ramparts of **a** fortified **town or castle. This last appearance is** so common that it is quite **unnecessary to specify instances.**

Hence it **will be seen** that the gritstone part of Derby-

* Except the Wye.

shire owes whatever boldness and grandeur it possesses to the highest parts of its hills, which, though they seldom, if ever, terminate in graceful peaks, or impressive bluffs, present very striking lines of rugged fragmentary cliffs. Such are the edges of Kinder Scout, Bamford, Derwent, Stanage, Froggatt, and Curbar, all of which, except the first mentioned, overlook the valley of the Derwent on the east side. In the limestone regions, on the contrary, the tops of the elevated portions are dull and uninteresting to a degree; all the beauty and boldness commences at the water's edge, and seldom attains a greater height than 300 or 400 feet. The absolute sheerness, however, of the cliffs gives them an imposing effect quite out of proportion to their actual height. They are also brighter and altogether more taking in appearance than the gritstone cliffs, and the vegetation which finds a genial soil in their chinks and fissures, materially assists their picturesqueness. Ivy and the sable yew, in particular, love to trail along or grow out of this rock, which possesses yet another advantage over the rival " grit " in the vertical appearance which its crags present as opposed to the less noble horizontal "lie" of the latter.

In its original state perhaps Matlock afforded the finest grouping of limestone rock in Derbyshire. Utterly reckless building, however, petrifying wells, lock-and-key caverns, and a score other amenities of a cheap-tripper's paradise, sadly handicap one's chance of enjoying its natural beauty, and the tourist who wants to see the best of this class of scenery, must go to parts of Monsal Dale, Millers Dale, and Chee Dale, or better still to Dove Dale, where the rock, if hardly so massive as at Matlock, is more varied and beautiful in outline, and has no lovers' walk or petrifying wells at its foot.

Roughly speaking, the line of separation between the gritstone and limestone parts of the Peak district may be drawn from Dove Holes—three miles north of Buxton—eastward to Castleton, thence over Bradwell Dale to Eyam and Stoney Middleton. From Stoney Middleton it turns west again, rounding Longstone Edge, and passing from Bakewell to the Lathkil valley and behind Winster to its most easterly out-crop at Matlock—the only point at which the limestone occupies the Derwent Valley. Thence it turns westward again and re-enters Staffordshire at the south end of Dovedale.

The most remarkable conjunction of the two rock systems is at Crich Hill, above Ambergate, where an isolated mass of limestone has been lifted up through the gritstone. A description of this will be found on page 105.

Colour is a very important factor in the effect produced on the mind by all kinds of scenery. We have commented on the characteristic dullness of the gritstone formation in this respect on page 33. The limestone is lighter and brighter, but still rather cheerless, except in the bolder cliffs, where there is an abundant relief of parasitic vegetation.

The Hills. As may be gathered from the foregoing remarks, hill-climbing for its own sake is dull, if not stupid work in Derbyshire. Every visitor who wishes to carry away with him a just appreciation of the district, must necessarily spend a large part of his time on high ground, from 800 to 1,500 ft. above sea-level, and by making from time to time judicious little divergences from his main routes to this and that view-point, or by ascending a few hundred feet to the top of some little green hillock, he may see all that is worth seeing. Of the so-called mountains the best known are Kinder Scout (2,080 ft.), Axe Edge (1,810 ft.) and Mam Tor (1,709 ft.). The "Edges" and skirts of Kinder Scout are well worth scrambling up, but the moorland waste constituting the summit-level, and reaching from one to four miles every way, is intolerable to every body except sportsmen—who will, we are sure, be grateful to us for mentioning the fact. As for Axe Edge, it is no edge at all, but merely one hogs-backed summit which the Ordnance Surveyors have selected for the honour of a cairn from a range containing several similar ones, almost, if not quite equal to it in elevation, though they have omitted to give its height. It is pleasant enough as the bourn of a stroll from Buxton, and those who drive or walk between that town and Leek or Macclesfield, must, perforce, reach an elevation little inferior to that of the hill itself, but the view from it is as dull and uninteresting a one as we remember to have seen from any other hill in the country, except, perhaps, the Cornish Brown Willy.

A distinct exception to the general rule must be made in favour of Mam Tor, and the range stretching eastwards from it to the Derwent Valley, and including Back Tor and Lose Hill. This range approaches the razor-back in shape, and the ridge commands, from end to end, views of some of the best valley scenery in the country. Still more beautiful, however, is the prospect from the isolated peak of Win Hill, which is separated from the Mam Tor and Lose Hill range by the narrow opening into Edale. Every one should cross Win Hill. It is, as it were, the axle of a wheel, whose spokes are valleys radiating in every direction except eastward.

View-Points. Admitting that, with the above reservations, there is little remunerative hill-climbing in Derbyshire, we add a rough list of easily attained points which command the best views. First come the numerous gritstone terraces or platforms, which we have already mentioned (p. xv). Beginning from the north we have Derwent, Stanage, Froggatt, and Curbar Edges on the east side of the Derwent valley, all of them traversed in one or more places by roads from Sheffield. In the last named Edge, the Wellington Monument, a sandstone cross just above Baslow, commands a specially fine view southwards down the valley. The green wood-capped hill east of Rowsley, and crossed by the Chesterfield road, should also be mentioned. Near Matlock, the Black Rocks and Masson both afford fine prospects, and the hill on which Riber Castle stands, an extensive one. The High Tor and the foot-track to Bonsall will delight the pedestrian, and no will regret paying a special visit to Crich Stand. Oaker Hill in Darley Dale is also a very pleasant little climb.

None of the hills near **Buxton** afford such varied or beautiful prospects as the ones we have enumerated above. The best perhaps is the one called Grinlow, on which stands the heap of stones called Solomon's Temple.

In the Ashbourne and Dovedale district we decidedly advise the visitor to stroll up Thorpe Cloud from the "Peveril," or Bunster from the "**Izaak Walton.**"

Geology, &c. As in the other volumes of our series, we only profess to handle the scientific bearings of our subjects in so far as they affect them from a picturesque point of view. This does not arise from any disrespect for the various "ologies" which are so copiously treated of in many guide-books, but simply from an unwillingness to smatter of things with which we are imperfectly acquainted. Geological tourists will find all they want in the works of Woodward and Ramsay on the Geology and Physical Geography of England, and, in a more compact form, in Mello's "Handbook to the Geology of Derbyshire;" while Mr. Cox, in the "Tourist Guide" has not left a square yard of ground unoccupied for the would-be archæological writer.

Hotels and Inns. There is a great variety of accommodation for the tourist in the Peak district, ranging from the palatial hotels of Buxton to the homely inns of the region of the Upper Derwent. The hotel charges hardly display that evenness which characterizes them in the English Lake district, though the scale does not in the main greatly vary from the ordinary one in tourist resorts. Of the country inns we may fairly say that they are, almost without exception, comfortable, clean, and reasonable in their charges. Cleanliness is a feature of Derbyshire dwellings of all kinds, and in no part of the county is it more conspicuous than in the hill-country of the north. The inns in this part are frequented by fishermen, but that fact does not in any way lessen the welcome accorded to ordinary tourists.

Fishing.—The principal fishing streams of the Peak district are the Dove, the Derwent, and the Wye. Several tributaries of the last named river—the Lathkil and the Bradford, to wit—afford excellent sport, the reason being, that they are strictly preserved by their ducal owners. The principal fish are trout and grayling—the latter a speciality of the district.

Where fishing is permitted, as it is along a considerable part of the three above-mentioned rivers, there is oftener than not a charge not exceeding half-a-crown a day for the privilege. The following are the principal inns, at which tickets may be obtained :—

On the **Dove** :—*Izaak Walton*, Ilam; *Charles Cotton*, Hartington.

On the **Derwent** :— *Snake* (on the Ashop: stream very small), *Ashopton* (for the Derwent and Ashop); *Lady Bower* (Ashop and Lady Bower Brook); *Yorkshire Bridge* and *Sickleholme*, Mytham Bridge (Derwent); Baslow (*for inns, &c., see p.* 132); *Chatsworth Hotel*, Edensor; *Peacock*, Rowsley; Matlock (*for hotels, &c., see p.* 98); *Greyhound*, Cromford; *Bull's Head*, Whatstandwell. The Derwent is strictly preserved about Hathersage, and the Wye about Ashford.

On the **Wye**:—Buxton (*see p.* 60; *Rutland Arms*, Bakewell; *Peacock*, Rowsley.

_{*} **Hotel-keepers** and others interested in the prosperity of the districts about which we write, as tourist resorts, will do a favour to us, and we venture to think, a corresponding benefit to themselves, by kindly informing us of any alterations affecting tourists which may from time to time take place in their particular localities. A few weeks ago we were compelled to make a journey of a hundred miles in order to verify one or two small matters of detail respecting a well-known "wonder" of the Peak district, of which we had sent a description, in proof, to the proprietor, as the person most interested in having it properly described. After our visit he returned our proof with the curt remark that he did not "want to advertise." We are glad, of course, to receive suitable advertisements, but let us, once for all, assure those to whom we write for information, that we are not "touting" for advertisements, but merely trying to ensure that accuracy of detail which is essential to a "thorough" guide-book.

SKELETON TOURS.

Resting places for the night printed in *italics*. *rd*, road; *rl*, rail; *fp*, footpath.

THREE DAYS.

From Derby.

1st Day.	m.	2nd Day.	m.	3rd Day.	m.
Wirksworth, rl.	14	*Longnor, fp.*	5	Abney, fp.	5
Cromford (by		Buxton, rl.	12	Eyam, fp.	12
Black Rocks)	17	Dove Holes, rl.	16	*Edensor, rd.*	15
rl.		*Castleton, rd.*	24	Rowsley, rd.	18
Matlock Bath, rl.	18			*Derby, rl.*	40
Rowsley, rd.	21½				
Haddon Hall, rd.	25				
Ednsor, fp.	28				

From Manchester.

1st Day.	m.	2nd Day.	m.	3rd Day.	m.
Whaley Br., rl.	16	Dovedale, fp.	8	Bonsall, fp.	4
Buxton, rd.	22½	Tissington, fp.	10½	Grange Mill, fp.	8
Longnor, rd.	30½	Ballidon, rd.	14½	Ballidon, rd.	12½
Hartington, fp.	35½	Grange Mill, rd.	17½	Tissington, fp.	14
		Bonsall, fp.	20½	Dovedale, fp.	17
		Matlock, fp.	22	Ashbourne, fp.	18½
				Manchester, rl.	74

From Sheffield.

1st Day.	m.	2nd Day.	m.	3rd Day.	m.
Baslow, *coach*	12½	Bonsall, fp.	1½	*Longnor, fp.*	5
Chatsworth, fp.	14	Grange Mill, fp.	4½	Buxton, rd.	12
Haddon Hall, fp.	17	Ballidon, rd.	7½	Dove Holes, rl.	15
Rowsley, fp.	18½	Tissington, fp.	11½	*Castleton, rd.*	24
Matlock, rd.	24	Dovedale, fp.	14	Sheffield,	
		Hartington, fp.	22	(coach), rd.	41

or by coach
from Baslow } 31

SIX DAYS.

From Buxton.

I.

1st Day.	m.	2nd Day.	m.	3rd Day.	m.	4th Day.	m.	5th Day.	m.	6th Day.	m.
Longnor, rd.	7	Tissington, fp.	2½	Darley Dale, rd.	3	Chatsworth, fp.	½	Win Hill, fp.	1½	Millers Dale, rd.	8½
Hartington, fp.	12	Ballidon, fp.	6½	Winster, rd.	6	Baslow, fp.	2	Mam Tor, fp.	6½	Cheedale, fp.	9½
Dovedale, fp.	20	Grange Mill, rd.	9½	Alport, fp.	11½	Eyam, rd.	6½	Blue John Mine, fp.	7½	*Buxton, rd.*	15
		Bonsall, fp.	12½	Upper Haddon, fp.	13½	Froggatt Edge, fp.	8½	*Castleton, rd.*	10		
		Matlock, fp.	14	Bakewell, rd.	15½	Fox House, rd.	12				
				Haddon Hall, rd.	18	Hathersage, rd.	15				
				Edensor, fp.	21	*Ashopton, rd.*	20				

II.

1st Day.	m.	2nd Day.	m.	3rd Day.	m.	4th Day.	m.	5th Day.	m.	6th Day.	m.
Hayfield, rd.	22	Win Hill, fp. & rd.	3½	Chatsworth, fp.	1½	Bonsall, fp.	1½	Hartington, fp.	8	Monsal Dale, rd.	3½
Edale, fp.	28½	Ashopton, fp.	5	Haddon Hall, fp.	4½	Grange Mill, fp.	4½	Monyash, rd.	13	Litton, fp.	6
Mam Tor, fp.	31	Hathersage, rd.	10	Winster, rd.	9	Ballidon, rd.	7½	Lathkil Dale, fp.	16	Tideswell, rd.	7
Castleton, rd.	34	Fox House, rd.	13	*Matlock, rd.*	15	Tissington, fp.	11½	Upper Haddon, fp.	17½	Millers Dale, rd.	10
		Froggatt Edge, rd.	16½			*Dovedale, fp.*	14	*Bakewell, rd.*	19½	Cheedale, fp.	11
		Baslow, 19, or *Edensor, rd.*	20½							*Buxton, rd.*	16½

From Matlock.

I.

1st Day.	m.	2nd Day.	m.	3rd Day.	m.	4th Day.	m.	5th Day.	m.	6th Day.	m.
Darley Dale, rd.	3	Eagle Stone, fp.	1½	Ashopton, rd.	5	Mam Tor, fp.	3	Longnor, rd.	7	Tissington, fp.	2½
Winster, rd.	6	Curbar, fp.	3	Win Hill, fp.	6½	Hayfield, fp.	12	Hartington, fp.	12	Ballidon, fp.	6½
Robin Hood's Stride, fp.	8	Eyam, rd.	6	Hope, fp.	8½	*Buxton, rd.*	34	*Dovedale, fp.*	20	Grange Mill, rd.	9½
Alport, fp. & rd.	10	*Hathersage* (over Eyam Moor)	10	*Castleton, rd.*	10					Bonsall, fp.	12½
Haddon Hall, rd.	1[illegible]½									*Matlock, fp.*	14
Chatsworth, fp.	16										
Baslow, fp.	17½										

II.

1st Day.	m.	2nd Day.	m.	3rd Day.	m.	4th Day.	m.	5th Day.	m.	6th Day.	m.
Bonsall, fp.	1½	Hartington, fp.	8	Monsal Dale, rd.	3½	Hayfield, rd.	22	Caves, &c.		Fox House, rd.	3
Grange Mill, fp.	4½	Monyash, rd.	13	Litton, fp.	6	Edale, fp.	28½	Win Hill, fp.	3½	Froggatt Edge, rd.	6½
Ballidon, rd.	7½	Lathkil Dale, fp.	16	Tideswell, rd.	7	Mam Tor, fp.	31	Ashopton, fp.	5	Eyam, fp.	8½
Tissington, fp.	11½	Upper Haddon, fp.	17½	Millers Dale, rd.	10	*Castleton, rd.*	34	*Hathersage, rd.*	10	Chatsworth, rd.	14½
Dovedale, fp.	14	*Bakewell, rd.*	19½	Cheedale, fp.	11					Haddon, fp.	17½
				Buxton, rd.	16½					Rowsley, fp.	19
										Matlock, rd.	24½

*** *Distances are in all cases accumulative.*

Hints to Cyclists.

———:o:———

The following are the principal routes through the Peak District, arranged alphabetically:

(1) **Ashbourne to Tissington**, 4 *m*; **Newhaven Inn**, 10 *m*; **Duke of York Inn**, 15½ *m*; Buxton, 21 *m*.

——**Newhaven Inn to Bakewell Station**, 7½ *m*.

—— ,, ,, **Youlgreave**, 4¼ *m*; **Rowsley Station**, 8 *m*.

—— ,, ,, **Winster**, 5½; **Matlock Bath**, 11¼ *m*.

(2) **Ashbourne to Grange Mill**, 10 *m*; **Cromford Village**, 14 *m*; **Matlock Bath**, 15 *m*.

Remarks. Cyclists passing through Ashbourne may with advantage take to their wheels either at Derby or Uttoxeter. The road between Derby and Ashbourne (13 *m*.) is hilly. That from Uttoxeter is flat as far as Rocester (4 *m*.), and afterwards rather hilly, but the landscapes between Rocester and Ashbourne (8 *m*.) are very charming. The road passes through Ellastone and Mayfield, places associated with the names of George Eliot and Tom Moore respectively.

All the Peak-ward roads from Ashbourne involve long though not very steep ascents, to heights of from 800 to 1,200 feet. That to Buxton almost gains its summit-level two miles short of Newhaven Inn, whence it is a good and easy run to Buxton. The branches to Bakewell, Rowsley, and Matlock descend rapidly during the last few miles of their courses.

The direct road from Ashbourne to Matlock reaches its summit at the crossing of the High Peak railway, 1½ miles short of the inn at Grange Mill, whence it is a fine run down the Via Gellia to Cromford.

(3) **Buxton to Ashbourne**, *see above*.

(4) **Buxton to Castleton**, 11¾ *m*. A dull but fair road. Fine descent for last 2⅓ *m*. into Castleton.

(5) **Buxton to Tideswell**, 9½ *m*; **Eyam**, 14½ *m*; **Stoney Middleton**, 16 *m*; **Baslow (for Chatsworth)**, 19 *m*; **Edensor Hotel (for Chatsworth)**, 20¼ *m*; **Rowsley** Station, 24 *m*. Two long hills between Buxton and Tideswell. From Tideswell, direct route to Stoney Middleton (5 *m*.) better than the Eyam diversion. Level from Stoney Middleton to Rowsley.

(6) **Buxton to Bakewell**, 12 m; **Rowsley**, 15½ m; **Matlock Bath**, 21 m. One long hill between Buxton and Taddington, 6 m. Level beyond Bakewell.

(7-8) **Buxton to Leek or Macclesfield.** *See reverse routes below.*

(9) **Buxton to Whaley Bridge Station**, 7½ m. A sharp rise for the first 1½ miles; then a very fine gradual descent. Road admirably engineered.

** Buxton being 1,000 feet above sea-level is a harder place to reach than to get away from on a cycle.

(10—13) **Castleton to Buxton, Chapel-en-le-Frith, Matlock, or Sheffield**; *see reverse routes.*

(14) **Chapel-en-le-Frith to Castleton**, 8 m. (*L. & N. W. Station*); 7½ m. (*Mid. Station*). Up hill for 3 m; fine descent for last 2½ m.

(15) **Derby to Belper**, 7½ m; **Ambergate**, 10 m; **Cromford**, 15 m; **Matlock Bath**, 16 m; **Rowsley**, 21½ m; **Edensor**, 25 m; **Baslow**, 27 m; **Calver**, 28½ m; **Hathersage**, 34 m; **Castleton**, 40 m.

—— **Rowsley to Bakewell**, 3½ m; **Ashford**, 5 m; **Taddington**, 9 m; **Buxton**, 15½ m.

—— **Baslow to Sheffield**, 13 m.

—— **Calver to Stoney Middleton**, 1 m; **Eyam**, 2½ m.

—— **Hathersage to Ashopton**, 5 m; **Snake Inn**, 11½ m; **Glossop**, 18½ m.

This main road is the only level one through the Peak District. Except for one or two steepish rises and falls between Baslow and Hathersage, it follows the river-level nearly all the way to Castleton and Ashopton. Of the branches the one to Buxton is level as far as Bakewell, and hilly beyond, Taddington being one of the highest villages in England; that to Eyam involves a sharp rise between Stoney Middleton and Eyam, but the main road may be regained in 2½ miles, near Grindleford Bridge, 3 miles short of Hathersage, by a capital road.

The Baslow and Sheffield road rises by a long hill of nearly three miles to the top of the moor, after which it is good running all the way.

Between the "Snake" and Glossop the road rises to a height of 1667 feet.

(16) **Glossop to Ashopton**, Sheffield, &c., *see routes from Sheffield.*

(17) **Leek to Buxton**, 12 m; and

(18) **Macclesfield to "the Cat and Fiddle"**, 7 m; **Buxton** 12 m.

The character of these roads is given on page 17. In both the ascent is severe, and the descent begins from 3 to 4 miles short of Buxton.

(19) **Matlock to Ashbourne**, *see reverse route.*

Matlock to Buxton, Castleton, &c., *see* (15).

(20) **Matlock to Chesterfield**, *see remarks on* pp. **107**, **108**.

(21) **Sheffield to Ashopton**, $11\frac{1}{2}$ m; &c. (p. 41).

(22) „   **Baslow direct**, $12\frac{1}{2}$ m. (p. 33).

(23) „   „ **by Froggatt Edge**, $16\frac{1}{4}$ m. (p. 35).

(24) „   **Castleton**, 17 m. (p. 37).

The routes from Sheffield are described and compared on page 32. They all involve a long ascent to the summit-level of the moorland intervening between the town and the Derwent valley. For Baslow the ascent commences at Dore, 5 miles on the way, and continues for 3 miles; for Castleton it is almost continuous for five miles, commencing 2 miles out of Sheffield and ending at Stoney Ridge toll-gate, half a mile short of Fox House Inn. The Ashopton road is a trying one because it involves two long hills with a dip into the deep Rivelin valley between them.

Approaches.

The walks and drives which lead up to a picturesque district possess a peculiar interest. Not only do they themselves share in the picturesqueness of the district, but they are, oftener than not, on an increasing scale of beauty which, instead of jerking the tourist, as it were, into the vortex of the scenery he has come to explore, leads him to it, step by step, by an easy and agreeable transition from ordinary rural landscape to the region of hill, valley, rock, and rushing stream which together constitute Nature's recreation grounds. The new-comer, too, is fresh and easily pleased. His appetite for the beautiful cannot have been cloyed or rendered fastidious by a prolonged enjoyment of it.

For this reason we have been at special pains to enable visitors to the Peak country to hire their carriage or don their knapsack, as the case may be, at any one of the numerous outlying towns which are within easy reach of the favourite places of resort therein, with as little trouble as possible. All these towns are easily accessible from the busy manufacturing centres which cluster round the Central Highlands of England; and in the long summer days any one may leave his place of business after a morning's work, and by sun-down reach one of the pleasant inns within the pale of the Peak, cheered and invigorated by a 12 mile walk or drive over the moors which encompass it on every side except the south.

Visitors from the south will do well to make Ashbourne or Matlock their starting-point, remembering that the routes to Ashbourne or Dovedale, from Rocester or Alton on the Churnet Valley branch of the North Staffordshire Railway, are worth a much more close exploration than can be made from the window of a railway carriage, and in the case of Matlock, that the real interest of the Peak scenery begins at Ambergate, 6 miles short of the favourite Derbyshire Spa. From the west the pleasantest approaches are by Ashbourne, Leek, or Macclesfield. The walk from Leek to Buxton along the ridge of the Roches and by Lud's Church, is a delightful one of 16 miles. The Macclesfield and Buxton road passes over the highest ground of any main road in England, but lacks cheerfulness. Visitors from Lancashire may conveniently commence their explorations at Glossop, Hayfield (pedestrian routes only), Chapel-en-le-Frith (for Castleton), or at Whaley Bridge (for Buxton). From Yorkshire and the north-east, Sheffield is not only the most convenient but also by far the most artistic **starting-point, the various coach** roads across the moors from that **town presenting** during **their** descent into the Derwent **valley some of the finest** views **in the** country. The roads from **Chesterfield also drop into the** Derwent valley, **but the** views from **them are neither so bold nor so** extensive **as those** from **the Sheffield routes. Pedestrians who like a** rough **walk to** begin with **will find one after their own** heart in the **15** mile track from **Penistone to Ashopton inn,** which crosses **the** wildest English **ground south of Westmorland.**

FROM THE SOUTH

Derby.

Hotels. *Midland,* adjoining the Midland Station; *Royal,* St. James', *Bell,* &c., in the town.

Post Office. Victoria Street. *Box closes for night mails:*—6 p.m. *(for S.W. counties and S. Wales)*; 9.20 p.m. *(N.W. counties, North Wales, Scotland, and Ireland)*; 11 p.m. *(other parts).*

Derby itself is a large and flourishing town of 80,000 inhabitants, but of no special interest to the tourist. The *Midland Station,* which is also used by the North Western and North Stafford Companies, is on the outskirts of the town, nearly a mile from the centre, with which it is connected by a tramway. Cars run every few minutes. The *Great Northern Station* is on the opposite or north-west side of the town, about half a mile from the centre. The tramway extends to this station also. Of the hotels the "Midland" is a house of high repute, and the others are all good without being obtrusively pretentious.

In its **churches** Derby well exemplifies the old saw that "distance lends enchantment to the view." The fine Perpendicular tower of **All Saints**—one of the highest in the kingdom; the smaller, but perhaps more beautiful one of the Roman Catholic Church, **St. Mary's,** and the tapering spire of **St. Alkmund's** rising between the two, are effective objects both in themselves and in their contrast with one another, from all points whence a general view of the town is obtainable, but the body of St. Mary's is scarcely worthy of its tower, that of St. Alkmund's is commonplace, while that of All Saints' besides being ugly in itself, is, in its relation to the tower, simply barbarous.

A pleasant stroll may be obtained in the Arboretum, about a mile south of the centre of the town, on the Osmaston Road.

For more explicit information regarding Derby, visitors should consult one of the local guide books, obtainable from Messrs. Bemrose, at the corner of Sadler Gate, or other booksellers.

Derby to Ashbourne. *By rail,* 30 m. *Fares,* 2s. 6d., 2s., 1s. 3d. *By road,* 13m.

We shall not describe the road route from Derby to Ashbourne, because, pleasant though it be, there is no special feature upon it to induce a tourist to devote the extra time and labour required to perambulate it. The railway route, on the contrary, though it only passes through ordinary scenery until its last few miles, possesses an interest quite commensurate with the time spent upon the journey – 1¼ to 1¾ hours, to wit. The pedestrian may, with advantage, quit the rail at Rocester, and walk thence to Ashbourne (8 m.), or, instead of taking the Ashbourne branch at Rocester, he may proceed for three more miles along the main Churnet Valley line to Alton, and thence walk by **Alton Towers** and the Weaver Hills to Dovedale or Ashbourne, a delightful ramble of about ten miles.

The Route. The North Stafford line from Derby runs over the main western line of the Midland for nearly 6 miles. From the point of divergence the tall, slender spire of Repton attracts attention on the left. Seven and a half miles from Derby we cross the Staffordshire extension of the Great Northern system at *Eggington*, and shortly afterwards converge with the Burton branch of the North Stafford, obtaining hereabouts our introduction to the pleasant companion and counsellor of the rest of our journey— *the River Dove.* The lower waters of this famous stream, vagarying hither and thither through flat green pastures in alternate pool and eddy, will sorely tempt the angling tourist to linger awhile ere he proceeds to explore the hills and dales which cluster round its head. It is famous, by the bye, for grayling.

Beyond the junction we pass on the right the pretty church of Marston-on-Dove, and then a mile's straight run brings us to **Tutbury** (Inns, The *Castle*, near the station, &c.), famous for its castle, its priory church, and its mediæval partiality for bull-baiting. The ruins of the *Castle*, strikingly placed on a green knoll above the river, are well worth a visit. As seen from the railway, the three towers, one of which is called *John of Gaunt's Gateway*, present a remarkably picturesque outline. Little else remains except fragments of the walls. The castle has a royal history. The original building existed before the Norman conquest. It was given by William I. to an ancestor of the present Lord Ferrers, in whose family it remained till the time of Edward I., when it became crown property, and was held by the Dukes of Lancaster as long as the house of Lancaster continued in the ascendant. The present buildings date chiefly from that period. They claim a special, if not a unique interest from having been one of the countless prison-houses of Mary Queen of Scots, who was held captive here with but little intermission for 15 years. We need scarcely add that the castle in its present condition is one of the many picturesque legacies bequeathed to us by "Old Noll." There is free admission at all times.

The **Church of Tutbury** was once in thorough harmony with the Castle. Restoration and addition have made it the reverse. Anything more discordant than the present conspicuous barn-shaped building, as seen in passing, we **can** hardly conceive. The west **door-way** is a remarkably fine **example of** Norman architecture, with its characteristic zigzag or "chevron" tracery. It is almost worthy to rank with that glorious trio of Norman arches which are the pride of Furness Abbey.

Between Tutbury Station and the village, the Dove is spanned by a handsome bridge.

Four miles beyond Tutbury we notice on the right hand (Derbyshire) side, among the trees, *Sudbury Hall*, a red brick mansion, the seat of the Vernon family. It was occupied for a short time by the late Dowager Queen Adelaide.

Beyond Sudbury the capricious course of the Dove is more than ever noticeable, and as we approach Uttoxeter Junction, the spire of *Doveridge Church*, and *Doveridge Hall*, the residence of S. C. Allsop, Esq., come into view on the right, and looking up the valley to the left of them we discern the *Weaver Hills*, an obtusely peaked ridge, which marks the commencement of the Peak country in that direction.

At Uttoxeter Junction (*refreshment* room; Hotel, *The White Hart*) the Churnet valley section of the North Stafford line branches away abruptly to the right. Pursuing it we note on the left the spire of Uttoxeter Church (the only object of any interest whatever in the town*), and continue along the strath of the Dove to Rocester, where the Ashbourne branch diverges to the right.

From Rocester (inn, *The Red Lion*, in village) by Alton Towers to the Weaver Hills and Dovedale or Ashbourne.

Rocester to Alton (rail) 3½ m; (road through grounds of Alton Towers 4 m). Alton to Dovedale, about 8 m. Alton to Ashbourne about 10 m. Two or three trains a day stop at Denstone Crossing on notice being given at Rocester. Denstone is a mile on the way. It contains a beautiful little church.

From Rocester either the train may be taken to Alton, or a pedestrian route chosen, the better half of which is through the grounds of Alton Towers. The *Grounds*, after having been closed to the public for some time, were re-opened in 1882. The charge for admission is 1s. each, and the chief entrance is close to Alton Station. The *House*, though strictly speaking private, is, we believe, occasionally shown to visitors.

The village of *Rocester* is half a mile east of the station, close to which is a small inn. For Alton Towers turn to the left about half way to the village, just short of the bridge over the Churnet, and 1¼ m. further enter the grounds at the Quixhill Lodge, after passing Denstone Church and crossing the Churnet. This approach to the Towers is called the *Earl's Drive*. Hereabouts the valley of the Churnet narrows, the railway winding

---

* The highest praise ever accorded to this town was by a native poet:—

"In all the country round there's nothing neater
Than the pretty little town of Uttoxeter."

alongside of the stream all the way to Alton. The drive, after crossing a meadow, ascends gradually till it reaches the level of the high ground on the east side of the valley, along which it continues all the way to the Towers, affording beautiful glimpses into the sylvan dell below. In this dell, which is a lateral depression of the main Churnet valley, are situated the gardens, conservatories, &c. of the Towers. Presently we reach a favourite view-point, called the "*Gothic Temple*," from which the mansion is well seen over and beyond the gardens. The chief feature of the latter is evergreen foliage. The drive then proceeds round a lake, and passing on the left the "*Modern Stonehenge*," as a group of sandstone blocks, piled one above another in the same way as a child builds up a pack of cards, is absurdly called, it enters the main drive from Alton to Farley just opposite the Towers. The fanciful and somewhat cockneyfied names given to several of the artificial adornments of Alton are apt to make one underrate in anticipation the part which Nature has played in establishing the fame of the locality. It was, however, the natural beauty of the site which, at the beginning of the present century, induced the then Earl of Shrewsbury to set about the building of the Towers. How he "made the desert smile," to quote from the inscription on his cenotaph at the entrance to the gardens, visitors will judge for themselves. Even the old local libeller who wrote—

"Alton and Calton and Waterfall and Grin,
The four fowest" (ugliest) "places you were ever in,"

would repent of his audacity if he could now take a walk through the country he thus stigmatised.

The external appearance of Alton Towers is very fine, and in thorough keeping with its physical surroundings. The sky-line is diversified with towers, pinnacles, and battlements, and the main body of the building, though it follows no regular plan, presents a combination of solidity and lightness which is seldom equalled in our more modern mansions. The general style may, perhaps, be called Baronial Gothic. The original building, called Alton Lodge, was occupied by the steward of the estate. The present one was commenced in 1814 by the fifteenth Earl of Shrewsbury, and completed by his son, to a great extent from the designs and under the superintendence of Pugin.

The interior of Alton Towers not being authoritatively open to public inspection, it would be presumptuous to attempt any description of it. A full one is given in Black's Shilling Guide and other local ones. All the movable objects of interest which it once contained—and they were many and magnificent—were sold by auction many years ago.

From the junction of the Earl's Drive with the Farley Drive, the route to Alton village bends to the left and crosses a bridge which spans the broad walk to the gardens, conservatories, &c. The view down the gardens from the bridge is very good. Close at hand is the "*Choragic Temple*," a copy of the Temple of Lysicrates at Athens. Cedars, rhododendrons, araucarias, and the fir tribe generally, almost cover the smooth undulating greensward. From the bridge the drive **passes** through the gateway and courtyard on the left hand of the mansion, whence a walk descends beneath butting cliffs of red sandstone, and down **one** or two flights **of** steps to the main entrance, close to the Alton railway station. The distance from Rocester to Alton by **this** route **is about four** miles.

Alton itself (inns, the *Shrewsbury*, **in** village, **5** min. from station ; *Talbot*, 2 min. from station), **is** almost on the top of **a** a steep **hill on** the opposite side of the valley **to the towers.** The village **has** no speciality **except the** *Hospital of St. John*, which occupies a bold and **picturesque position on a red sandstone** cliff, overlooking the valley. **The Castle, which occupied almost the same site, was dismantled in the Parliamentary war, and what remained was suffered to go to further ruin. The Hospital buildings,** which are now **partly occupied as a Roman Catholic school, are in** Pugin's **best style, and eminently in accord with the character of** their situation. **The whole scene carries you in spirit far away from the midland counties of England.**

Alton to Ashbourne (*about* **9** *m.*) **Enter the grounds of Alton Towers at the gate close to the station, and passing through a** wicket on the right, and **up some steps, reverse the route we have** just described as far **as the mansion.** Hence, crossing the bridge over the broad walk which **leads into the gardens, keep straight on to the stables**—a quadrangular **block with square ivy-covered towers at two of** its corners. Thence for **Ashbourne keep** straight on, and when you enter the lane **turn to the right. The** route onward is by *Plumpton*, *Wootton Grange* **(by a path near to** a private drive), and *Ellaston*, where the **Uttoxeter and** Ashbourne high road is joined, 5m. short of Ashbourne (*see p.* 8.) Upwards of a century ago Wootton Hall **was** inhabited **for a year** by the celebrated Rousseau.

Alton to Dovedale over the **Weaver Hills**, 3 *hrs. good walking.*

This is an interesting, **but intricate walk. Modern philanthropy** has made a clean sweep **of refreshment houses on the way. The** points **to** make for **are** *Farley cross roads*, *Ramsor*, the *Calton Moor cross roads*, and *Blore*. **The Weaver Hills lie between** Ramsor and Blore. **Their height is from 1,200 to 1,300 feet, and** they **are** easily ascended. **The view is extensive and varied,** especially towards the south **and west. Beyond them the high** ground of Calton Moor **is crossed. From Blore** a rapid **descent** is made by **a** road through the fields to *Ilam*, ¾m. short of **the** *Izaak Walton Inn*, **at the entrance to Dovedale.**

Rocester to Ashbourne (*by road*), 8 m. Turn to the left in the middle of the village of Rocester, after which the road is unmistakable. In 3½ miles we reach **Ellaston** (*Bromley Arms Inn*), where was the joiner's shop of the fictitious Adam and Seth Bede, and the real one of the relatives of the author of that book. Hence as we proceed, with the Dove below us on the right hand, the views are very charming. At *Mayfield* (*Inn*) where is the cottage in which Moore wrote the greater part of "Lalla Rookh," we cross the stream, and in another 1½ miles enter *Ashbourne*. For a description of the town see p. 46.

The **Railway route from Rocester to Ashbourne** takes the south side of the Dove, and is on a lower level than the road. Two miles from Rocester it passes **Norbury**, where the *Church of St. Mary* is well worth visiting. It contains a great deal of stained glass of the fourteenth century, and several monuments of the Fitzherbert family. Close to the Church is the old *Manor House*, the front part of which has been cased with brick. It also contains much old glass, and an oak-panelled room called "Sir Anthony Fitzherbert's study."

The rest of the journey calls for no comment. Four miles beyond Norbury we reach *Clifton Station*, and in another mile we enter the *Ashbourne terminus*, which is close to the church, and about ¼ mile distant from the principal inn—the "Green Man."

For a description of Ashbourne see p. 46.

Derby to Matlock and Buxton (*by rail*). Route 2.

Derby to *Ambergate Junction*, 10 m; *Matlock Bath*, 16 m; *Matlock Bridge*, 17 m; *Rowsley* (*for Chatsworth*), 21½ m; *Bakewell*, 25 m; *Miller's Dale Junction*, 31 m; *Buxton*, 36½ m.

Fares. 1st cl. 1⅞d; 3rd cl. 1d. a mile. Return, double.

Time. 1 hr. 5 m. to 1¾ hr.

In breadth and grandeur of scenery the railway from Derby to Buxton is surpassed by the Callander and Oban, the Highland between Perth and Inverness, and between Dingwall and Strome Ferry; the Settle and Carlisle, and by parts of the Furness line; but in picturesque combination of rock, wood, and river, it is second to none in the kingdom. Those in a hurry to reach Buxton will find such of the Manchester and Liverpool expresses as stop at Miller's Dale amongst the most comfortable and best appointed trains running. The carriages are of the smoothly running "bogie" type, and a Pullman car is attached to the evening trains. The leisurely traveller, however, who is not too dignified to gratify his eyes from the window of a railway carriage, may be excused for preferring the slower trains, as there is scarcely a station between Ambergate and Buxton which does not command a more or less romantic prospect. As far as Rowsley the line never deviates from the Derwent Valley, and from Rowsley the Wye is only lost to sight for a few miles between Bakewell and Monsal Dale.

The Route. Issuing from Derby Station we at once cross the River Derwent, along whose green, woody banks and those of its tributary, the Wye, lies the whole of our journey. The name Derwent probably signifies "fair water" (from the Celtic *dwr gwent*), and indeed wherever it occurs—in Cumberland, Yorkshire, and Derbyshire—it is a true index to the character of the surrounding country. If nomenclature goes for anything, our barbarous forefathers were far superior to our civilized selves in genuine appreciation of Nature. Nowadays, if we had the naming of a river, we should probably call it after the biggest man that lived upon it.

Beyond the Derwent the towers and spires of Derby town appear on the left of the line, its racecourse and the county cricket ground on the right, beyond which we pass under the Staffordshire branch of the Great Northern Railway. The valley now becomes more clearly defined. On both sides gentle wood-crowned eminences appear, which mark the limit of the wide plain of central England, those on the left growing gradually higher and higher till they culminate in that long moorland ridge which forms what is called the "backbone of England," and stretches far northwards with but few breaks to the waters of the Forth and the Clyde. The first station is **Duffield**, whose pretty little church and church-yard are adjacent to the line on the right hand. A tunnel succeeds, and then the line cuts through the town of **Belper**, between which and Ambergate it crosses the Derwent four times. At **Ambergate** ("the passage of the Amber," a small tributary of the Derwent) we diverge to the left from the main line to the north, and the hills close in on both sides—steep, high, and profusely wooded to their summits. That on the right is *Crich Hill*, an eminence of great geological interest. The next station—**Whatstandwell**—is popularly supposed to owe its name to native solicitude respecting its bridge, the constantly repeated query at the time of its erection "Wu't stand well?" having grown into a formula. We give this explanation for what it is worth. More erudite scholars than ourselves derive the name from a certain Walter Stonewell, who lived here five centuries ago. In any case the natives have grown too wise to perpetuate tradition at the expense of breath. They call Whatstandwell "Whatsall," and the neighbouring hamlet of Alderwasley "Arrerslee."

From Whatstandwell the railway continues to follow the windings of the Derwent, revealing a good view of *Crich Stand* above a semi-circular combe on the right, and then passing through a short tunnel almost underneath the beautiful greensward on which is Lea Hurst, the occasional residence of Florence Nightingale.

On the left hand, immediately beyond the tunnel, the High Peak mineral line sets off in earnest at a gradient of about 1 in 8 for its 30 miles of twisting and burrowing across the bleak limestone uplands of the district after which it is named. It is worked by the North Western Company in short lengths, several of the intermediate gradients being surmounted by the aid of stationary engines and ropes.

A little short of Cromford Station, 5 miles beyond Ambergate, we obtain a charming glimpse of the bridge, village, and church of the same name, on the left hand. Beyond the bridge the Derwent issues from the narrow gorge along which it flows from Matlock. On its north bank are seen the grounds of *Willersley Castle*, the seat of the Arkwrights. The cotton mill, also visible, was built by Richard Arkwright in 1770, and was the first erection of the kind in Derbyshire. We must not say a word against cotton, of course, but there is bad as well as "good in everything," and cotton and other mills have played sad havoc with the native beauty of the Derwent, the necessary weirs and dammings up having converted in many places, notably at Matlock, a sparkling stream into a sluggish pool.

From Cromford to Matlock the distance is 1 mile, mostly underground. Above our heads, and hidden from our profane gaze by the black tunnel, is a beautiful knoll, overlooking the Derwent, on whose grassy sward happy lovers " walk," and from whose headlong crags despairing ones " leap." A few yards beyond the tunnel, **Matlock Bath** bursts into view on the left hand, in a cup-shaped hollow, from which rise the *Heights of Abraham* and *Great Masson*. The station commands an excellent view of the whole, but, if our train be express, we have scarcely time to catch a glimpse of it before we enter another tunnel at the foot of the perpendicular face of the *High Tor*. Out again in a few seconds, another peep into the narrow defile on the left—a third tunnel— and, again crossing the Derwent, we pass or stop at Matlock Bridge. The High Tor has retired on the right to make room for the strath of Darley Dale, up which we travel for the next 4 miles. The village of **Matlock Bridge**, pleasantly placed on the green hill-slopes, is well seen as soon as we have passed the station. The square, fortress-like mansion crowning the hill to the south of the village is *Riber Castle*, built by the late Mr. Smedley, whose famous hydropathic establishment is conspicuous in the village.

Darley Dale affords space for quiet contemplation after the hot haste and rapid alternations of Matlock. It is wide, green and quietly beautiful. Half-way up it we pass the station of the same name, and note on the left hand its church and churchyard, in which is a veritable patriarch of trees—a yew said to be more than 2,000 years old. If it be so, it is second only to the famous yew of Fortingall, in Perthshire, which has seen between 2,500 and 3,000 summers, and is pronounced on the best authority to be the " oldest authentic specimen of vegetation in Europe." Though second in antiquity, however, the Darley Dale veteran is by no means second in the way it carries its years. It still stands erect without the aid of such crutches as serve to prop its poor crippled elder brother in the north. Just beyond Darley, on the right of the line, is *Stancliff Hall*, the residence of Sir Joseph Whitworth, known to all the world, and riflemen in particular. The house is built behind the site of a quarry, which is conspicuous from the way in which the stone has been utilized in the formation of rockeries.

As we approach **Rowsley** a vast breadth of siding accommodation is passed on the left of the line. Between it and the station the meeting of the **Derwent** and Wye, two of England's fairest streams, may be seen on the same side of the line. There is something as pleasant as it is foolish in the thought of the river which has hitherto cheered our way, thus gracefully introducing us to its sweetest tributary, before itself bidding us farewell, as it does a few yards beyond the station, where we cross it for the fourteenth and last time. Giving a last look, we have a short vista on the right hand of the valley down which it flows from the highest moorlands of the Peak, through the lovely vale of Hathersage, and past the resplendent domain of Chatsworth. The last-named is three miles up the valley, and the only part visible is the Hunting Tower on the hill behind the house.

From Rowsley, sweeping round to the left, we enter the Wye Valley at once. *Haddon Hall* is a mile and a-half on our way, but the *railway* passes behind it through a tunnel, the construction of which was a condition insisted upon before the iron monster was permitted to invade such sacred territory. Emerging therefrom we have left Haddon behind and still invisible, but we gain ample amends in the beautiful valley spread below, and the town and spire of **Bakewell** coming into prominence on the left. A pleasanter-looking town than Bakewell we know not. It distinctly asserts itself without being in any way pretentious. The stream in front and the woody hills behind are in thorough harmony, graceful and unobtrusive. Before entering the station the railway presents an effective view of the whole.

From Rowsley to Buxton it is almost all "collar work." Beyond Bakewell we leave the Wye valley, and proceed through a somewhat less interesting country past **Hassop**, under *Longstone Edge* on the right, by **Longstone Station**, and then through a tunnel, at the end of which, with a suddenness characteristic of this route throughout, a full-length view of the most beautiful reach of Monsal Dale breaks upon us *on the left*, the viaduct over the river —the Wye again—being crossed almost before we leave the tunnel. Here the valley sweeps abruptly round to the north-west, and the railway follows its course past **Monsal Dale Station**, immediately beyond which a very pretty vista of the sweetly-wooded little glen called *Cressbrook Dale* is presented on the right. The Wye valley between this and Miller's Dale is sadly spoilt by mills and dams, but for which it would vie with any in Derbyshire—except Dovedale—for striking beauty.

Two tunnels, a very short distance apart, succeed Monsal Dale. From between these and immediately beyond the second the river is seen far below on *the right hand*, winding between steep wood-covered hills on one side and sheer limestone cliffs on the other, **both** lovely peeps. Beyond the latter the valley straightens, and the railway ascends high above **it on the left.** At **Miller's Dale Station** we may have **to change carriages.** Then **comes** another **tunnel, and** immediately **beyond it on the right hand a** glimpse, **beautiful as it is momentary, down** the gorge **of** *Cheedale.* This **is the finest bit of scenery within** 10 miles **of Buxton, but from the railway it comes and goes like a** flash **of lightning. We are** in another **short tunnel at once, and** then **follow the course of the** Wye between **steep limestone cliffs,** graced **with yew and mountain** ash **and other trees, all the way** to Buxton, **branching off from the main Manchester line at a** triangular **opening of the valley 4 miles short of our destination.** The **most faithful disciple of Ruskin and Wordsworth can** hardly **fail to be struck with the great engineering skill which has** pushed **as easy**-going **a line of railway as any in the country** through this **most** rugged of valleys, **as well as by the character of the** principal works upon it, **which by their light and** elegant appearance often enhance **rather than detract from the** natural beauty of the **scenery. If the days of picturesque Derbyshire are numbered it will be** due rather to **mines and mills than to railways.**

APPROACHES FROM THE WEST.

Leek to Buxton. *By high road,* 12 *m; by the Roches, Lud's Church, and Flash,* 16 *m;* 5—6 *hrs.* Route 3.

Leek (Hotels: *Red Lion,* in Market-place; *George,* opposite **church, &c.) is an excellent** starting-point **for** tourists to the Peak **district from the populous towns** of **the** Potteries, the railway **journey from** Stoke **being** accomplished in about 40 minutes. **The town itself, well-built and** thriving though it be, has little **to detain the visitor. The** *Parish Church* has **recently been beautified by the addition of a handsome** chancel. **The** *Roebuck Inn* **is apparently one of the oldest** buildings in the **town, and preserves the characteristics in architecture** of the early **Tudor period. The suburbs of the** town, however, contain scenery which will prevent **any knight of** the knapsack **re**gretting that **he** has donned his impedimenta **at a place so little known** to his fraternity, and in **no** direction **do they afford better views or more** agreeable walking **than in that which points to the Peak of** Derbyshire.

Turning to the right at the north end of the market-place, **which is about half a mile from the station, we** quickly emerge **into the open country. Our road is wide** and, **in** places, pleasantly **fringed with** grass. **Carefully** guarded saplings on either side promise in time to complete what **is** already a partial avenue. In less than a mile **we** reach the brow of a hill, where we draw breath for a minute to admire the rich retrospect of the town and its green environs of meadow and woodland. Our voluble and usually discriminating friend, "Strephon," has dubbed Leek "unlovely." Even from his view-point—the distant Roches—its one or two towers and spires are effective objects in a landscape of universal beauty, and we have, alas! far too many really unlovely towns in England to pass over without protest the wrongful addition of a single one.

At this point we pass, on the right, the *Moss Rose Inn*—why so called is not apparent. Then the road has a pleasant fringe of grass till it descends to a tiny dell, at the bottom of which the water glints through a tangled web of thorn and briar and brushwood, which the writer was prevented from duly admiring by the threatening movements of a brindled collie with one grey and one green eye. By the way, when will the British rustic learn that his dog has no more right than himself to molest travellers on public thoroughfares? and that if he cannot teach it to discriminate between men and sheep, he ought to keep it off the roads altogether? Towards the latter timid and docile animals it is too often trained to display an unnecessary ferocity, which we can only wonder that it does not extend even more than is the case to strangers of human kind. You meet the yokel and his canine follower on a public road. The latter erects his bristles and pauses within a few yards of yon, snarling. Then he wheels slyly round and approaches you from the rear. You fling imaginary stones at him, or threaten him with your stick. Then, and not till then, his lord and master says "Come awa,' or "Down, lass," and carelessly adds as you pass him, "He'll no bite." We have more than once had triangles cut in our trousers and the flesh below incised by these animals who'll "no bite," and we vow that the next time we will summon the yokel at all costs. But *allons!*

From the top of the next rise the long rocky ridge of the Roches reveals its rugged gritstone cliffs on the left with greater distinctness. In front is a rude pinnacle as much out of the perpendicular as Chesterfield Church. If North-East Staffordshire were, like Westmorland, a "poet's corner," this singular excrescence would have been called "Sage Sidrophel," or by some other fanciful name. In fact, the gritstone assumes the grotesque in shape much more readily than any other rock.

About 2½ miles from Leek we pass the *Three Horse Shoes Inn* on the left, and then a little short of the third mile we cross another little brook and begin to climb in earnest. The hamlet of *Upper Hulme* on the left is picturesque, but when once it is passed there is little for the next four or five miles to charm the eye or engage the pen. Limestone uplands, smooth and bare, rise on the right, and on the left all distant prospect is barred by the uninteresting side of the Roches. Let us rather strike off at the bridge over the aforesaid little brook, and make the round of the Roches, taking Lud's Church on our way, and rejoining the high road after a desperate struggle up the long and steep three miles between Gradbach and Flash. Our walk from the Three Horse Shoes to Flash will, perhaps, take 3 hours, and except for such modest fare as may be obtained at Rock Hall, 1½ miles on the way, we shall find little or no chance of refreshing ourselves. Possibly a *rencontre* with that formidable maintainer of territorial rights, the keeper, may oblige us to deviate somewhat from the route as described below, but a "soft answer turneth away wrath," and a "wee bit siller" is, we believe, fairly demanded for the privilege of progress, as much as a safeguard against encroachment by that rough element of humanity who hold the apostolic view that all things are common, as for any other purpose. Special leave to trespass is only obtainable at the other end of the private property, as explained in the description of the route taken the reverse way, in our Buxton Section. (p. 66.)

Détour by the Roches and Lud's Church. From the little bridge, 3 miles from Leek, a footpath strikes up the hill to the left, and cuts off the corner formed by the high road and the lane which we are about to follow. The footpath joins the lane in the hamlet of *Upper Hulme*. Then we pass on the right a conspicuous villa, whose completion was prevented by the death of its proprietor, and, leaving on the same side a cyclopean outlier of the Roches, separated from the main ridge by a grassy depression, we soon detect a cottage—a tiny fortress so closely embedded in the rocks as to be scarcely distinguishable from them. This is **Rock Hall**; a pathway leads up to it. The sword of Damocles hung scarce more threateningly over the Sicilian tyrant than do the millstone crags over this little rock fortress. From the small greensward in front of it there is a beautiful view over the country we have just traversed. The bold bluff due west and to the right of Leek is *Congleton Edge*, and the green peak northwards, which has for some time attracted our attention by reason of its contrast with the regular outline of the adjacent heights, is *Shutlings Low*. Taking these two landmarks, the map will enable us to identify any other objects in the prospect.

The way onwards is through a wicket to the left of the cottage, and by a path which leads upwards to a projecting rock, whence, as an inscription thereon informs us, Prince and Princess Teck viewed the scene in 1872. To this visit we probably owe the railing placed at the edge of the rock to prevent us from tumbling over; but we have no suicidal proclivities, so continue our route through fir, bracken, and bilberry, with here and there a rhododendron, till in a few hundred yards we strike across a path which climbs through a tiny ravine to the summit ridge of the Roches. Further guidance is for a time unnecessary. On the highest point, nearly a mile to the left, is the Ordnance Cairn, and to it the narrow path defiles through the stunted heather, now and again crossing a stone wall, which, with a few breaks, runs the length of the ridge. Half-way to the cairn is a small reedy tarn, whose waters are of peat peaty. From a picturesque point of view the attainment of this ridge does not greatly enhance the prospect. On the Derbyshire side the dull monotone of the limestone country with its fir and beech-clumped summits commences. Many of the houses visible might, with some show of reason, claim to be the highest inhabited houses in England; so at least we think until we have travelled another hour or two, and seen the adventurous cottages which almost crown the summit of Axe Edge, and that strangely placed "Cat and Fiddle," which from every point of the compass stands out against the skyline more like a rectangular cairn than a country inn. An interesting feature of the scene is the Congleton Viaduct, on the North Stafford line, a little to the right of Congleton Edge.

Railways, in regard to their effect on natural scenery, have been abused wholesale. Poets have led the way, and " Mrs. Grundy " has followed; and yet, setting aside the futility of the attack, there is surely a strange lack of discrimination in it. There are railways and railways, and a man who describes an express engine on one of our great lines in terms which would excuse an intelligent Fijiean's mistaking a hideous traction-engine for one, not only stultifies himself, but also does harm to the cause which must be at the heart of every true lover of nature—its preservation to the utmost extent, compatible with a fair regard for commercial interests. This cause is not furthered by crying out against such obvious needs as direct communication between Manchester, Derby and Nottingham, between Perth and the North of Scotland, and between the western counties of England and the coast of Mid-Wales. The constructors of such lines, dependent as they are to a great extent for their traffic on the attractions which they offer to visitors in search of the picturesque, must make them in such a way as to inflict as little injury as possible on the scenery through which they pass. Besides, railways are not necessarily devoid of all elements of the picturesque —the curve is graceful in art as well as nature, and the stone bridge or viaduct is not a more unsightly object when a railway than when a road crosses it. Opposition to railways would be more effectual if it were less diffuse, and confined itself to attacking those schemes which, without the excuse of public demand or convenience, are promoted for purely speculative purposes, and involve the certain ruin of the natural beauty of the region invaded by them—such wanton schemes as have lately been happily repelled in the Lake District, where a profit from passengers is impossible, and from minerals an off-chance;—and now for Lud's Church.

This singularly-named curiosity of scenery is usually visited from Buxton, whence the way is easy enough to find, and in connection with which town we shall more fully describe it. Going from Leek it is otherwise, and if the right of way is challenged, a considerable circuit must be made.

In proceeding down the ridge from the cairn on the top of the Roches, you will reach in less than a mile a depression, beyond

which the ridge again slightly rises. At the depression a road
is crossed, at the far side of which is a stone step-stile; cross
this and another a few yards further on. Then keep the wall
along the summit of the ridge on your left hand. A densely
wooded valley lies below some way on your right. A little above
the upper edge of this wood, and nearly a mile a-head, you may
have detected, in descending from the cairn, a few stunted oak
and beech trees. These mark the exact locality of Lud's Church,
which is on the eastern side of the range of the Roches. When
the wall along the summit of the ridge (as above described) bends
down to the left, continue along the ridge till you reach another
wall surrounding a plantation. Descend from this plantation to
the right through the heather. If you meet the dreaded keeper
speak him fair, and he will tell you the way round. From the
gritstone rocks at the top of the plantation, projecting into mid
air like so many field guns, there is a splendid prospect across the
fertile valley westwards.

By this route you enter **Lud's Church** at its upper end. A
rude flight of stone steps leads into the narrow ravine, which grows
deeper and deeper until you emerge through an opening which has
been almost blocked by the fall of its right-hand portal. A path
then strikes away to the left and in a few hundred yards joins
a cart-track almost opposite the **Castle Cliff Rocks**. Turn
to the right down the cart track and through the wood. At the
bottom you will come to a square cottage. Take the foot-track
past the far side of this cottage and cross the foot-bridge, whence
the track proceeds by the side of the left-hand stream to *Gradbach
Mill*. Hence the road on to Buxton is unmistakeable. A mile
beyond the mill, after joining a more important thoroughfare, it
forks. From the fork the nearer and steeper way is by the lane
to the left; the longer (by ¼ mile or more) keeps straight a-head.
The route up the short cut can only be likened to the famous
"struggle" from Ambleside to the Kirkstone Pass, in Westmorland. The distance to Flash (*two inns*) is nearly 1½ miles.

A quarter of a mile beyond Flash we rejoin the Leek and
Buxton main road, a little short of its highest point—that is,
some 1,700 feet above the sea level. There is a wide but bleak
view to the right across the limestone country, which contributes
the main waters of the Dove. Several conical hills, of no great
height, pique our curiosity in this direction. The green one is
High Wheeldon; the more rocky ones, nearer at hand, Chrome
Hill and Park Hill.

After passing another small inn, "The Traveller's Rest," we
descend the eastern slope of Axe Edge to Buxton. A *détour* of
twenty minutes or so will take us by the Ordnance Cairn on the
top of *Axe Edge*, and in clear weather it is worth while to make
it. To the cairn it is very tiresome walking, but beyond it there
is a fair path which hits the main road again at a point where
a cross road diverges, and just opposite the second milestone from
Buxton. Then we cross the High Peak railway, and pass the

huge limestone quarries, **and** reach a fork at *Burbage*, whence, if our bourne is Old Buxton, we keep the right-hand branch; if the railway station or fashionable Buxton, the left hand.

For Buxton, see p. 60.

Macclesfield to Buxton by the "Cat and Fiddle."

Macclesfield to the Setter Dog **Public House, 3 m; Cat** *and Fiddle* **Inn,** 7 *m;* **Buxton,** 12 *m.* **Route 4.**

Macclesfield (Hotels, *Queen's*, opposite **Central** Station, *Macclesfield Arms, Bull's* **Head,** Market Place. *Letter Box closes* 9.30 *p.m.*) is a smoky, manufacturing **town, with** nothing in it to prevent the pedestrian shouldering his knapsack and setting off at once. There is **no** public conveyance between Macclesfield and **the** Cat and Fiddle, but **a break travels twice a** day **during the season between the Cat and Fiddle and Buxton (*see* p. 63).**

This **road is the highest public highway in England, except,** perhaps, **the companion one from Leek to Buxton. Both of them** attain **to within 100 feet or so of the altitude of Axe Edge, which** is **accounted about 1800 feet above sea-level. So far, however, the Ordnance Survey has been very sparing of its heights in this part of the country, and many of the most important ones—that of Axe Edge amongst the number—are omitted altogether. The occupants of the Cat and Fiddle consider themselves to be 1,966 feet above the sea, but we venture to deduct some 250 feet from this reckoning, and even then we leave them the proud satisfaction of beating the reputed "highest house"—the Traveller's Rest on the Kirkstone Pass in Westmorland—by fully 200 feet, and of rivalling, if not overtopping, a still greater celebrity in point of** height—**the shooting box of Corrour Lodge in Perthshire, between** which **and the sea level the perpendicular measurement is 1700** odd **feet. Even higher than the Cat and Fiddle stand some** quarrymen's **cottages on the other side of Axe Edge, which we** believe to be **really the highest inhabited houses in the country. If** not, **we shall be thankful to any correspondent who will kindly undeceive us.** *

As to these **two roads over Axe Edge, the only highway in the** kingdom **attaining a greater elevation is, we believe, that from Braemar to the Spittal of Glenshee, which climbs to a height of 2,250 feet.**

The **road from Macclesfield to Buxton is more** wild, but less **rich and** diversified **in the views it commands than that from** Leek **over the Roches** (p. 14). **The country** is intersected in every direction **by** stone **walls,** and there is throughout a marked scarcity of foliage **in** the foreground. The distant landscape, however, is continually widening as the road ascends to the Cat and Fiddle, and the bracing character of the walk will commend it to **many** tourists.

* **The 6 inch Ordnance is now published (1887).**

The Route. The Buxton road strikes eastwards out of Macclesfield from the railway arch near the north end of the central station. It begins to rise at once, and in about a mile forks, the left hand branch being the main road, and the right hand a somewhat shorter but more hilly one. As we ascend by the former there is a good retrospect between the hills on each side over Macclesfield to Alderley Edge. With regard to Macclesfield, distance gives distinct enchantment to the view. On the left hand a sharply-ridged picturesque group of hills strikes away. At the *Setter Dog* public house (3 *m.*) the two roads re-unite. The ascent continues, and in front one of the highest ranges in the Peak country appears. It is called the *Tors*, and is an extension of Axe Edge. A striking feature on the right is the conical hill called *Shutlings Low*, one of the most clearly defined hills in a district which is not remarkable for distinctive outlines. Eastward of this hill the *Valley of the Dane* imparts a softness to the scene which it has hitherto lacked. Round the head of this valley the road takes a wide sweep, slightly descending and then mounting along the side of the Tors to the **Cat and Fiddle**. If the weather be clear there is a marvellously fine view westwards from this part of the road. The Mersey, dotted with its varied craft, is seen across the plain of Cheshire, and south of it the dim outline of the Welsh hills *may* appear. Local tradition asserts that the Peak of Snowdon is sometimes included in the panorama. If so, it cannot rise much above the summit of the Glyders, which lie close to it in the line of sight.

The Cat and Fiddle and the road between it and Buxton are duly described in the Buxton Section (*p.* 64). Either the regular highway may be taken, or the old road, which is somewhat shorter, or a descent may be made by a rough track into the Goyt Valley (well worth visiting) on the left, to near Errwood House, whence a rough road ascends very steeply into the high road from Whaley Bridge to Buxton*; or Axe Edge may be crossed. The two latter routes involve the addition of from half an hour to an hour in time. Inquiries should be made at the Cat and Fiddle. In descending to Buxton direct, the road passes underneath the High Peak Railway, and through the village of Burbage, 1 mile short of Buxton. At Burbage the road forks, the right hand branch leading to Higher Buxton, and the left to the fashionable part of the town and the railway stations.

* A good cart-track to Goyts Bridge (Errwood House), quits the old road to Buxton by a gate on the left hand, 1 mile beyond the Cat and Fiddle, and at the head of the main Goyt valley. Hence it is a good 2 miles to Goyts Bridge—the last half is very beautiful—and 5 miles to Buxton.

Macclesfield to **Buxton** by rail. (*L. & N.W. and N. Staff. joint*) 22½ *m.*; 3s. 9d., 2s. 9d., 1s. 10½d.

This route, the most convenient one to Buxton from the Potteries, joins the Manchester and Buxton (L. & N. W.) line (*p.* 19) near **Disley** (9½ *m.*).

From Manchester.

Manchester to Chapel-en-le-Frith—for Castleton—and Buxton (by L. and N. W. Railway); Route 5.

Manchester to Whaley Bridge, 16 m; *Chapel-en-le-Frith*, 20 m; *Buxton*, 25 m.

Fares to Whaley Bridge, 2s. 9d., 2s. 3d., 1s. 3½d.; Buxton, 3s. 9d., 2s. 11d., 1s. 11½d.—*Whaley Bridge to* Buxton (road), 7½ m.

The characteristic scenery of the Peak district by this route may be said to be entered a few miles short of Whaley Bridge, at a point where skirting the southern end of the ridge on which Marple stands, we look down upon the Goyt valley, sadly spoilt by mills and factories, on the left, and it would be absurd to attempt any description of the alternation of genteel suburb, smoky factory and pastoral landscape which is presented to the eye up to this point. Pedestrians should certainly get off at Whaley Bridge and follow the road route, which is so good, and commanding in its views, that in these days of amateur Jehuship it is a wonder that no one has been found enterprising enough to start a Manchester and Buxton express coach.

The Route. A mile beyond **Stockport**, which, as seen from the high level of the railway, with the Mersey rolling its turbid waters through the centre of the town, looks almost picturesque in its blackness—reminding one slightly of Newcastle from the High Level Bridge—we turn sharp to the left from the main North Western line, and follow almost a straight course as far as **Disley** (12 m. from Manchester), a little short of which a square turreted building crowns a conspicuous upland on the right. It is called *Lyme Cage*, and commands a wide view westwards. Beyond Disley the line is carried at a considerable elevation along the west side of the *Goyt Valley*, the rival Midland route running parallel at the bottom of the valley. About **New Mills** we catch a glimpse of Kinder Scout up the Hayfield valley, and then descending almost to the level of the river we reach **Whaley Bridge** (inns, *The Jodrell Arms*, close to the station, good and moderate, &c.) Here the railway quits the Goyt Valley and turning eastwards to Chapel-en-le-Frith (p. 21) station, which is a mile from the town, allows a good view of the Kinder Scout range, stretching away towards Castleton. Half-a-mile east of Whaley Bridge, high up on the hill-side, is an old Roman chariot-course, called **Roosdych**. It is more than half-a-mile long, and nearly 50 yards wide, and is flanked throughout by trees, chiefly oak, ash and beech. At Chapel-en-le-Frith we pass over the Midland line, and then climbing round the hill on the right, double back so as to recross it over and above the *Dove Holes* Tunnel. Then turning south we descend a bleak upland with Combs Moss on our right all the way to Buxton. *Dove Holes Station*, 3 miles short of Buxton, is one of the highest in the kingdom, being over 1,100 feet above sea-level.

Carriage or Pedestrian Route *from Whaley Bridge to Buxton.* This forms part of the old London and Manchester coach road. It is admirably engineered so as to maintain a gradual ascent all the way until the fall commences, 1½ m. short of Buxton, and it commands beautiful longitudinal views of the Goyt valley. A healthier or pleasanter road walk can hardly be wished for. Up to the present time Whaley Bridge is on the boundary line between the town and country—smoke and rusticity—God and Mammon, we might almost say, reversing the order, unless the *High Peak railway*, which also threads the upper Goyt valley, be held to establish the claim of Mammon to the beautiful glen. The railway, which is a single line and used for goods and mineral traffic only, commences by a junction with the Buxton branch at Whaley Bridge, rising at once to a high level by a steep gradient which is worked by a stationary engine with ropes. It is about 30 miles long, and at its other end joins the Midland near Cromford, after a course whose abrupt curves and breakneck gradients are only rivalled by the equally eccentric Dartmoor railway from Princetown to Plymouth. A great part of the country traversed by it is of unmitigated bleakness. The traffic is chiefly limestone. Passengers are not carried.

Quitting Whaley Bridge by the road, we pass under the Buxton Railway, and begin to ascend at once, rising higher and higher above the river at every step. The *Goyt* comes down from the mountainous uplands west of Buxton near the Cat and Fiddle. Its course, as far as Whaley Bridge, is due north. The bed of the valley down which it flows is abundantly wooded throughout, and the hills on its western side are also crowned with wood for a considerable distance above Whaley Bridge. Our road, at first flanked with trees on both sides, takes us past the little village of *Taxall*, whose church presents to the road the most primitive of east windows. Then rising to the open hill-side, we pass the *Shady Oak Inn* and cross the High Peak railway. A lateral valley on the far side of the stream, deeply embowered in foliage, wears a very tempting look. Then we pass the lodge at the entrance to the private road to *Errwood House*, a turreted mansion which rises above the woods near the head of the valley, more like a shooting-lodge in a highland glen than a gentleman's seat in the midland counties of England. Opposite Errwood House our road sweeps sharply round to the left, and takes a wide circuit so as to avoid a deep depression in front. The circuit may be avoided by following the old road, which drops into the deep depression and, after climbing a steep pitch on the other side, rejoins the highway at the top of the pass, where the descent for Buxton begins. From this point there is a good all-round view. An

Rte. 6.] MANCHESTER TO CHAPEL-EN-LE-FRITH. 21

opening to the **north** reveals, over the extensive **farm-house of** *White Hall*, a **view of** the Kinder Scout ridge and the intervening pointed hills between Chapel-en-le-Frith and Hayfield. Buxton and **its** bleak **background of** limestone hills, **on** which **trees** only seem **to** thrive **under** protest, appears **in front, and to the right of** it Axe Edge is recognisable by it **cairn. The descent of the** *Long Hill*, as it is called, to Buxton, passing **the Corbar Woods on the** **left,** reveals no fresh **feature.** *For Buxton* see **p. 60.**

Manchester to Chapel-en-le-Frith—for Castleton—and Buxton (by *Midland Railway*.) Route 6.

Manchester (Central) to Marple, 14 m ; *Chapel-en-le-Frith*, 23 m ;— (*Castleton*, 31 m.)—*Buxton (direct)*, 33 m. (by *Miller's Dale*), 37 m.

Fares. To *Chapel-en-le-Frith*, 1st class, 2s. 9d., 3rd, 1s. 6d. ; to *Buxton*, 1st class, 3s. 9d., 3rd class, 1s. 11½d.

Passengers starting from the London Road station, Manchester, by the M. S. & L. trains have to change at Marple.

The **direct** Midland route from Manchester to Buxton is 8 miles, and to Chapel-en-le-Frith about 4 miles longer than the London and North Western. The Midland station at Chapel-en-le-Frith is about half a mile nearer to the town than the L. and N.W. At Buxton the stations adjoin one another. The fares are the **same in all cases.**
The Midland lines **from the Central and London Road stations** respectively join one **another at Romiley, 3 miles short of Marple.** The county of Derby, **and with it the Peak district, is entered a little beyond** Marple **by a viaduct which crosses the river Goyt at the** commencement **of what must once have been an extremely picturesque** valley. Mills and factories have, however, played their usual part, and rendered any description of the first few miles quite out of place in a holiday guide-book. Smoke and poisoned water do not cease until **New Mills** is passed, after which we continue along the Goyt valley for another 2 miles to Bugsworth. Hereabouts, just after the completion of the line in 1866, a huge landslip occurred, causing the present viaduct to be substituted for the original one, which was nearer the bottom of the valley. Thence, passing on the left *Chinley Churn*, a commanding eminence of 1,500 feet, and crowned by a camp, we cross, by a viaduct 100 feet high, the *Black Brook*, a mountain streamlet which descends from the south part of the Kinder Scout range, and in another mile reach **Chapel-en-le-Frith**. (*P. p.*, 3,500. Inns, *King's Arms*, *Bull's Head*, &c.) The town is dull and featureless, and the church equally devoid of interest. Agriculture, mills, and calico works provide the staple occupation of the people.

Chapel-en-le-Frith to Castleton, 7½ m. (*high road.*) This route is more interesting than the one from Buxton to Castleton, but less so than the pedestrian one from Hayfield, which we shall next describe. There is no public conveyance.

For the first few miles the road is on an almost continuous ascent, affording very pleasing views, both retrospective and into the depths of the valley on the left. One and a-half miles from "Chapel" we pass on the left hand *Slack Hall*, an old farm-house, and once an inn, beyond which the road continues to rise to *Rushup Edge*. On our left rises the long moorland ridge called *Cowburn*, a southern prolongation of Kinder Scout, and behind us the isolated peak of Chinley Churn. There is nothing further noteworthy until the road reaches its highest point, about 4¼ miles (less than 4 by the milestones) from "Chapel." Hence a by-road starts to the left for Edale. It is quite worth while to follow this road for about a quarter of a mile till it attains the narrow *col* overlooking Edale. The view from the *col* is one of the most impressive in the Peak district, and gains great effect from the suddenness with which it bursts upon the eye. To describe it in detail would spoil the *coup*. The summit of *Mam Tor* is only a few hundred yards from the *col*, on the east side, and easily attained. You may regain the Castleton road by a path across a field from the *col*, and then proceed either by the Winnats, *i.e.* the old road from Buxton to Castleton, or by the newer one, along which you have already been travelling. The map is the best guide to both. To the right of the latter, a little way down the hill, is the entrance to the Blue John Mine, and the Speedwell Mine is near the foot of the Winnats (*see Castleton Section.*)

Main Line to Buxton (*continued*). Beyond Chapel-en-le-Frith the line continues to ascend, and passing under the L. and N. W. Buxton branch, enters the *Doveholes Tunnel*. This tunnel is more than 1½ miles long, and took three years in construction. It passes under *Caw Low*, in the midst of which the millstone grit of the northern part of the peak district, gives place to the limestone of the southern. High as is the course of the line here, the North Western, which recrosses our route above the tunnel is still higher by nearly 200 feet. Emerging from the tunnel we reach the summit level of the line (985 ft.) at **Peak Forest Station**. Thence, we descend continuously for nearly five miles, first through a rocky waterless valley called *Great Rocks Dale*, and then, after passing the Buxton Junction on the right, through *Chee Dale* (p. 64), wherein are three short tunnels. Between the second and third there is, *on the left hand*, a lovely but momentary glimpse of the best part of the dale. Another couple of minutes and we pull up at **Miller's Dale Station**. For the route thence to Buxton, which is a retrograde one for the first 1½ miles, see page 12; for that on to Bakewell and Matlock, see page 70.

Manchester to Hayfield, for the ascent of **Kinder Scout** or for the pedestrian route to **Castleton,** viâ **Edale.** Route 7.

Manchester (London Road) to New Mills, **13m.;** *Hayfield,* **16m.;** about ten trains a day each way.

The *Hayfield* line is worked by the Manchester, Sheffield, and Lincolnshire Company. It branches off from the Midland route (*p.* 21) at New Mills.

Hayfield (*pop.,* 4,000. Inns :—*Royal, George*) is only interesting from its position as a convenient starting point for pedestrians who wish to dive at once into the wildest regions of the Peak country. It possesses large calico print works, besides cotton and paper mills. The inns are comfortable. The walk which we are about to describe to Castleton, &c., is one of the most enjoyable in the county, and the ascent of Kinder Scout is better made from Hayfield than from any other place. By a slight divergence from the Castleton route, the highest point of the mountain may also be reached, but the route described below is a much more interesting one to such as wish for a real mountain climb, the moorland walking from all other sides being heavy and wearisome in the extreme. Pedestrians must not forget that Kinder Scout is a grouse moor, and that promiscuous wandering about it at particular seasons is very reasonably objected to. Enquiries on this point should be made before starting.

Ascent of Kinder Scout. *3-4 hours, there and back.*

Leave Hayfield by the passage on the left (north) side of the Royal Hotel. Turn almost at once to the right, and keep along the road with the Kinder stream on the right hand. In less than a mile, and after passing the *Kinder Print Mills,* the track for Edale stretches to the right, across the stream. That for Kinder continues straight a-head for another quarter-mile or so, and then crosses the water, rising at once to a small group of houses, approached by two gates. Pass through the left-hand one, and a little further on, just beyond a second gate, you may either pursue the worn track leading to *Kinder Head*, the highest farm in the valley, or you may diverge to the left, down a green lane, which descends to *Low Kinder Farm.*

At both these farms the cart tracks cease, and from either of them the ascent of Kinder is easily made. After heavy rain it is worth while to follow the course of the stream all the way up, for the sake of the **Kinder Downfall** as it is called, diverging a little where the direct course is too rough or steep. There can be no mistaking the way. The mountain ridge as seen from below is shaped like a horizontal V, with the Downfall at its angle. The proper time to see the latter is when the wind is blowing from the south-west after a " downfall " of rain. Then we are told that the water is blown back and upwards, in such quantity, and to such a height, as to be visible for many miles. One gentleman informed the writer that he had himself seen it from Stockport, a distance of 10 miles in a bee line.

The *summit ridge* of Kinder is reached just above the Downfall. An easier way to it from the Kinder farms is along the shoulder which runs parallel with the stream on the north side of it, and which gains the ridge about half way between the "Downfall" and the *Ordnance Cairn* at the north-east extremity of the mountain. This Cairn is 1,981 feet above sea level, lower, by perhaps 100 feet, than the highest ground at the southern extremity of the ridge, which, strange to say, has not had its height recorded by the Ordnance Surveyors. There is, however, but little difference in the views from this side of the plateau of Kinder, and a walk along the ridge from end to end (*from* 2 *to* 3 *miles*) is only to be recommended for its bracing effects. Those, however, who undertake it may strike the highest point of the Castleton route, described hereafter, at Edale Cross.

The wide table-land which constitutes the top of Kinder Scout, is, according to the Ordnance Map, the "Peak" par excellence, though, oddly enough, it does not contain a single feature to justify the name. It extends for about 4 miles from west to east, and in its widest part, 1½ miles north to south. It consists of millstone grit, and its scarped edges, when seen from the valleys immediately below, display the bold and fantastic appearance, as well as the dull colouring peculiar to that formation. The chief escarpment is on the western side, up which we have been climbing, but both northwards and southwards, over Ashop Dale and Edale, respectively, hang steep and rough-hewn edges. The walking over this plateau is the worst imaginable. The vegetation consists of rank long grass and stunted heather, and the floor is of deeply rutted peat.

The *views* from Kinder Scout are only worth noticing where standing on one of its edges, you look down into the valley immediately below. The distant prospect in every direction except westwards consists of billowy ranges of featureless hills. Westwards the eye ranges as far as the state of the atmosphere or the smoke of the Cheshire towns will permit. Far or near there is little sweetness about Stockport, but beyond it on the left, the busy estuary of the Mersey *may* be seen, and the Welsh hills, even Snowdon coming within the range of possibilities.

Let not the tourist waste time in hunting for the *Kinderlow Cavern*, which is now, we are told, blocked up. It lies near the south-west extremity of the mountain. Two gentlemen, it is said, once set about a thorough exploration of the subterranean labyrinth which goes by this name. The Ariadne of one of the Hayfield inns supplied them with thread and candles. The candles, however, went out, and the clue was lost. A night was spent in vain efforts to regain it, and had it not been for the apprehensive solicitude of Ariadne, which caused a search to be made on the following day, the upshot might have been serious. We tell these tales as they were told to us, *on the spot*.

From Kinder a pretty direct descent may be made to **Glossop** (1¼ hrs.) by crossing the *col* at the north-east extremity of the ridge, and following for a little way a line of poles over the subsidiary ridge beyond. It is, however, a wearisome trudge, and in any case not worth the risk of being stopped for trespass.

Descent to the **Snake Inn.** From the above *col* you may also descend, in about an hour, by the side of the Ashop Brook to the Glossop and Sheffield road, which is entered close to the Snake Inn (*p.* 27). A more interesting route, however, to the same inn, is to keep along the edge eastward for about 2 miles to *Fairbrook Naze*, one of the boldest, and certainly the most peak-like scarp of the crag-girt Kinder. The walking is very rough, but the view down Ashop Dale is of increasing interest as the valley grows deeper and richer. From the Naze you may descend to the Snake, a comfortable and well-supplied inn.

Hayfield to Castleton by Edale Cross and Upper Edale.
Bridle path and road. Route 7 (continued).

Hayfield to Edale Cross (summit of ridge), 3½ *m*; *Barber Booth*, 6½ *m*; *Castleton*, 11 *m*.

This route affords short and telling access to the centre of the Peak District, and is specially to be recommended to pedestrians from Manchester and the busy towns of Lancashire and Cheshire who wish to see the best part of the country in a few days. The walk presents a much greater diversity of scenery than the carriage route from Chapel-en-le-Frith to Castleton, with which it converges about 3 miles short of Castleton. There is no inn on the route.

Starting from Hayfield we take the Kinder Scout road (*p.* 23) behind the Royal Hotel and past the Kinder Print Mills. In front the top ridge of Kinder comes into view. A mile from Hayfield a guide post ("*Edale*, 6 *m.*") tells us to cross a bridge and pursue the narrow valley on the right. Hereabouts is the boundary line between the unsightly chimney country and the wilds of the Peak. The hills around assume some boldness of outline, and are well wooded. In another mile the road rises abruptly to the left from the bottom of a prettily wooded dingle called *Coldwell Clough*. The green conical hill bringing the valley to a sudden end southwards is *South Head* (1,633 ft.). Beyond the farm house at Coldwell Clough our road becomes a cart track, rising between two walls and skirting the southern shoulder of Kinder Scout till it reaches its highest point, about 1,800 feet, at **Edale Cross**. The Cross itself, a block of gritstone, with one arm nearly chipped off, is hidden from the road by the left hand wall close to a gateway. What special purpose it was intended to serve we cannot say.

Probably, like other similar erections in the district, it was a guide post for pack-horses, set up when tracks were faint and enclosures unknown in these wild uplands. A quarter of an hour's divergence to the left, starting by the wall side, will place the tourist on the highest part of the long and monotonous *Kinder Ridge*. In the grouse season, however, it is flat trespass, and except for the view of the rest of the V-shaped ridge itself and the deep combes below, it is hardly worth the attendant exertion.

So far our walk, since quitting the valley, has been rather dreary. Peat bog, rank grass, bilberries, and dull coloured heather do not form the most attractive carpet for mountain sides, and these, together with a sensation of smoke in the west, and a dull line of limestone heights in the south-west, comprise the whole prospect. Weariness, however, quickly vanishes as we commence our descent for Edale. The edges, instead of the slopes, of Kinder rise above us on the left, topped by many a quaintly-shaped block of grit, and a multitude of tiny rills course down the deep ravines to the bottom of the valley, which gradually reveals itself—in its upper reaches narrow, green, and sylvan. Beyond it rises Mam Tor, round whose crest the circular earthwork, broken where the side of the hill has slipped away, may be detected in clear weather.

In descending to the valley, the track eases the steepness by taking a wide sweep to the right. This may be avoided by crossing a step-stile in the wall, and dropping down by a footpath locally called *Jacob's Ladder*, as shown on the map. At the point where the two converge again, a stone bridge introduces us to green pastures over which, on a gradually improving road, and past, here and there, a group of picturesque farmsteads, we proceed, noting, if the summer be far spent, the brilliant glow of the bracken, which covers on this side many of the deep cloughs of Kinder, and the richly tinted foliage of the birch and other trees fringing the merry streamlet on our right. The traveller down Edale, by the way, should keep a sharp look-out for dogs, who, as usual in the remote corners of the land, are less partial to new faces and more inquisitive as to strange legs than in populous parts.

As we approach *Barber Booth*, whence the Castleton road, which we have seen before us for some time, commences the ascent for Mam Tor, the wider portion of Edale opens on the left. Barber Booth is a mere handful of farmsteads, with, if we recollect right, a little shop. The road over the bridge threads the valley the whole distance to Hope ($6\frac{1}{4}$ m). Our route, now become a good carriage road, winds upwards, affording views of the whole of Edale, except its lowest two miles, constantly increasing their interest till the climax is reached at the top of the narrow *col* which separates that valley from the less interesting one leading down to Chapel-en-le-Frith.

The rest of Edale, Mam Tor, and other hills visible from here, are more fully described in the Castleton Section. The summit of Mam Tor is close at hand, only a hundred feet or so above the *col*, and the tourist who is not in a hurry to reach Castleton, or who does not wish to descend the Winnats or to visit the Blue **John Mine** on his way, may with advantage ascend to it, and continue as far as he likes eastward along the ridge, which, from its comparative sharpness, affords simultaneously the most comprehensive views possible of Edale **on the left and Hope** Dale on the right, including the hideous chimney which blisters the beauty of the latter between Hope and Castleton. The ridge walk may be continued the whole way to Lose Hill, and down to **Hope** (*good inn*, **4** *m. from Mam Tor*, 1½ *m. short of Castleton*), or a direct descent may be made upon Castleton, by a footpath, from a depression 1¼ m. from **Mam Tor, and just** short of the rugged face of Black Tor.

From the *col* the road bends back a little towards Chapel-en-le-Frith, but there is an obvious cut across a field to a point near the convergence of the roads from Chapel-en-le-Frith and Buxton, whence, for the Blue John Mine (*see map and Castleton Section*), keep the high-road for Castleton; for the Winnats follow the Buxton road for a few hundred yards till it turns sharp to the right. The track through the Winnats turns with equal sharpness to the left, being, in fact, itself the old road from Buxton to Castleton.

Manchester to Glossop, Snake Inn, and Ashopton Inn.
Route 8.

Manchester (London Road) to Glossop (rail), 13 *m. Glossop to Snake Inn (road)*, **7** *m; Ashopton Inn*, 13¼ *m.*

The last part of this route, between Snake Inn and Ashopton Inn, is along, perhaps, the most romantic valley of its kind in Derbyshire, that of the Ashop. The pedestrian part of the route —between Glossop and Ashopton—is fully described the reverse way on page 45, so we shall here confine ourselves to an abstract of its salient points.

The railway from Manchester to Glossop is entirely outside the **Peak** district, and calls for no description.

The town of **Glossop** (*pop.* nearly 20,000; Hotel, *Howard Arms*, close to the station) lies in a deep recess, one mile south of the main line, the junction with which is at *Dinting*. The appearance of the town suggests a much smaller population than it possesses. The neighbourhood abounds in cotton factories and print works.

Quitting the town, the road rises at once to the bleak moorland which connects **Kinder Scout with the high ground of the** West Riding. The highest point (1,667 *feet*) is reached 4 miles from Glossop, after which the road winds down a narrow ravine to the **Snake Inn**, itself some 1,000 feet above sea level, and one of the most remote hostelries in **the country, the nearest town to it** accessible by road, with the exception of Glossop, being Sheffield, which is 17 miles distant. For all that, it is quite capable of giving comfortable entertainment to man and beast. Kinder Scout may be easily ascended from it in 1½ hours.

Beyond the "Snake" cultivation recommences, and the road winds down the *valley of the Ashop* through scenes growing less wild but more beautiful throughout, the northern edges of *Kinder Scout* beetling above the valley with great effect. The boldest and most striking of them is *Fairbrook Naze*, which projects from the main ridge opposite the Snake. As we descend the valley numerous farmsteads appear. The *Ashopton Inn* is an excellent one in itself, and a good centre for excursions. Fishing tickets for the Derwent and Ashop are obtainable at 2s. 6d. a day.

Penistone to Ashopton Inn by Derwent Head. Route 9.

Penistone to Langsett (Inn), 3¼ *m*; *Slippery Stones (Derwent Dale),* 8½ *m*; *Derwent Chapel,* 13½ *m*; *Ashopton Inn,* 15 *m. Time* 4½—5¼ *hrs.*

The wildest English scenery, and the most bracing air south of Westmorland, are the reward of the adventurous pedestrian who undertakes this walk. From the point on the summit level, between the basins of the Don and the Derwent, where the head waters of the latter stream are first seen, the view is one of the most remarkable in the country. Standing within 20 miles of Manchester and 12 of Sheffield, the spectator has presented to him a wide prospect of hill ranges, scarped rocks, profound depths, and rushing streamlets, without a sign of human existence or a vestige of cultivation. In the gloaming of a late autumnal afternoon, when the rich tints of the dying bracken, with which the hill sides are abundantly carpeted, pervade the atmosphere, it is difficult to imagine a more impressive scene. The track is but faintly marked in places, but with the aid of the general map, on which we have carefully marked it out, and the following directions, it cannot well be missed in clear weather. The road is plain enough when once the Derwent valley is reached, but the tourist should not stint himself in daylight. "Featherbed Moss," over which the highest part of the route passes, affords not only the softest of couches, but also the dampest of sheets.

Penistone (Inns.—*Wentworth Arms,* close to the station; *Rose and Crown, Old Crown,* and *Spread Eagle* in the town) is a dull little upland town, with a conspicuously placed church. It is 30 miles by rail from Manchester, 13 from Sheffield, and 800 feet above sea-level.

The Route. A carriage may be taken to Langsett, 4 m. by road, but pedestrians should proceed as follows. Pass southwards along the main street of Penistone, and take the first turn to the right. A short ½ mile further turn to the left. An upright stone in a field on the right, beyond the next turning in that direction, is an old guide post for travellers before the moor was enclosed. A little further, we reach the brow of the hill, and look down over the valley of the *Little Don* to the main ridge of fells which we have to cross. The village of Langsett is visible from 1 to 1½ miles in our right front. To reach it pass through a gate opposite the and of the road you have ascended, and follow a footpath which passes about half way between two farm houses—the one on the left occupying a singular position on the top of a knoll, so exposed as to appear itself thrown out of the perpendicular by the westerly gales only to a less degree than the solitary birch which grows in front of it. This path drops into the road along the Little Don Valley, about half a mile short of the " *Waggon and Horses* " at Langsett. From this small hostelry descend by a narrow lane to the *Little Don*, which is crossed by a new footbridge built above some ancient stepping stones. From the lare you will have seen in front, high up on the opposite hill, a solitary farm, locally known as " North America." The way is by this farm, to reach which you cross the stream either by or below the footbridge and climb the hill by a path that goes to the right of some stone-wall enclosures. Continuing straight, in front of the farm, you find yourself almost at once in line with a wall, alongside which there are scraps of a rough track. Keep straight on with the wall on your right, till it turns obtusely to the right. The track, fainter and fainter, keeps on with a tendency to the right. When it vanishes entirely, keep straight ahead through the heather and bilberries, and in a few minutes, just over the crest of the hill, you will strike square into a narrow but well-marked path running north and south along Mickleden Edge high up above a stream. Turn left along this path and in a mile you will be level with the stream, and in *Black Dyke*, where stream and path pass between peat-banks with generally a firm sandy floor. The highest part is called *Cut Gate*, and the scene is dreary in the extreme until, ¾ hour or so after entering the path, you reach the edge of the moor, and look down into the Derwent valley on the scene we have described in the introductory remarks, as perhaps the most wildly beautiful in the centre of England. The descent into the valley of the Derwent is rapid, along a spur between two deep ravines—*Bull Clough* on the right, and *Cranberry Clough* on the left. At the bottom we cross the streams of both, and soon enter—at *Slippery Stones*—a fair cart track, two miles above the highest house in the valley. The spot called Slippery Stones derives its name from a landslip, the locality of which is still noticeable. On the top of a hill, higher up the valley and due north, are the *Rocking Stones*, so called from a loose boulder which has somehow got wedged in between two firm crags; whether it will rock we cannot from experience say, but the ordnance surveyors are evidently of opinion that it will.

At Slippery Stones the public road, or rather right of way—for there is neither bridge nor stepping stones, and the traveller must get through the stream as he can—crosses to the west or Derbyshire bank of the Derwent, and continues along it for the next 3 miles, after which it recrosses to the east side by Ouzelden Bridge. There is, however, a fair cart-track—the last part of it green—along the east or Yorkshire side of the river, from Slippery Stones to *Howden Farm* (2 m.)—the first house we pass after leaving Langsett—and from Howden a carriage road continues all the way to Ashopton. This is the shortest route, and the trespass, if any, involved in adopting it, is of the most innocent kind.

The walk from Slippery Stones to Ashopton is beautiful throughout. The bottom of the valley soon begins to be cultivated, and a goodly sprinkling of trees to diversify the landscape. Several lateral valleys contribute their waters to the main stream—a V shaped one on the west, half way between Slippery Stones and Howden offering its "quota" in a succession of charming little falls,—but the chief contributor is the Westend stream, which is big enough to be styled a river, and falls into the Derwent opposite Howden after a course of several miles.

Half a mile beyond Howden we come to *Abbey Farm*, and enter Derbyshire, the river having thus far marked the boundary between that county and Yorkshire. Our road takes a little sweep to the right, and then clings to the water-side all the way to *Ouzelden Bridge* (¾ m. further), where the through public road rejoins it.

Abbey Farm, Derwent Chapel, and other objects of interest are more conveniently described in the return route from Ashopton (*see p.* 43), to which we refer our readers. It is a short 4 miles from Ouzelden Bridge to Ashopton. The road is somewhat hilly as far as Derwent Chapel, but unmistakable throughout.

N.B.—The route described in previous editions of this book takes the tourist over a part of the moor—between the Little Don and Black Dyke—where the right of way is doubtful, and unnecessary annoyance is given to the shooting tenants. We hope this revision will satisfy both tourists and sportsmen.

From Sheffield.

Sheffield. Hotels, *Victoria*, M. S. and L. Station; *Wharncliffe, Royal, King's Head, Angel*, &c., &c., 7-10 min. walk from stations.

Post Office, Haymarket; *Box closes (for* **Scotland, Ireland,** *and N.W. Counties)* 8 **p.m.** *(other parts)* 10.30 **p.m.**

General Remarks.—Hitherto it has not **been fashionable** with guide-book writers **to associate** Sheffield **in any way with the** Peak district. That **industrious class of public benefactors has** shunned **not only the town itself, as it would shrink from touching a red hot coal, but also every highway and by-way by which the country they have written about is connected with it.** We shall so far fall in with established custom as to confine our description of the **cutlery metropolis within the narrowest limits.** Words cannot well paint **it blacker than it has** painted **itself, and any** remarks upon the praiseworthy attempts which it is **now making** to assume an outward appearance more in **accordance with its size and commercial importance** would **be out of** place **in a guide-book to the** picturesque. **At the** same **time, there** is **no more convenient or remunerative starting-point for the Peak** district than **Sheffield.** The moment its smoke-vomiting chimneys and **ugly red-brick streets are** left behind, the tourist**'s interest commences. He** forgets at once " the spreading **of the** hideous town.'' **Luckily, it does not spread in** this direction. Whether he climb **the hills or thread the** valleys leading into Derbyshire, **the** town disappears at once, and no indication of its existence remains except its suburbs. Finer ones no large town **in** England, not **even** Bristol, possesses. All the roads lead gently up to the summit **ridge** of that **long line of** upland which, dropping abruptly **into the valley of the Derwent, affords a** series of **the** finest landscapes **in the centre of England, and** brings before the **eye at one** *coup* **the full beauty of the Peak district.** This peculiar **" lie" of the hills** " striking**" westwards in the direction of the best** scenery **gives a** special piquancy **to the views which is** not to **be obtained** by approaching the district from **any other** direction. **Pedestrians** may choose from half-a-dozen **routes more or less interesting, and** carriage-folk **may either hire or avail themselves of the coaches** which ply **daily** between Sheffield **and the favourite resorts of the Derwent valley** at fares not exceeding 1½d. **a mile. We append a list of the** different **routes** by which the **district is reached from Sheffield.**

Coach Routes.

Sheffield to Baslow, *direct by* **Owler Bar**, 12½ m.
,, ,, *by* **Owler Bar** and **Froggatt Edge**, 16 m.
,, **Castleton**, *by* **Fox House** and **Hathersage**, 17 m.
,, **Ashopton**, *by the* **Manchester Road**, 11½ m.

Other Routes.

Sheffield to Baslow, *by* **Fox House** and **Froggatt Edge** (*carriage road*), 15 m.
,, **Baslow**, *by* **Fox House** and **Grindleford Bridge**, (*carriage road*), 15 m.
,, **Hathersage**, *by* **Ringinglow** (*pedestrian route*), 10 m.
,, **Ashopton**, *by* **Redmires Reservoirs** (*do.*), 12 m.

N. B.—The distances are all reckoned from the New Market Hall at Sheffield, the starting place of the coaches. The various milestones seen on the way reckon from points from ½ to ¾ mile nearer the outskirts of the town. At Baslow we have calculated to the principal inns, which are close to the entrance to Chatsworth Park, rather than to the village itself, which is half a mile further by the direct route from Sheffield, and half a mile nearer by the Froggatt Edge and Grindleford Bridge routes.

Comparison of Routes.—Of the above routes the finest are:—the one which drops into the Derwent valley from Fox House to Hathersage, and the one by Froggatt Edge, which, as our table shows, may be commenced by either the Owler Bar or Fox House road. These two form kinds of terrace roads descending smoothly but quickly beneath the sharp gritstone edges which abut on to the valley, of which they command complete and beautiful views in both directions. The direct road to Baslow *viâ* Owler Bar is far less interesting, because it drops to the Derwent valley through and not alongside of the hills, thus limiting the view on either hand to the ravine by which it descends, until it reaches the level of the valley close to Baslow itself. The Ashopton road presents a very charming vista as it descends to Lady Bower and Ashopton. The Ringinglow route is a deservedly favourite one with pedestrians, not only from its bracing character, but also for the views it commands nearly the whole way, and specially for the fine descent into Hathersage from the highest ridge of rocks overlooking the village. The route by Redmires and Stanage Pole to Ashopton or Hathersage is of the same character as the last mentioned in so far as it is a kind of ridge walk until the descent commences, but it is neither so picturesque nor so enjoyable. The Grindleford Bridge route passes through a charming glen a mile beyond Fox House.

* Besides the many public ways we have mentioned, there is quite a system of private drives, broad, green and velvety, across the moors. These drives where, as is often the case, they skirt the edges overlooking the Derwent Valley, present a continual feast to the eye of the wayfarer. They belong to the Duke of Rutland, and can only be walked over by privilege.

We are anxious not to overrate the attractions of these routes, and it is only fair to add that there is one drawback from which, in the eyes of most lovers of natural beauty, they one and all suffer—and that drawback is one of **colour**. In this respect the millstone-grit formation, of which these hills almost entirely consist, compares ill with most other mountain formations. Dull and insipid to begin with, it weathers a dark, dusky brown, which the liveliest play of sunshine can hardly quicken into cheerfulness. A casual observer might imagine that it was infected with the smoke of the neighbouring towns, but the sympathy thus displayed is, in reality, purely spontaneous. Smoke or no smoke, it is everywhere the same. Wherever the bracken grows plentifully ,here is a constant relief to this colour-gloom, which the heather, when in flower, helps further to dissipate, though it does not show the same vigour and brilliancy of bloom which make it dominate whole hill-sides in Scotland. Out of flower, it wears under a clouded sky an almost funereal aspect. The light green of the bilberry is not pervading enough to materially influence the scene:— and now we have said our worst.

Sheffield to Baslow, direct route by Owler Bar. (No. 10.)

Sheffield (New Market) to Abbeydale Hotel, Beauchieff, 4¼ *m; Dore and Totley Station,* 4¾ *m; Totley Inn,* 6½ *m; Peacock Inn, (Owler Bar),* 8 *m; Baslow,* 12½ *m. No tolls.*

Omnibuses daily, at 1 *p.m.; Saturdays,* 2 *p.m.; returning from Baslow at* 7 *p.m. Fares: single,* 1s. 6d.; *return,* 2s. 6d.

Pedestrians may save 4 *m. by taking the train (Mid. Sta.) to Dore and Totley.*

Quitting Sheffield by the London road, we travel side by side with the River Sheaf and the Midland Railway as far as Dore and Totley Station. *Abbeydale,* along which our route lies, is so called from *Beauchief Abbey,* the remains of which, consisting of part of the western tower and a small portion of the nave, are situated about half-a-mile up the road which strikes to the left at the *Abbeydale* Hotel, close to Beauchief Station. The Abbey is seven centuries old, and there is an unlikely legend that it was founded by an accomplice of the murderers of Thomas-a-Becket.

Steep, wood-covered hills descend into Abbeydale on the left, and on the right the ground commences to rise gradually for the moors which we are about to traverse. At *Dore and Totley Station* the railway bears away to the left, and, entering a tunnel, parts company with us for good. A bill was passed some years ago for a connecting branch from Dore to Chinley, on the Derby and Manchester line between Chapel-en-le-Frith and Marple, but so far the scheme hangs fire. This line may become a great boon to Sheffielders by enabling them to explore the inner recesses of the Peak district, which they have at present only just time to reach **in a day and** get home again, pleasant as the journey is. The **only fear is** that it will be made a lever for "developing **mineral resources,**" in which case the **longer** it remains unmade **the better.** *Di, prohibete nefas!*

The long and low Gothic building opposite Dore Station is the *Licensed Victuallers' Asylum*, built in 1878, for the infirm members of their association. A little beyond it we **commence** the ascent for Owler Bar, passing in less than two miles the village of Totley, where the *Cross Scythes Inn* makes a decided pretence of the æsthetic about its exterior. The valley now on our right sinks low, and a wide stretch of deeply troughed moorland hints at the character of the country we are about to traverse for the next few miles. A sharp pitch of the road brings us to Owler Bar and the *Peacock Inn*. The "bar" remains in name only. At it the road from Dronfield and Holmesfield, whose humpty-dumpty church has long been visible, perched high up on the hill, joins ours. Hereabouts many decayed guide-posts testify to the anxiety of former generations and the indifference of the present one about directing travellers on their way. From the "Peacock" there is a charming peep down a valley on the left, through which a country lane leads to Sheepbridge and Chesterfield. Here also the moorland road to Fox House and Hathersage (p. 35) diverges.

We are now on the high level of the moors, some 1,200 feet above sea level. The air is bracing, but the scenery monotonous, and it is a relief when, a couple of miles further, we begin to wind down the rapidly deepening ravine which opens on to the Derwent valley at Baslow.

By Curbar Edge to Calver, Stoney Middleton, and Eyam.
(*Calver*, 2½m; *Stoney Middleton*, 4m; *Eyam*, 5½m.) An old cross-road, in parts grass grown, turns to the right out of the highway. 600 yards or so beyond the tenth milestone. After a gradual ascent for half the distance, it reaches the top of *Curbar Edge*, whence a splendid view up and down the Derwent Valley breaks upon the eye. At the very top, to the right of the road, is one of the old stone pillars which served as guides in the pack-horse days before the moors were enclosed. It bears an inscription on all sides, the decipherer whereof would be cleverer than ourselves. The rock-scenery to the right of the edge is very wild.

At the top of the edge the road is crossed by one of the Duke of Rutland's Drives (p. 32). It then makes an abrupt descent through the hamlet of *Curbar* into the Baslow and Hathersage road, which it enters close to the new *Church of Calver* and just opposite the *Bridge Inn* (p. 36). Hence to *Stoney Middleton* is 1½ and to *Eyam* 3 miles. This is a pleasant alternative route for those who are familiar with the main ones.

Just beyond the divergence of the Curbar Edge route, one of the aforesaid grass drives leads in a short mile to a sandstone cross inscribed "Wellington, 1866," whence there is a charming view down the Derwent Valley. (*See* "*Matlock*" *Section*.) Behind it is the "Eagle Stone," a huge isolated block.

Gritstone crags and boulders, lying **in the** most admired confusion, now diversify **the bare** hill-side, and the new-born stream, babbling louder and louder as it leaps from stone to stone is a doubly welcome fellow-traveller after the dead silence of the moor, broken only by the whirr and "quck—qu-r-r-r-r," of a disturbed grouse or two. Presently, *Baslow* with its numerous inns.

and new Hydropathic Establishment, overlooking the village from an eminence on the right, appears below us. A few yards short of it is the **main** northern entrance to Chatsworth Park. For a description of the **village, see** *Matlock Section*. The inns in this part of it are the *Royal*, the *Wheatsheaf*, and *White's*, while a little farther on the *Peacock*, with its trimly kept coat of ivy, offers equally good accommodation **to those who wish to reach** Chatsworth with as little delay **as possible from this direction.** Chatsworth **House** is a good **mile from the entrance gate, and** besides the main drive there **is a footpath to it from the loop of the road to the** left beyond the **inns.**

For **a** full description **of** *Chatsworth* and *Baslow Village*, see p.p. 110, 132.

Sheffield to Baslow by Owler Bar and Froggatt Edge.
Route **11.**

Sheffield (*New Market*) **to** *Owler Bar* (*Peacock Inn*) **8 m;** *Chequers Inn* (*Froggatt Edge*), 12½ m; *Calver* (*Bridge Inn*), **14 m;** *Baslow Village*, 15½ m ; *Baslow* (*entrance to Chatsworth*), **16 m.**

Coach daily at 9 a.m. **Returning from Baslow at 6 p.m. Fares, single,** 1s. **6d.;** *return*, 2s.

Pedestrians may **save** *half a mile between* **The Chequers Inn and** *Calver.*

This route is the same as the one last described as far as *Owler* **Bar.** Hence the road crosses the moor for nearly two miles in a north-westerly direction, **and presents no feature of special interest until it turns to the left, and commences the descent into the Derwent valley, across** which a very fine view is at once revealed up the Hope valley, in the direction of Castleton. Hathersage, backed by Win Hill, is seen **far below, and Mam Tor rises in the background.** Westwards, **a road wonderfully made, straight as a die, and apparently steep as a house-side, climbs the** opposite hill. This is *Sir William Road* leading from Grindleford Bridge to Tideswell, **over Eyam Moor.** Gradually descending, we pass a wayside inn, and **then swerve sharply to the right, so as to double the** cliffs **of** *Froggatt Edge*. **The view across and up the valley now becomes very beautiful. Above us impend the towering crags,** and below, the hill, **strewn with loose boulders, drops steeply to the river** side, **beyond which the hills, broken by one densely wooded combe** rise with **equal abruptness. Then the** green **pastures rising to** Eyam appear, **and a glimpse is** caught of the limestone **cliffs of** Middleton Dale. **The transition from** gritstone to limestone **about** Eyam and Stoney **Middleton is very** sudden, and the character of the country undergoes **a** corresponding change. The gritstone escarpments crown the hills, the limestone ones are their footstool.

Half a mile short of the bottom of the valley is the **Chequers Inn**, an old-fashioned and deservedly favourite resort of pleasure seekers. It is beautifully situated in a shady part of the road and overlooks a charming reach of the Derwent.

Foot road between the Chequers and Calver. Pedestrians may save half a mile by taking a lane on the left hand about a quarter of a mile beyond the "Chequers," and in another half mile descending by a private road (*public f.p.*) to the river-side. The private road rejoins the highway close to Calver Bridge.

The Chequers to Eyam (*foot-road*) 2½ m. Descend by the lane which commences a little north of the inn to Froggatt Hamlet. Cross the Derwent by Froggatt Bridge, and proceed up the shady lane opposite, with Stoke Hall on the right hand, till you join the main road from Baslow to Hathersage. Cross this road and continue straight on by a footpath which ascends steeply through two fields, and then strikes into the Hathersage and Eyam high-road, a mile short of Eyam village. (*For Eyam, see p.* 81.) This route is all but straight from end to end. After entering the Eyam road it commands a fine view over Middleton Dale and Village.

Half a mile beyond the Chequers we cross the Derwent by *New Bridge*, as it is called, below which the free course of the unfortunate river has within the last year been still further curbed for commercial purposes. There are footways on both sides of the bridge going direct to *Calver Bridge*. Our road makes a wide *détour* round a grassy knoll, joining the Hathersage and Baslow road at a point whence those who wish to visit Stoney Middleton may take a field-path along the brook-side. A quarter of a mile further, the high-road from Stoney Middleton converges, and the Bakewell road climbs the hill to the right. There is a small inn at the junction.

Calver to Bakewell. (4⅜ m.) The road ascends the narrow green valley which separates Longstone Edge from the heights between Chatsworth and Bakewell. In about 2 miles it reaches the village of *Hassop*, shady and picturesque, with a hall which was garrisoned for the King in the Parliamentary War. A road branches off to the right here for *Longstone Village*, (1¼ m.) beyond which it reaches in another mile the Bakewell and Tideswell road at a point from which there is a very beautiful view of Monsal Dale. (*p.* 71.)

From Hassop Village the road descends to *Hassop Station* (*good inn*) where it crosses the railway, and in another 1½ miles passes over the Wye Bridge **into** *Bakewell*.

Passing to the left of *Calver*, we cross the Derwent again, close to a huge mill. On the other side of the bridge are the new *Church* of Calver and the *Bridge Inn*. The rest of the road to **Baslow** along the east side of the Derwent needs no description. The village is entered close to the Derwent bridge and the church. The situation of the latter, close to the river-side, and encompassed by lime trees, is extremely picturesque. The fabric is 3 centuries old, and is remarkable for its short, stumpy tower. Considerable additions have lately been made. The principal Baslow inns are ¼ mile further, on the Sheffield road, and close to the entrance to Chatsworth.

Rte. 12.] SHEFFIELD TO CASTLETON. 37

Sheffield to Hathersage and Castleton. Route 12.

Sheffield to *Fox House*, 8 m; *Hathersage*, 11 m; *Hope*, 15½ m; *Castleton*, 17 m.

Four-horse Coach (*Monday, Wednesday, Friday*), at 8.30 a.m. Fares, 2s. 6d.; return, 5s. Passengers for Buxton may proceed by afternoon Coach from Castleton (p. 95).

A very interesting drive or walk all the way. The descent from Fox House to Hathersage affords one of the finest prospects to be obtained from any carriage-road in the country. But for this particular view, which should be missed by no tourist who wishes to return home with a correct appreciation of the district he is visiting, the alternative route herein described by Ringinglow is a preferable one for pedestrians, and not impracticable for carriages.

Quitting Sheffield by the Ecclesall road, we pass for more than a mile along the dead level of the *Porter Valley*. On the left is the pleasant suburb of *Sharrow*, and on the right, as soon as we begin to ascend, the statelier mansions of *Ranmoor* come into view. Between them and ourselves we leave the Porter as it debouches from its prettily wooded little glen, a favourite strolling ground with Sheffielders. As we rise to Ecclesall church, a public-house on the left, called the *Banner Cross Hotel*—every little pot-house in and about Sheffield, is an hotel—reminds us unpleasantly of the notorious Peace, who committed one of his most detestable crimes in this neighbourhood. Ecclesall church is the mother church of a considerable part of Sheffield.

Sheffield to Hathersage by Ringinglow. 10 m. The Ringinglow road strikes to the right out of the main Hathersage road a few yards short of Ecclesall Church, which it passes on the left hand. It maintains a high level all the way to Ringinglow, and during the leafy season of the year, commands a very attractive retrospect over the Porter Valley and the Ranmoor suburb. At **Ringinglow** (5¼ m. Inn: *Norfolk Arms*), it enters the moorland. There is an old road, now little better than a cart-track, leading directly over the moor from Ringinglow to Fox House (2½ m.).

From Ringinglow we proceed for 2 miles along a road, now little used for vehicular traffic, to *Upper Burbage Bridge*, whence a view opens southwards down the wild Burbage Valley. On the right of it rises the rocky wilderness which contains the old British Fort called *Carl Wark* and *Higgar Tor*. Cael or Carl Wark gives unmistakeable evidence of the purposes which it once served, but there is nothing whatever artificial about the appearance of Higgar Tor, or to justify the Ordnance Survey marking it as a Druidical Remain. The latter height is easily reached from the road about half a mile beyond Burbage Bridge, and the *détour* to it should be made, not only for the closer inspection of the fantastic rocks which constitute it, but also for the fine view commanded by it to the west and south. In the former direction, the Castleton Valley, extending to Mam Tor is seen, and in the latter, the richly wooded stretch of the Derwent valley between Hathersage and Baslow. From it a direct descent may be made to Hathersage by a rough road, down a steep wood-girt valley. Between Burbage Bridge and Hathersage there are obvious short cuts.

Leaving *Ecclesall Church* on our right, we proceed for 2 miles to **Whirlow Bridge,** where our road enters Derbyshire. Here is a good inn by the side of the Whirlow brook, which descends from the higher ground on the right, near Ringinglow, through the sweetest dingle within 5 miles of any large town in England. For a full mile the little stream descends between steep hills, on which the trees do not leave a bare spot, and whose floor is carpeted with brake, **male fern and** lady fern, and in summer time with bluebells **innumerable.** There is a good path from the inn, keeping the brook **on the left hand** until the wood is left behind, after which **half-a-mile's further** ascent by the water-side brings us out close to the inn at Ringinglow.

From Whirlow Bridge the road continues **an upward course,** passing *Dore Moor Inn*, and affording a wide view over Abbeydale on the left hand. The church tower about a mile to the left is that of Dore, and the squat little one on the top of the high ridge beyond it, Holmesfield. At the bottom of the valley the railway may be seen entering the Dronfield tunnel. As we proceed the country becomes more and more wild. We shall probably hear the qu-r-r-r of a grouse or two, and we cross here and there a deepening ravine. At the very highest part of the road, in the bleakest position imaginable, and some 1,250 feet above sea-level, stands the *Stony Ridge* toll-gate.* This is the only Derbyshire road out of Sheffield on which tolls have not been abolished. The venerable keeper of it seldom leaves his eyrie—" there's so many draughts," he says, " i' Sheffield," he " allers catches cold." Hence a view opens up in front to Eyam Moor, Mam **Tor,** and the Kinder Scout ridge, with Higgar Tor and Carl Wark nearer at hand on the right. A slight descent leads to the time-honoured **Fox House Inn.** Here is a wonderful piece of oak carving in the shape of a cabinet, on whose panels are represented in bold, not to say grotesque, fashion various scenes from the New Testament. In the window-recess of the same room with it is an old oak table from Haddon Hall, and the landlord has several other interesting antiquities.

Fox House to Baslow by Froggatt Edge. This route joins the one from Sheffield to Baslow by Owler Bar (*p.* 35) in ¾ mile.

Fox House to Grindleford Bridge, 2½ m ; and **Eyam, 5** m. This road, branching to the left a few yards beyond Fox House, passes *Longshaw*—a shooting-box of the Duke of Rutland—and descends by the *Burbage* **Brook**, through one of the sweetest little glens in Derbyshire. A mile from Fox House a gate opens on to a green track running parallel with the road. From this you may in a few hundred yards descend and cross the stream by the second wooden bridge, ascending again on the other side to the *Surprise* (*p.* 39), or on re-entering the road you may take a cart-track to the right and go by the old chapel of Padley and the riverside to *Hathersage.*

From **Grindleford Bridge** (*Inn*) the road rises rapidly, and affords beautiful views over the Derwent and Middleton Dales. (*For Eyam, see* p. 81.)

From Fox House the **Hathersage road turns** abruptly to the right, and after descending for half a mile crosses *Lower Burbage Bridge.* During the descent some exceedingly bold rock-scenery appears in front. Its culminating ridge is **Higgar Tor**—a corruption according to an enthusiastic writer on Derbyshire scenery of Hu-Gaer, " the city of God." Cavillers at this derivation should bethink themselves of Ben Ledi, in Perthshire, which is thought by **many to mean the "** Hill of God," and upon which, we are told,

* Abolished (1887).

the worshippers of the god "Bel" were wont to receive from their Druids the "need fire" annually on the 1st of May. The Ordnance surveyors have regarded the huge and strangely placed blocks of gritstone which crown the summit of Higgar Tor, as "Druidical Remains," and though their present arrangement, however extraordinary, has nothing artificial in its appearance, favourers of the druidical theory may gather a grain of comfort from the apparently analogous case of Ben Ledi which we have quoted.

Higgar Tor, which, by the way, is best visited from the Ringinglow route to Hathersage (p. 37), is recognisable from our present route by the circumstance of its highest block being arched so as to admit daylight through it.

Between Burbage Bridge and Higgar Tor, and approached either by the green drive, a little short of the bridge, or by a footpath just a little beyond it, is a lower group of rocks which, on close examination, betray much stronger evidence of human interference. This is Carl Wark (derivation very uncertain)—said to be an ancient British stronghold. Oblong in shape it covers several acres of ground. To the north and east Nature has built impregnable buttresses of rock, but westwards the rampart is almost entirely artificial, consisting of small uncemented boulders, at the south end of which is an entrance between the débris of two walls. There are two short cuts from Carl Wark to Hathersage by roughish roads, but both miss the view-point we are about to describe. The tracks to Carl Wark, by the bye, are by grace and not by right; and when the Duke of Rutland is at Longshaw, trespass is not winked at.

A few yards from the bridge, on the right of the road, is the *Toad's Mouth*, a block of gritstone, bearing before and behind a marvellous likeness to that interesting reptile.

From Burbage Bridge, our road turns south-west again, and rises slightly for nearly a mile. Then, at a sudden turn to the right between two rocks called *Millstone Edge Nick* or the "Surprise," there bursts upon the eye the handsomest view in the midland counties. The main features are Hope Dale, wide and pastoral, in front, and the valley of the Derwent, narrow and beautifully wooded, reaching far away to the south. Between the two is a sylvan V-shaped glen down which the Highlow brook flows to its confluence with the Derwent. The principal hills are Win and Lose Hill on the right of Hopedale, the narrow ridge of the latter stretching westwards to Mam Tor, behind which rises the still loftier ridge, uniting it with Kinder Scout; Offerton Moor, between Hopedale and the Highlow brook; Eyam Moor south of the latter, and the long line of edges flanking the Derwent on the east. In the foreground green meadows slope steeply to the river-side and here again as we look down upon a beautiful reach of the river spanned by a rustic bridge, our thoughts hark back to the Teith and Callander Bridge, as seen from Ben Ledi—twin scenes of beauty, such as an artist might make his name and fortune by faithfully depicting.

Hathersage, to which we now descend, is a small village which certainly might turn to better account the great advantages of its situation. At present it is dominated by two or three hideous chimneys, and is mainly dependent for its prosperity on needles and shackle **pins**. The principal inns (small but comfortable) **are** the *George* and the *Ordnance Arms*. The *Church* is graceful in itself, and most picturesquely placed on rising ground **north of the village**. In the churchyard, south of the church, is the **reputed grave of " Little John,"** who is also said to have been born **here. It is marked by two** small stones, which **by their** position **make " Little " John to have** been ten feet high.

There are many pleasant walks and drives from Hathersage.

(1.) **Higgar Tor and Carl Wark,** 5—6 m. Take the old road to Sheffield **which climbs** steeply up a narrow valley due east, and diverge on to the moor as soon as you get underneath the Tor. *For a description of the Tor, see* p. 37. **Carl Wark** is the lower rocky platform half a mile further south, and has already been described, as well as the return from it to Hathersage, on page 37.

(2.) **To Eyam, Stoney Middleton,** &c. See route from Castleton to Rowsley, p. 96. Go over Eyam Moor and return by Grindleford Bridge.

(3.) **To Ashopton, Lady Bower,** &c., going or returning over Win Hill. See below.

The road from Hathersage to Castleton keeps along the **bottom of Hope Dale** all the way, and the valley when thus seen does **not** show **to** the **same** advantage as from the different heights which overlook it. In 2 miles we reach *Mytham Bridge* (inn), **where the** main Derwent valley diverges to the right between Win **Hill** and Bamford Edge. The **inns** about here are favourite fishing resorts.

Win Hill and Ashopton. From Mytham **Bridge the Derwent Valley** turns northwards to Ashopton, distant by road 3 **miles.** The route **calls for** little description. It passes (¾ m.) the charmingly situated village of *Bamford* and (2 m.) *Yorkshire Bridge Inn*, beyond which it forks, the left branch leading to *Ashopton Inn* and the right to *Lady Bower Inn*, both on the high-road between Sheffield and Glossop. The pedestrian should cross **Win** Hill on his way to Ashopton and return by road. From Mytham Bridge to Ashopton by this route will take about 1½ hours. There is also an inn at Bamford.

Leave the Castleton road by a footpath about 200 yards **beyond** the milestone on the west side of Mytham Bridge. This path leads in ¼ m. to the hamlet of *Thornhill*, on a spur of Win Hill, where it enters a lane passing through the hamlet. Continue upwards first along a grass-lane and then across fields, skirting the S.W. corner of a plantation just before reaching the steep pitch which leads to the top of Win Hill. For the view from the summit see p. 43. The descent to Ashopton is at first eastwards for a short distance along the spur, and then northwards till you strike a path which takes **you off the moor to a** wall, whence you may drop directly into Ashopton. If **bound for Castleton, you** may descend from the summit to Hope as directed **on p. 43.**

Between 2 and 3 miles beyond Mytham Bridge is the village of **Hope**, with several inns (The *Hall*, &c.) Hence the Edale road diverges on the right. The *Church* of Hope is noticeable for the thickness of its spire. The present chancel was built in place of the old one in 1881. Between Hope and Castleton the most noteworthy object is a huge chimney, which materially detracts from the beauty of the valley. Mam Tor, the " shivering mountain," is the monarch of the scene as we approach **Castleton**, for a description of which village see p. 84.

Sheffield to Ashopton and Glossop. Route 13.

Sheffield to Norfolk Arms, **6** *m*; *Lady Bower Inn*, **10½** *m*; *Ashopton Inn*, **11½** *m*; *Snake Inn*, 18 *m*; *Glossop*, 25 *m*.

Coach *from Sheffield to Ashopton daily* **from about** *Whitsuntide to end of October at* **1 p.m.**; *Saturdays*, **2** *p.m. Returning at* **6 to 7 p.m.** *Fares*: *single*, **1s. 6d.**; *return*, 2s. 6d.*

The direct road from Sheffield to Glossop threads the valleys of the Rivelin and the Ashop, between and at each end of which it crosses three considerable ridges, the highest,—that between the "Snake" and Glossop—being 1,667 feet above sea-level. The valley of the Ashop is one of the most beautiful in the Peak district, and that of the Rivelin, though somewhat marred by its proximity to Sheffield, is by no means devoid of interest.

The Route. Leaving Sheffield in a westerly direction by the Glossop road and Broomhill, we ascend continuously for about 2 miles. The fashionable suburb of Ranmoor and the Porter valley lie below us on the left. A corresponding descent then takes us into the depths of the Rivelin valley.

Route *vid* **Redmires and Stanage Edge** to Ashopton (13 m.), or Hathersage (10 m.). Instead of descending to the Rivelin Valley, we may turn to the left at the highest point between it and Sheffield, and follow a good high-level road to the 3 reservoirs at *Redmires* (distance from Sheffield 6 m.). This road commands fine views into the Rivelin Valley on the right, and the green glade of Whiteley Wood on the left. On the road-side by the reservoirs there is a small public-house, called the "Grouse and Trout." Beyond it the road skirts two sides of the last reservoir, from the side of which an enterprising caterer offers what is called an "Ocean View,"—and then ascends a dreary stretch of moor by a rough cart-track to the highest ground (7½ m. *from Sheffield*). Here, just beyond a gaunt wind-swept plantation, is a little cluster of boulders, on which **Stanage Pole**, a long-standing landmark, has lately been re-erected. A wide panorama extending to Riber Castle over Matlock in the south, to Axe Edge and its associate hogs-back ridges beyond Buxton in the west, and to the table land of Kinderscout in the north-west, suddenly breaks upon the eye, but there is no happy contrast of verdant vale and wood-fringed stream until we have walked nearly half-a-mile further, to the edge itself. Then we obtain a charming and characteristic view. Immediately in front the ground sinks only to rise again to the top of Bamford Edge, beyond which the clear-cut outline of Win Hill rises in front of the over-topping ridge of Kinder, but southwards a charming view reveals itself of Hathersage and the Derwent Valley, and westwards, too, the village of Castleton may be seen with the "Winnats" beyond it and Mam Tor on its right hand. From our point of observation, the road onwards may be seen taking a wide sweep to the right round the head of the valley, whence one branch crosses the southern slope of *Bamford Edge*, and drops into the Hathersage and Ashopton road, ¼ m. short of *Yorkshire Bridge Inn*, and another goes due south to *Hathersage*. The Ashopton Inn is 1¼ m. beyond Yorkshire Bridge Inn. The pedestrian will probably "make tracks" from Stanage Edge.

Dropping to the Rivelin Valley, we cross, a little short of the bottom, a picturesque little glen threaded by a streamlet called

* Except (perhaps) Tu. and Th.

Black Brook. Thence we pursue the valley, closely hemmed in by steep and rocky hills, past a couple of reservoirs. Into the first of them the *Wyming Brook* falls through a rocky dell, musical with countless cascades, shaded with fir and birch, and so blocked with rough boulders and undergrowth as to be well nigh impassable. Hereabouts we come to the *Norfolk Arms Inn*, a pleasant little house of call, boasting among its treasures some old ale which might convert Sir Wilfred Lawson. Beyond it the road climbs the north side of the valley to the scattered hamlet of *Hollow Meadows*. Rising from the heathery moorland on the left are a few isolated stacks of rocks, to which such fanciful names as "Stump John," the "Cock-crowing Stone," have been given. Then, 8½ miles from Sheffield, and at a height of 1,181 feet above sea-level, the road enters Derbyshire. Right a-head appear the pimply crest of Win Hill and the grassy peak of Lose Hill, to the right of it, with Mam Tor and Lord's Seat in the space between. The tame side of Derwent Edge is immediately in front of us on the right hand of the road, and crowned by a castle-like group of rocks, called *Hurking Stones*. A few yards further, we pass on the right hand the shooting-box of *Moscar Lodge*, beyond which a moorland road to Penistone strikes off on the same side. Then, as our road descends, the sameness of the heather-clad upland gives place to a valley rapidly deepening and growing in picturesqueness. A pleasant stream babbles down it, passing under the road at "*Cut-throat Bridge*." The repulsive story in connection with this bridge, is that a man killed his horse upon it because the animal could not or would not proceed any further.

Footpath to Derwent Edge (1¼ m.), &c. From this bridge a footpath strikes upward to the right, and in a few hundred yards taking the second sharp turn to the left, is faintly maintained to a point from which *Derwent Chapel* and *Dale* burst upon the eye with a most effective suddenness. From this point a round-about path may be pursued by the side of the wall northwards to the *Village*; a hap-hazard descent may be made through the nick in front into the road between Ashopton and the village. or the brink of the Edge may be followed southwards by a narrow path from the end of which you may zig-zag down by a couple of cottages to the back of *Ashopton Inn*, or descend upon *Lady Bower Inn*. Northwards, along the Edge at irregular intervals are isolated bosses or excrescences of rock, which with more or less reason have received such fanciful names as the "Cakes of Bread" "Lost Lad," the "Salt Cellar." The Salt Cellar, 1½ miles north of our present view-point, has a very singular shape, consisting of a number of horizontally placed slices, very much screwed in at the waist. All these, we are told, have been worn into their present form by the action of the sea. A walk along the Edge as far as the Salt Cellar, is very interesting, but in the breeding and shooting season, at all events, the tourist must not forget that promiscuous wandering about these heathery wastes is not permitted. An obvious descent may be made from the "Salt Cellar" to Derwent Chapel.

Our road now continuing its descent at some height above the stream, which flows through a ferny dingle overshadowed by birch, mountain-ash and other trees, reaches the **Lady Bower Inn**, a clean and comfortable hostelry in a situation of great natural beauty. Fishing can be had for half-a-crown a day in the Lady Bower Brook and the Ashop. (*See Introduction, p. XVIII.*)

Rte. 13.] SHEFFIELD TO ASHOPTON. 43

From Lady Bower *Hathersage* is 5 m. distance by a good road which follows the course of the Derwent past the *Yorkshire Bridge Inn*, 1 m., the delightfully placed village of *Bamford* with its modern church (2 m.) and Mytham Bridge (3 m.). At the last named place the high-road from Sheffield or Baslow to Castleton (4. m) is joined (p. 40). *Inns also at Bamford and Mytham Bridge.*

At **Ashopton** we enter the main Derwent valley, just where the waters of the Ashop, coming down from Kinder Scout and the Glossop moors, join it. The inn and one or two farm-houses constitute the hamlet, which is, as it were, the axle of a wheel, of which the roads to Sheffield, Hathersage, Glossop, and Derwent Chapel are the spokes. In all directions the scenery ranks amongst the finest of the Peak district, and the ascent of Win Hill is **as** pleasant **and** remunerative **a** little climb as any in Derbyshire. The inn **is excellent.**

Win Hill, 1532 *ft*; 950 *ft. above Ashopton.* ½ *hr.* Cross the Derwent and the Ashop by the bridges a few yards beyond the inn. Then, passing through **a** gate beyond **a** farm-house, turn into the field on the right and follow the footpath till it forks, **a** little **short** of another farm-house. **Take the** left hand **branch, pass** through **one stile** and over another, **then through** the second **gate-way, leaving** the **farm-house** 150 yards below **on the right.** Here the top **comes into view, and** the path, indistinct for **a few yards,** makes straight **towards it, reaching** the **open moor close to a trespass**board. *Win Hill* **forms a** sharp ridge from east to west. It commands, on the south-west, a full panorama of the wide pastoral **valley of Hopedale, with** Castleton lying beneath the famous **Castle of the Peveril, the Winnats and Mam Tor at** its upper end, and a frightful **brick** chimney **in the** middle. **In the south-east the** valley of the Derwent extends beyond Hathersage. **East and north are the lofty** Edges separating the Derwent from Yorkshire, while to **the north-west and west,** the lower parts of the valleys **of** Ashopdale and Edale **contribute a full share to** the beauty of the panorama, which, without being **either grand or wildly ro**mantic, **is** thoroughly beautiful. The hill opposite Win Hill **on the far side of the** entrance **to** Edale, by the **way, is** called Lose Hill, though **it is manifestly some**what **the higher** of the two. How they got their respective **names is matter for** curious speculation. **Arrow-heads found in the** neighbouring **heights give** colour to **the local tradition that a great battle was once won and lost on the** two ! **The date was something between 500 and 1500 A.D. You may** descend Win Hill directly either to *Hathersage* or *Hope*. **For** the former, **make for** the corner **of a plantation, follow a** wall **southwards for a** short distance, and then keep **along the top of the spur of the hill, through the** hamlet of *Thornhill*, whence **a** footpath leads **straight down to** *Mytham Bridge* **on the** Castleton and Hathersage road, 2 m. **short of Hathersage.** *Time from the top,* 1¼ *hrs.* For *Hope*, continue along the top-ridge **for 5 minutes, and then descend by an** obvious footpath into the Edale **road, about** ¼ **m. north of Hope.** *Time* ¾ *hr.*

Ashopton to Penistone by the Upper Derwent Valley.

Ashopton to Derwent Chapel, 1½ *m*; *Ouzelden Bridge,* 3¾ *m* ; *Abbey Farm,* 4¼ *m* ; *Howden Farm (end of carriage road),* 5 *m* ; *Slippery Stones,* 7 *m* ; *Langsett (Inn),* 12½ *m* ; *Penistone Station,* 15½ *m*. *Time,* 4½—5½ *hours.*

There is no public right **of way between Howden Farm and** Slippery Stones. In case of objection it is necessary to **cross the Derwent** at Ouzelden Bridge and recross at Slippery Stones, where there **is a right of** way, but neither bridge nor stepping stone. This walk is **a little** longer, and by it you risk a wetting.

We have fully described the route between Penistone and Abbey Farm—the reverse way—on page 28, where the tourist will find some general remarks upon it. Taken this way the grand "coup" **of** the Derwent Valley from the ridge between **it** and Penistone is missed, but the walk for **the** first 10 miles, at all events, is of a most interesting character. Afterwards the scenery falls into that of an ordinary upland district. No **one** should attempt **the walk in this direc**tion without a good margin of daylight before him.

The Route. A **few** yards west **of the** Ashopton Inn, the upper Derwent Valley road strikes northwards **up** the narrow pass down which its waters flow to their confluence with **the** Ashop. In a long 1½ miles we reach **Derwent Chapel, a** village which possesses besides its charming situation, some traditional interest. In monkish time a large portion of the valley was given to the **Abbey of Welbeck in Notts.** The farmstead called Abbey Grange, 2½ miles higher **up** the **dale, is close to one of** four **chapels** which once testified to the proprietorship. *Derwent Hall,* **by the** river-side, belongs to and **is an** occasional residence **of the** Duke of Norfolk. **It is** about 2 centuries **old, and has** recently **been enlarged. Adjoining the house is a** Roman Catholic **chapel. A** drive has **also been lately made, rejoining the public** road three-quarter miles north **of the village.**

From the entrance to the Hall the road leaves the river-side **and climbs a little to the right, passing on the same side the** modern church, an **unassuming, but well proportioned little fabric with a** graceful spire. **It contains two relics of the former chapel,—a font, 200 years** old, and a finely **engraved chalice half as old again.**

Mill Brook, **after descending through a deep and impressive clough from Derwent Edge, flows into the Derwent** close to the chapel. **Our road onward continues for nearly two miles** some way above the main stream **from which it is separated by the hall and** its grounds. **The flanking hills are for a time somewhat lower and** tamer, the main ridge **of** Derwent Edge having **retired behind the Mill Brook** depression, and there is nothing specially noteworthy until **we drop by a steep pitch to** Ouzelden Bridge, where, as before stated, the strictly orthodox **route to Penistone crosses to the** west side of the river. **Continuing, however, along the east side we reach in another half** mile **the** *Abbey Farm,* **where are the remains of the** old chapel above mentioned, **in appropriate proximity to a grove of yew trees.**

In another half mile the carriage road ceases at *Howden Farm,* **and we pass through a gate on to a green cart-track, which becomes a** fair road again **after crossing one or two fields, and degenerates into a rough** foot-track at *Slippery Stones* **(see p. 29).** Here we leave the **Derwent side and follow for a** few yards **the deep ravine called** *Cranberry Clough.* **Tourists who wish to hear the very first infant lisp of the Derwent, may continue along its side and make their way in a few miles over the moors to the** *Woodhead Station* **at the west end of the Woodhead Tunnel on the main M.S. and L. line, but there is no track, and the writer can well believe a by no means encouraging description of the route which he obtained from a local authority.**

In crossing from Slippery Stones **to Langsett, care is required. The track, at first unmistakeable,** crosses **the Cranberry stream at once, and a few yards further, that of** *Bull Clough,* **a short and deep ravine coming down from the north. Then turning abruptly to the left it climbs the spur between the two, keeping Bull Clough in view for some time, and reaching the top of the ridge at a spot known as** *Cut Gate.* **The retrospect during the ascent is very fine ; for a description of it see p. 29. From the summit the path enters a well defined pass through the peat bog, which is called on the Ordnance Survey** *Black Dyke.* **On both sides there are banks of peat a few feet high. The footing is generally firm and sandy, and as we proceed we find that our route is in reality a water-course, the bed of which we follow for about 20 minutes, and then skirt its left hand side. Gradually the prospect in front opens** up—**a somewhat dull one—and in a few minutes more the track crosses to the** right hand **side of the stream, a few yards short of a lateral ravine on the left.** Continue **along the track, with the deepening ravine on the left, for about a** mile, and then, **about 500 yards short of a gateway seen in front, strike across the** moor **to the right. You will see almost at once a wall that comes up from the gateway and makes an obtuse angle ¼ mile in front of you. Make for this angle and then, keeping a rough track alongside the wall, you will in another half-mile reach a moorland farm called "North America." Hence the position of Langsett is seen at the top of a lane across the Little Don – nearly a mile away. Descend to the stream by a path and cross it by or below a footbridge.**

N.B. If you have any doubt as to the point at which to quit the path beyond **Black Dyke, keep on it as far as the** gateway **and then turn sharp and follow the wall all the way to "North America."**

At **Langsett** there is a fair **little inn**, the *Waggon and Horses*. Hence to reach Penistone by the shortest **and easiest** way, follow the main road down the Little **Don** Valley, till you cross a **brooklet** about half a mile distant. A few yards further take a footpath which commences at a stone step-stile on the left, and ascend half-way between two farm-houses, the right hand one of which is placed high up on a projecting knoll. At the top of a hill you will enter a road which will take **you** directly into Penistone. All these paths and roads have been carefully marked upon our general map. For *Penistone* see p. 28.

Crook Hill. This hill occupies the angle between the Ashop **and** the Derwent dales, and is easily reached in about twenty minutes from Ashopton Inn. The way up is by a footpath starting from the far **side of** the Derwent Bridge. There are two tops—knobs of rock—both of which **command** charming views into and across the valleys below.

From Ashopton **the Glossop roads ascends** the *Ashop Dale* all the way to the Snake **Inn. This is the most** beautiful part of our route. Indeed, **in simple and happy combination** of wood, hill, and water, **the valley of the Ashop may vie with any of** its kindred dales. Less **stern** than Edale, **and less wild than** the upper part of Derwent **Dale, it** produces **on the mind a more pleasing impression of varied and picturesque grouping than** either.

Ashopdale into Edale. At the farm-house of *Grimbo Car*, 1½ miles beyond Ashopton, **the** Ashop is crossed by a foot-bridge from the far side of which a path starts up the hill **to the lowest part of the ridge between these two** valleys. An old Roman road **runs along the ridge, and on** it, ¾ mile from the foot-bridge **and 1,064 feet above sea-level (***see map***) is** an old guide-post, inscribed "Sheffield, Hope, Edale, Glossop, 1737," **and** called the "**Pillar.**" It is **of sandstone, and 8** feet high. The **nearest cut into** Edale is some way south **of this pillar, and an** interesting **way on to Castleton is** by a footpath which crosses **the ridge between** Edale **and Hopedale just beyond** Back Tor, the precipitous **face of rock** between **Lose Hill and Mam Tor.** *Distance, Ashopton to Castleton*, 7—8 m.

As we proceed, the bold northern edges of Kinderscout appear prominently on the left. The first is *Black Dean Edge*, and beyond it is *Seat Edge*, separated by a short clough from the bold bluff of *Fairbrook Naze*, one of the most effective escarpments in the district. Beyond *Allport Bridge*, where the pretty Allport valley opens on the right, the country becomes less cultivated, and at the **Snake Inn** we are on the verge of the wilderness. The Snake is a clean and comfortable inn, though not in the most cheerful of situations. From it Hayfield may be reached in about 6 miles by climbing to a height of about 1,800 feet round the northern spur of Kinderscout; or the northern cairn of Kinderscout (1,981 *ft.*) may be reached in 3 miles by following the same route until you are immediately beneath it. We can hardly recommend either route. There is no authorized track, the scenery, except during the descent on the far side of Kinder, is monotonous, and there is the risk of being stopped by the gamekeepers.

Beyond the Snake, **the valley** contracts, and **the** road rapidly ascends through it till it reaches the bare unlovely top of the moor at the highest point on the journey (1,667 *ft.*). We are now fairly out of the Peak district, and the descent to Glossop, which is a convenient station for getting on to Manchester or back to Sheffield, calls for no comment. For *Glossop* see p. 27.

Ashbourne and Dovedale Section.

Ashbourne. (*Pop.* 3,500. Inns, the *Green Man and Black's Head*, ¼ m. from station; *Wheatsheaf, White Hart*, &c.) *Letter Box closes* 6.30 *p.m.*

Ashbourne is, perhaps, next to Bakewell, the most pleasantly situated town in Derbyshire. Not that it possesses, either in itself or in its immediate neighbourhood, any special claim on the tourist's attention—always excepting its church. It does not even boast a river. The Dove, which has been making straight for it all the way from its rise amid the bleak uplands of Buxton, suddenly turns aside after issuing from Dovedale, to wander through the green meadows of Mayfield and Ellaston, and leaves Ashbourne on a siding. Nothing but a stern sense of duty to the public as a guide-book writer, enables us to remember that the insignificant tributary which runs the length of the town is called the Henmoor. For all that, Ashbourne is a most satisfactory place for a comfortably disposed tourist to commence his wanderings from. To begin with, he has a really good old-fashioned inn, the "Green Man," with a sign swinging all across the street, and the joint for his dinner or supper, as the case may be, hanging from the rafters of the open passage by which he enters. Then he has green hills, crowned with rich foliage, all around him, and close at hand a church, which is as graceful and picturesque in its general appearance as it is weak and incongruous in many of its details.* No other building in Ashbourne calls for special description. The town is amongst the oldest in the midland counties, but the only historical record of any interest in connection with it is the proclamation of the Young Pretender as King of Great Britain in its market-place a few days before the famous "Black Friday" of 1745.

Ashbourne Church, close to the railway station, is more than six centuries old. Its shape is cruciform, and its style mainly Early English and Decorated. The most beautiful portion is the spire, upwards of 200 feet high, eight-sided, like that of Bakewell, but much lighter and more pleasing in appearance. The spacious chancel is Early English, and was restored by the late Sir Gilbert Scott. The interior contains many antiquarian features, but is chiefly interesting for its monuments, one of which—that of a child of the Boothby family—displays as great a triumph over the cold inexpressiveness of marble as a sculptor ever achieved.

Note, 1881. The church has been well restored.

The figure tells its own history, and we will only repeat the last sentence of a well worn description of it, which we have noticed in every recent guide-book—" The man whom this does not affect wants one of the finest sources of genuine sensibility; his heart cannot be formed to relish the beauty either of nature or of art." Of its sculptor, **T.** Banks, R.A., it may be truly said, " Vivos duxit de marmore vultus."

Ashbourne to Dovedale, Tissington, Hartington, Bakewell, Buxton, &c.   Route 14.

Ashbourne to south end of Dovedale (viâ Thorpe), 4 m. (*footpath, viâ Mappleton*, ½ *m. longer); Dove Holes (north end of Dovedale footpath*), 6 m.; *Mill Dale* **Hamlet,** 7 *m*; *Buxton road*, 8½ *m*; *Newhaven Inn*, 12 *m*; *Bakewell*, 19 *m*.

Détours. *Ashbourne* **to south end** *of Dovedale, viâ Tissington,* 6 *m*.

Mill **Dale to Wetton and Thor's Cave, 3** *m. Thor's Cave to* **Izaak Walton Inn (***south end of Dovedale***), viâ Ilam,** 5 *m*.

Mill Dale to Hartington, viâ Beresford Dale (footpath), 5 *m*.

Return from Mill **Dale to Ashbourne by Buxton Road and** *Tissington*, 7 *m*.

Newhaven Inn to Rowsley Station, by Youlgreave, 8 m.

Newhaven Inn to Buxton (*high road***), 11** *m*.

General Remarks. The attraction of **all these routes centres in** Dovedale, without traversing which from **end to end no one** can fully appreciate the beauty of **Derbyshire scenery.** Well worthy **of a** visit, too, are Tissington, **Ilam, Thor's Cave, Beresford Dale, and some** of the river bits between **Hartington and Buxton.** The general level **of the country between Ashbourne, Buxton and** Bakewell **is very** high, **especially in the immediate** south **of** Buxton, **where it is as much as 1,500** feet **above the sea.** The hill scenery, as **is frequently the case in** limestone districts, is tame and featureless—a **wide area of pasture** and meadow land, intersected **by numberless stone walls, and varied only by green** knolls **upon whose summits desolate groups of fir and beech trees** carry **on a brave but unequal contest with the winds which attack** them **from every quarter. It is only along the river-courses that** real **richness and beauty of prospect is to be found, and these** coming **suddenly upon the eye as it is growing wearied with the** upland **bleakness, and seen from the vantage ground of lofty hills,** give this **part of Derbyshire its claim to be regarded as a tourist** district. **The depth and steepness of the defile through which** the Dove **forces its way in its most beautiful part prevents its** extending **any influence on the scenery beyond its immediate** proximity, **but the wider valleys of the Wye and the Derwent with** their tributary **streams afford a number of exquisite landscapes** wherever we approach **the eastern side of the plateau we have** been describing.

Choice of Route. The quickest way of seeing Dovedale is to hire from Ashbourne to Thorpe or the Izaak Walton, and to walk or hire a pony thence to Dove Holes and back again (5 m). Those who wish to see as much as possible within the limits of a comfortable day's excursion are recommended to drive to Thorpe, viâ Tissington; thence to walk through Dovedale to Mill Dale, Wetton, and Thor's Cave, returning direct from Wetton to the Izaak Walton or Thorpe through Ilam. They may order their carriage to meet them at Wetton, thus reducing the walking distance to about 7 miles. Carriage folk bound to Buxton, Bakewell, or Matlock may leave their conveyance at Thorpe and rejoin it at the junction of the by-road from Mill Dale with the Buxton road, 5½ miles from Ashbourne, after a walk of 4½ miles through Dovedale. A study of the map, the foregoing distance table, and the remarks appended thereto, will enable pedestrians to settle their route without difficulty. If bound for Buxton they will find a charming bit of *bijou* valley scenery in Beresford Dale, and excellent quarters for the night at the Charles Cotton Inn at Hartington; if for Bakewell, they may comfortably repose in the old coaching days' hostel of Newhaven.

For convenience sake we shall divide our route into sections as follows: (1) Ashbourne to Dovedale; (2) Dovedale to Hartington and Buxton; (3) Dovedale to Newhaven and Bakewell, or Rowsley; (4) Dovedale to Matlock.

(1) **Ashbourne to Dovedale** (*a*) **by** Thorpe. Follow the Buxton high-road, which strikes northwards from opposite the Green Man Inn (*p.* 46) for the first mile, at the end of which turn to the left. A guide post directs to Thorpe. Crossing a tributary stream of the Dove, the road ascends the side of a finely timbered glade, and presently discloses a view of Thorpe Cloud— a more or less conical hill of 900 feet, with the features of a mountain, green to the summit, and standing as it were a sentinel at the southern portal of Dovedale. At the *Dog and Partridge* public-house, 3 m. from Ashbourne, our road diverges to the left, and descends to the picturesque little village of **Thorpe**, in which the ivy-mantled church, with its square tower, is rather a pleasing picture of the landscape than an attractive object in itself. A little short of the village an open drive, commencing under an archway, crosses a field to the "Peveril of the Peak" hotel, a time-honoured house of entertainment, which has been tastefully enlarged in the Tudor style. From the back of the inn a bridle-path descends directly into Dovedale through a combe on the right of Thorpe Cloud, which may be easily climbed on the way.

Those who wish to commence their exploration of the dale from the Izaak Walton, or to see Ilam before entering it, must descend from Thorpe by the *Dovedale Hotel* (smaller than the Peveril), and cross the river itself. During the descent Ilam is well seen in front, but Dovedale is hidden by Thorpe Cloud, opposite to which, on the Staffordshire side of the dale, rises the loftier, but less marked, height of Bunster. The *Izaak Walton*, also in Staffordshire, is well situated, a mile beyond Thorpe, and just past the bridge over the river. To reach it we pass under an arch formed by the jaws of a whale, and up an open drive. The hotel, which has a well-earned reputation, commands a view of the entrance to Dovedale, but of nothing particularly characteristic of its beauty. A path crosses a field to the foot of Thorpe Cloud, where—as soon as we have briefly described Ilam—we shall commence our walk up the dale.

The **Village of Ilam** is ¾ m. from the "Izaak Walton." It is what is called a model village, *i.e.*, the rude picturesqueness of thatched and whitewashed cottages has given place to well-built and trimly kept little Gothic tenements, which form an almost equally pleasing contrast to the square and hideous red brick boxes of which so many of our midland villages unfortunately consist. At the entrance to the village is an elegant *Cross* and *Fountain*, erected in 1840, in memory of the wife of the owner of Ilam Hall, Mr. Watts Russell. The Hall itself is Elizabethan in character, and was erected during the present century. In front of it stands the *Church*, which contains a beautiful monument by Chantrey, representing the last moments of David Pike Watts. His wife and children stand around him, the whole forming a group which moves the spectator by its wonderful purity and truthfulness.

In the grounds of the Hall the river *Manifold* issues from an unseen cavity in the limestone rock, through which it has pursued a subterranean course for several miles. A semicircle of wood climbing high up the hill-sides forms a background to the general scene. Nature, in short, has been profuse of her charms to Ilam, and Art has well supported her.

(2) **By Tissington.** To reach Dovedale by Tissington, continue along the Buxton road (*p.* 48) for 3½ miles, till you come to an avenue of lime trees on the right, a little beyond the *Blue Bell* public-house. Half-a-mile's walk along this avenue brings you into the village. Everybody with an eye for the beautiful has admired the pictures of Birkett Foster. We know not how better to describe Tissington than by saying that it looks more like the fount from which that artist drew his inspiration than any other village we have ever seen. Its essence is rustic simplicity and undesigned picturesqueness. On one side of a wide grass-edged road stands the old Elizabethan Hall, overshadowed by elm trees and characteristically sombre: on the other the church, restored to be sure, but as suggestive of antiquity as ever, is only partly visible through the abundant foliage of the churchyard; all about, little groups of cottages, kept with true Derbyshire neatness, but utterly innocent of arrangement or architectural design—in fact, the only building with any pretension in this way, except the Hall, is the post office, which seems to aim at being classical. Here and there are the famous wells, bubbling up their pure spring water. The *Well Dressing*, for which the village is famous, takes

place on Holy Thursday. The wells are tastefully decorated with
flowers and scriptural texts, and the villagers, after attending
church, go the round of them, performing various parts of the
service over again. More of Tissington we shall not say, except
that the Hall is the residence of the Fitzherbert family, and that
the church contains some interesting Norman details.

Footpath from Tissington to Dovedale. One way of reaching Dovedale from
Tissington is to follow a footpath which strikes westward from the north end
of the village just beyond the wood, and crosses the two roads, as marked on the
map. Beyond the second road the route onward resolves itself into a choice of
walls and gateways, but by bearing slightly to the left we shall reach the glades
which descend to *Sharplow* between the limestone crags called Tissington Spires.
The view down into the dale strikes the eye with almost magical suddenness,
and is exquisitely beautiful. The distance is about 2 miles.

Retracing our steps through the avenue by which we reached
Tissington, we cross the Buxton high-road, and a few hundred yards
further take a footpath to the left, at the bottom of a hill. This
path crosses a couple of lanes, the latter of which must be followed for a short distance, and squeezing through a succession of
stone walls, reaches Thorpe close to the *Peveril of the Peak* Hotel.
The distance from Tissington to Thorpe by this route is 1½ miles.
For the routes onward from Thorpe, see p. 48.

(3) **Footpath from Ashbourne to the Izaak Walton**,
4½ m. In hot weather and when the roads are dusty, this is the
pleasantest route to Dovedale. Starting up the hill from the
Green Man at Ashbourne, we take the first turn to the left and
the next to the right, travelling for the first three-quarters of a mile
by the Mappleton road, as far as the bottom of a hill, where the
road crosses a tributary stream of the Dove. To this point a
direct route, first lane and then footpath, leads from the station,
leaving the church on the left and the town on the right. A few
yards beyond the stream, the footpath again leaves the road, and
ascends a hill, on the right of a modern villa, whence it drops
again abruptly into the road, a little short of the village of **Mappleton** (Inn, the *Oakover Arms*). Mappleton Church is a curiosity,
well worth seeing for its supreme ugliness. Elaborate church
architecture is certainly not needed in scenes which Nature has
consecrated as her own, but surely Art is not called upon to act,
as it does in so many of the beautiful districts of our island, the
part of a mere foil to Nature. Mappleton Church has been face-
tiously called "Little St. Paul's."

The Mappleton corner (see map) may be cut off by another
footpath, which leads to the bridge over the Dove, whence it continues along the east side of the river all the way to the bridge by
which the road from Thorpe to the Izaak Walton crosses the
stream. The valley, closely hemmed in by soft sylvan heights,
presents a succession of pleasing prospects to the eye. Opposite to
Mappleton are the hall and park of *Oakover*.

Dovedale proper, which we now enter from any of the above
described approaches, extends northwards from Thorpe Cloud to

Dove Holes, a distance of 2 miles. The path leads up the Derbyshire side, and those who make the Izaak Walton their starting place must cross either the foot-bridge, a little north of the hotel, or the stepping stones still higher up, at the first bend of the river. A private cart-track, which leads up the Staffordshire side, comes to a sudden end at the narrowest part of the dale, where the rock descends so abruptly to the river-edge as to defy further progress.

In describing Dovedale let us at once ease ourselves of such epithets as "stupendous" and "magnificent." It is neither one nor the other, but simply the most beautiful and harmonious blending of rock, wood, and water within the limits of the four seas. In each feature, taken separately, it is surpassed by other scenes of similar character. Its waters have not the torrent rush and sparkling brilliancy of the glorious East Lyn, or of the streams which thread the glens of Scotland and Wales and the Lake district; its woods are less rich and varied than many in Scotland and Devonshire, and its limestone crags have not the massive grandeur of the Cheddar Cliffs, but it presents to the eye at one glance a happier combination of these essential elements of beautiful scenery than can be obtained in any of the districts we have mentioned. Perhaps its leading characteristic is consistency: the critical eye searches in vain from end to end for a bare spot or a dull outline. Once in it we are utterly unconscious of the wearisome limestone uplands by which it is surrounded. Pinnacled rock and wood-crowned knoll bound our vision on both sides, while the stream below, alternating between tranquil pool and rippling eddy, supplies a soft music thoroughly consonant with the spirit of the scene.

"Give a dog a bad name and hang him," says the proverb, and Staffordshire is a striking exemplification of its truth. The coal, iron, and pottery-ware which have placed the county so high from a commercial point of view, have damned it from an æsthetic. Whatever claim it may have on the notice of the lover of nature, or the devotee of country life, has been filched from it by Derbyshire. Even its cheese is called "Derbyshire." And yet no county in Central England boasts of more beautiful scenery. The Churnet Valley Railway is one of the prettiest in the country, and all that part of Staffordshire which lies between that line and Derbyshire, including Alton Towers, the Weaver Hills, and the Roches, is worthy of more attention from the lover of the picturesque than it has hitherto obtained. But the glory of Staffordshire is the one side of Dovedale, which lies entirely within it, more abundantly wooded than the Derbyshire side, and only a little inferior in the boldness and shapeliness of its rocks.

Forgive us, indulgent reader, for this digression on behalf of a much maligned county, whose sole contribution towards the well-being of humanity has hitherto been supposed to emanate from tall chimneys and smoke-dried towns—and let us take a walk up Dovedale.

Our starting point is the stepping stones at the foot of Thorpe-

Cloud, reached, as we have already indicated, either from Thorpe or the Izaak Walton. **At this** point **the** dale, which commences a few hundred yards back between the **steep** slopes of Thorpe Cloud and **Bunster,** takes an abrupt turn **to the** north west, and the scenery **commences.** The track, **which is** by the river side all the way, **first crosses** a narrow greensward, and then climbs to one of the best view-points in the dale—*Sharplow* **Point.** The stream is **broken by** a succession of little weirs—partly artificial—and hold-**ing back the water in** a manner which will only be appreciated by **the fisherman.** Around us **are** hawthorn, hazel, and **a** multitude **of other** trees, shrubs, and wild flowers, which may recall to the mind Scott's famous descriptions of the Lady of the Lake scenery, where

"Boon nature scatter'd far and wild
"Each plant or flower, the mountain's child."

In springtide, when every little knoll is carpeted with primroses, or in the late autumn when the foliage assumes its ruddiest tint, the dale wears its loveliest aspect. The preponderance of ash in its more thickly wooded parts defers till very late in the season the period at which winter utterly strips it of its leafy honours, and even then its undergrowth of bracken and the sombre yews, which take root in the crevices **of its steepest** crags, maintain a contrast of colour till the vivid **green of the** sprouting larch ushers in returning vegetation.

On the Staffordshire side as we approach Sharplow Point, the woods climb from the water's edge to the brow of the hills, but they are broken by a series of steep and rugged limestone crags which have been fancifully named the *Twelve Apostles*. *Sharplow Point* itself is a bare face of rock a few yards to the left of the path, and easily accessible. Occupying a sharp angle of the stream, and standing out a hundred feet or more above it, it **commands a beautiful vista** in both directions. Northwards the dale is seen growing narrower and narrower till there is only room for the river to pass between the perpendicular cliffs which hem it in. Southwards the cone of Thorpe Cloud rises most effectively, **and** secures **that entire exclusion of extraneous objects** which is **the characteristic** of Dove-dale views. Eastwards a grassy glade, by which Tissington **may be** reached in 2 miles, climbs steeply amongst an assemblage **of sheer and lofty pinnacles of crag,** called *Tissington Spires*. They some-what resemble the famous needle rocks **of** Cheddar, and though in reality they are only scarped projections **of** the high ground behind them, **they have** every **appearance from** below of being virgin peaks. A climb up this glade will amply repay the visitor.

Beyond Sharplow Point **the track** again descends to the water's edge, passing, on the Staffordshire side, **a** deeply fissured mass of rock, to which the name *Dovedale Church* **has been given.** A little further the track forks, **the** left hand **branch** keeping the river side, and the right hand ascending to *Reynard's Cave*. In any case the latter should be taken, for the sake of the lovely view it affords of **the** Straits of Dovedale, **as the narrowest part of the** glen is called. Close to the view-point, which is only a minute or two's walk from the fork, is a large natural arch perforating a ridge of rock only a few feet wide. About fifteen years ago this rock was the scene of a terrible accident. A school party from Derby was making holiday in the dale, and one of its members ventured along the giddy ridge. He missed his footing, and fell headlong on to the steep hill-side below, rolling thence to the bottom of the valley. The result, we need scarcely add, was fatal. In Dovedale, too, the Rev. W. Langton, Dean of Clogher, lost his life through a slip of his horse near Sharplow Point.

High up above the archway which we have just described, and approached by the steepest of paths, is *Reynard's Cave*, a wide-portalled alcove, which invites a visit chiefly from the difficulty of paying it. However, we cannot go wrong in Dovedale, and every climb between the rocks and tangled foliage which clings round their feet and up their sides repays the toil of making it.

Descending again to the river-side path, we approach the narrowest part of the dale, which is appropriately called the *Straits*. At this point the Staffordshire side is quite impassable, and the Derbyshire side affords only a narrow causeway between the stream and the impending rock. After heavy rain even this is flooded. The beauty of the glen hereabouts is of a very high order—foliage and water are brought into their closest contrast. Hawthorn, hazel and wilding creepers encroach on the track, and darkling yews grow out of the chinks in the perpendicular crags. A rock in front, on the Derbyshire side, is, with a fair show of reason, called the *Lion's Head*. Above it is a half-detached rectangular block, which seems ready to topple down on our heads on the slightest provocation. It goes by the name of the *Watch Box*.

A few strides further, and we have left the beauty of Dovedale behind us. It ends as it began, thoroughly unique. Nature has even given it a gateway, the posts whereof are two towering crags, one on each side. The Staffordshire one can never have been trodden by man or beast, so precipitous are its sides, and the Derbyshire one brings to an abrupt end the narrowest of ridges. Looking back between these rugged portals, after we have passed through them, we find ourselves posed for another remarkable view of the dale, scarcely inferior in beauty to any of those we have already described. We will not dilate upon it. The word "beautiful" has been repeated, we fancy we hear our reader say, "*ad nauseam*," but that epithet is really the only fitting one. Dovedale is neither grand nor awe-inspiring, and to call it pretty would be a libel on Nature.

From the portals our course bends to the right, and passing three huge-mouthed caverns, big enough to have accommodated the monster Cacus, and called *Dove Holes*, we enter *Mill Dale*. Steep hills still rise from the stream on both sides, but they are only scantily varied with rock, and there is very little relief of foliage. Most of us have heard the story of the Lancashire operative who accounted for his excessively dirty appearance by stating that he had not been to Blackpool that summer. He might have found a fitting consort in Mill Dale, where some years ago abode an ancient hag in a residence which Nature allowed her to occupy rent-free. In a cavern of limited dimensions she stored her pots and pans, and kept the vestal hearth a-blaze. Casually interrogated by the writer as to the whereabouts of her lavatory, she replied " down in t'river," " and when," pursued the questioner, " did you last wash yourself?" " Well," she answered, " a'll not be quite sartain whether it were last summer or t'summer afore." This eligible residence is now, we regret to add, in the market.

At the hamlet of **Milldale**, a short mile beyond **Dove Holes**, we reach the first carriage-road we have seen since entering **Dovedale**, and this is a very little one. Here, too, is a small " **tommy shop**," but no inn. Our exploration of Dovedale may be said to come to an end here, and we may retrace or continue our steps by various routes.

Back to the Izaak Walton by Thor's Cave and Ilam. A narrow lane rises to the left from Milldale hamlet, and leaving the village of Astonefield on the right reaches that of Wetton in a long two miles, as shown on the map. Here is a little inn, distinguished by characteristic cleanliness. The cottagers of this part of the country make a liberal use of whiting to embellish their hearthstones and stone floors, just as the fashion holds with gentry folk of having a fringe to their carpet. From Wetton, first a lane, then an open track leads in less than a mile to **Thor's Cave**, a wide cavity more remarkable for its commanding situation than any internal interest. What Thor had to do with it we know not, but it is big enough for him or any other mythological giant. From its thresholds we look down on the windings of the river Manifold, which a little way further vanishes, after the manner of streams in limestone districts, beneath the ground, only to re-appear some miles lower at Ilam.

Retracing our steps to Wetton, we may reach the Izaak Walton again in a short 5 miles by a road which runs parallel to Dovedale and about a mile from it, passing Bunster on the left hand, and the village of Ilam (*p. 49*) in the last mile.

Dovedale to Hartington and Buxton. *Mill Dale to Hartington (footpath) 5 m. Hartington to Buxton, vid Longnor (cartroad and high-road) 12 m.*

From Mill Dale hamlet a carriage-road skirts the Staffordshire side of the river as far as *Load Mill*, half-a-mile on the way, where it crosses the stream and ascends to join the Ashbourne and Buxton high-road. The pedestrian route is across the bridge to the Derbyshire side and thence along a footpath which follows the winding course of the stream till the hills recede on the left hand at the southern end of Beresford Dale. The scenery is more interesting than that we have passed through since leaving Dovedale, the hill-sides being in places varied by limestone crags and covered with brushwood. At the entrance to Beresford Dale a cart-track crosses the stream by a bridge, and for a few hundred yards we proceed along the Staffordshire side, recrossing at the far end of the dale. **Beresford Dale**, though less than a quarter of a mile in length, is one of the prettiest bits on the Dove. Steep limestone crags, finely overgrown with birch and other trees, enclose it on both sides, while laurel and rhododendron decking the pleasant greensward between the river and the rocks make it on a warm summer's day quite a domestic little Paradise. At its northern end a sharp pointed rock rises from the centre of a part of the river which has hence got the name of *Pike Pool*—described by the "Viator" of Waltonian days as "the oddest sight I ever saw." *Beresford Hall* lies behind the rock on the west side of the dale, which ends abruptly, giving place at once to open pastures on both sides of the river. Recrossing to the Derbyshire side, we notice on the side we have just left the famous *Fishing House* wherein Izaak Walton and Cotton smoked their pipes and fried their trout two centuries ago, heedless of Kingsman and Puritan, and of all the civil strife which embroiled that unsettled period. The "house" consisting of one square room with a pointed roof, and placed in a shady angle of the river, is kept in thorough repair.

Opposite the Fishing House we leave the river, which winds away on the left. Then, crossing a pasture, with one or two smooth green hills on our right, we enter the village of *Hartington* within a few yards of the *Charles Cotton Hotel*, a thoroughly comfortable house.

Hartington is a large village, or a small town, whichever you will. Remote from any leading thoroughfare, quiet and sombre in itself and in its surroundings, it chiefly recommends itself to the tourist as a convenient halting place, and to the fisherman as the best head-quarters for the upper waters of the Dove. Both fisherman and tourist will find excellent and reasonable accommodation at the *Charles Cotton Hotel*, where fishing tickets may be obtained for 2s. 6d. a-day. The town is two miles from the Ashbourne and Buxton road. The Duke of Devonshire is Lord of the Manor. The *church*, nearly three centuries old, and restored in 1858, contains several incised slabs and other relics dating much farther back than the present building. It is mostly in the Decorated style, and has a square tower.

Hartington Hall, ¼ mile east of the town, and of the Elizabethan period, has recently been restored.

Hartington to Buxton, 11 miles. The carriage-road to Buxton, which joins the main **Ashbourne-road on high** ground, 3 miles from Hartington, continues through a bleak stone-wall country, more or less near the High Peak railway, almost the entire distance. The pedestrian will eschew it, and take in preference the river-side route, which **starts on one** side of the hotel, and reaches the stream in about a mile.

Hartington to Buxton by Longnor. *Hartington to Longnor,* 5 m; *Buxton,* 12 m. After reaching the river-side, as above, the path keeps along it all the way to *Crowdecote Bridge* (4 m. from Hartington), where it enters the Longnor and Bakewell road. Longnor lies out of sight nearly a mile west of the river. During the steep ascent to it, a fine view up and down the dale is obtained. The smooth green hill on the far side of the river is *High Wheeldon;* the sharp-pointed ones higher up are *Park Hill* and *Chrome Hill.* Longnor and the road onward to Buxton are fully described in the Buxton Section (p. 77). The road descends to and crosses the Dove (here a mere rivulet) in 1½ miles, and passing on the left the precipitous *Park Hill* rises again through a narrow little limestone glen called *Glutton Dale.* Issuing from this it leaves the village of *Earl Sterndale* (small inn) on the right, and climbs to the high ground south of Buxton. Then passing under the High Peak railway, it joins the Ashbourne and Buxton high-road three miles south of Buxton.

For carriage people proceeding from **Hartington** to **Buxton**, the route through *Sheen* to *Longnor,* on the Staffordshire side of the river, is much to be preferred to the Ashbourne and Buxton high-road. Between Sheen and Longnor it forms a kind of terrace, commanding the valley with great effect. Pedestrians may also join this route by crossing the river at *Pilsbury,* 2½ miles north of Hartington.

Dovedale to Bakewell or Rowsley. *Mill Dale to Newhaven Inn,* 5 m; *Bakewell,* 12 m; ditto (*Station*), 12½ m.—*Newhaven Inn to Youlgreave,* 4½ m; *Rowsley Station,* 8 m. Either of these routes may be recommended as commanding beautiful views when once the eastern side of the limestone plateau is reached about 3 m. beyond Newhaven.

From *Mill Dale* take the road along the west side of the Dove, as in the route to Hartington (p. 54) to *Load Mill.* Here cross the bridge and ascend the road to the right, diverging up a stony lane to the left in about half-a-mile, and joining the Buxton high-road 5¾ m. from Ashbourne. Hence the road ascends slightly for a while and then maintains its high level to Newhaven and for 3 miles beyond. At first there is a pretty peep on the right over the little village of *Alsop-en-le-Dale* and down a valley whose stream is the same we may have already crossed on our way from Ashbourne to Thorpe (p. 48). Otherwise the prospect is only varied by the round fir-and-beech-topped eminences which characterize this part of Derbyshire. Approaching Newhaven we have a wide view on the left over the village of Heathcote towards Hartington, noticing in the distance the clear-cut little hills which rise near the source of the Dove between Longnor and Buxton.

Newhaven Inn—commodious and very reasonable—is a relic of the coaching days. Now the country round gathers to its fairs twice a year, but otherwise it is left almost desolate. Three miles from it, and one to the right of the Buxton Road, is the *Druidical Circle* of **Arbor Low** (spelt on the Ordnance sheet "*Arbelows*"). It is surrounded by a ditch and a mound, the latter measuring nearly 1,000 feet in circumference, and affording entrances at the north and south. The stones, of which there are about 30, lie prostrate, the largest of them measuring 12 feet in length, and the rest about half as much. A road passes within a quarter of a mile to the north of them by which the tourist may rejoin the route to Bakewell or Rowsley, having added about 2¼ miles to his route by the *détour*.

Newhaven Inn to Rowsley Station, 8 *m*. Taking the right hand road from Newhaven, we pass in half-a-mile under the High Peak Railway, a line used for mineral traffic only by the London and North-Western Company. One and a half miles further we may either continue straight on, or follow the leafy lane to the right, and reach Youlgreave by *Middleton*, a wood-embowered village, below which on the right hand flows the little stream called the River Bradford. This is, perhaps, the more picturesque route, but in either case the descent to Youlgreave is a pleasant relief to the ' lang weary" miles we have been travelling for the last hour or two. If we do not pass through Middleton, we turn right from the Bakewell road nearly a mile beyond the turn for Middleton. During this part of our walk we see in front the long ridge of gritstone hills which rises from the east side of the Derwent, separating it from the course of the main Midland line by Chesterfield and Sheffield. Riber Castle, overlooking Matlock Bridge, is conspicuous on our right hand, and lower down in the same direction, and about half the distance, we discern the twin rectangular rocks called Robin Hood's Stride. Descending to Youlgreave, we look down into *Bradford Dale*, a deep valley, which before the days of wholesale utilitarianism must have been strikingly picturesque.*

Youlgreave (Inns, *The Bull's Head*, recently enlarged, *George*, &c.) is an extensive village, with a fine church, whose tower is a conspicuous object from the country round. It contains several interesting monuments, and a remarkable font, 700 years old. It was restored in 1870. Hence the road descends to *Alport* (inn, the *Boarding House Hotel*), a hamlet at the junction of the Lathkil and Bradford streams, whose wooded valley it pursues till it joins the Bakewell and Matlock road, 1¼ miles short of Rowsley Station, and almost opposite Haddon Hall. *For Rowsley see p.* 127.

Newhaven Inn to Bakewell, 7 *m*. This road is direct all the way, and identical with the foregoing one to Rowsley for almost 3 miles. Then, after descending to the River Lathkil, (*p.* 129), which it crosses in a very picturesque part of the dale, and leaving the village of Upper Haddon on the left hand. it rises again somewhat, and finally drops into Bakewell near the church, and half-a-mile short of the railway station. *For Bakewell see p.* 123.

* It is a charming walk along the south side of the Bradford from Alport or Youlgreave to Middleton (*see map*).

Hartington or Newhaven to Buxton by high-road. 11 m.

These roads, which are identical after the first 3 miles, maintain the high level of the limestone plateau until the slight descent to Buxton is commenced, about 3 miles short of that town. The only inn on the route is the *Duke of York*, which is situated as nearly as possible half-way. The country throughout is bleak and barren of foliage, stone walls doing duty for hedges, and the table-land extending too far on both sides of the road to admit of a view into either the basin of the Dove on the left or of the Wye tributaries on the right. Buxton is entered through the High-town.

Dovedale to Matlock. *Pedestrian route* about 14 m. Thorpe to *Tissington*, 2 m; *Parwich* (Inn), 4 m; *Ballidon Moor* (Ashbourne high-road) 6 m; *Grange Mill* (public house), 9 m; *Cromford* (inn), 13 m; *Matlock Bath*, 14 m.

This is an interesting walk at its extremities, but somewhat dull in the middle. A footpath strikes out of the field containing the drive up to the Peveril of the Peak Inn, and after passing through a succession of stiles, which in the days of crinoline must have been prohibitive to the fair sex, crosses two lanes, and enters a third at a slight depression. A few hundred yards further the Buxton road is crossed, just opposite the avenue of lime trees leading into Tissington (p. 49). At Tissington enquire for the footpath to Parwich. It is some years since the writer travelled it, and his memory is treacherous. The path crosses an intervening valley, and presents no difficulty. The first part of it is, we think, down a narrow lane. *Parwich* is an extensive village with a new church pleasantly placed at the foot of a round hill.

From Parwich a footpath crosses a slight eminence to Ballidon (1 m.), a tiny village at the foot of White Edge. Hence the easiest way is by an unfenced cart track, which crosses the southern end of *White Edge*, and joins the Ashbourne and Bakewell road a little way up the ravine that lies between that hill and Brassington Rocks. The shortest and most effective route, however, is by a faint footpath, which turns to the left from the cart track, and crossing the centre of White Edge drops abruptly to the Bakewell road, about a quarter of a mile north of the point where the cart-track joins the same road. At about its highest level this path passes a little round pond, immediately beyond which the high-road comes into view at the bottom of the valley, winding up and up till it is seen passing under the High Peak railway at its highest point. On the opposite side of the valley and close at hand are the **Brassington Rocks**, a broken mass of limestone boulders, rising in graceful outline from the greensward of the valley, with ivy clinging to their sides, and fir trees growing out of their interstices, and crowning their summits. Their longest extent looks southwards towards the lane leading to *Brassington Village* from opposite the point on the high-road at which the above cart-track strikes it.

Rte. 14.] DOVEDALE TO MATLOCK.

To Cromford (6½ m.) and **Matlock** (7½ m.) *by* **Brassington Village.** This is a shorter route by nearly a mile, than the main one which we are now describing. It misses the Via Gellia, and in its place puts the Black Rocks overhanging Cromford, which should certainly **form an** item in the programme of every well arranged **tour.** They may, of course, **be easily** got at from Matlock, but the view from them **gains** effect if it is first **seen on the way thither.**

Brassington is rather an untidy village **with a poor inn, two** miles from Ballidon Village. **The dullness of the four** miles **between it and the Black** Rocks **is only** relieved **by the Harborough Rocks on the left, about** one-quarter, and the view **into the Wirksworth valley on the** right, about three-quarters of the way. Winding upwards **from Brassington the** road reaches the side of the High Peak Railway at the top **of an incline, and then** diverges slightly **to** the right for Wirksworth. For the *Black Rocks* **make for** the other side **of** the short tunnel visible in front. Beyond **it you will enter a** lane again, **which** joins the **Ashbourne** and Winster Road, and passing the southern end of *Middleton Village,* **enters the** Wirksworth and Cromford Road **almost** underneath the Rocks. *For the view* and *the* road on, *see page* 103.

An hour or two may be enjoyably devoted to a closer exploration of Brassington **Rocks,** especially as **the** road onward falls off in interest, **and after passing under** the High Peak railway, preserves a dull monotonous character all the way to Grange Mill. In ascending to the railway, **a peculiar** feature is the **number of** holly **trees** on the left hand. At **Grange Mill, where** many **roads** diverge, there is a public-house, **the** *Holly Bush*. Thence **the** descent to **Cromford** (4 m.) **is very** interesting. **The** road threads the *Via Gellia* (p. 122), **a V** shaped valley of **marked beauty.**

From the lower part **of this valley there are two pedestrian** routes to Matlock, which **avoid** the Cromford corner, **and deserve special notice** for the splendid views **they** afford in descending **to** Matlock. Those who adopt either have ample compensation for missing the **Black Rocks (***see above***).** We shall describe the higher and more toilsome one in **our account of the route** taken the reverse way. The lower, easier and equally picturesque **one, is by** a footpath which leaves the valley opposite the *Via Gellia Colour W rks*, 1¼ **miles** short of Cromford, and climbs through **the wood** into a lane. The lane **drops at once into** the *Bonsall valley,* whence **you ascend by** footpath **to Bonsall Church.** *For the rest of the route,* see *p.* 102.

Three miles beyond Grange Mill, **the Via** Gellia **comes to an end** at its junction **with Bonsall Dale. An** inn **with the strange sign** *Pig of Lead* **at this point suggests one of** the chief local industries. Then passing *Cromford* (p. 103), **the** road turns sharp to **the** left through **the** abrupt limestone **portals,** called *Scarthin Nick,* which admit **it to Matlock Bath.** (*p.* 98.)

BUXTON SECTION.

Buxton.

Stations:—*L. & N. W.* and *Midland*, close together.

Hotels. LOW BUXTON :—*Burlington, Crescent, George, Old Hall,* **Palace,** *Royal. St. Anne's* ; in or near the Crescent. Aver. Tariff :—Bed and Att. from 4s., Meat Bkft., 2s. 6d. to 3s., Din., 3s. 6d. to 6s., Board at table d'hôte, 8s. to 10s.

Lee Wood, Manchester-rd.; *Midland, Shakespeare,* Spring Gardens.

HIGH BUXTON :—(Commercial) *Eagle, King's Head, Swan.*

Hydros:—*Buxton House, Clarendon, Haddon House, Malvern House,* **Peak.**

Post Office, Quadrant, near stations. Open 7 to 9. Sun. 7 to 10 a.m. *Chief del. abt.* 7 a.m., *desp. abt.* 7.45 p.m., *Sun.* 7.35. **Tel. Off.** open 7 to 9. *Sun.* 8 to 10 a m., and 5 to 6 p.m.

Distances. (*Rail*):—Ashbourne, 66½ m.; Bakewell, 11½ m.; Birmingham, 76½ m.; Derby, 36½ m.; Liverpool, 53 m.; London, 163 m.; Macclesfield, 22½ m.; Matlock Bath, 20½ m.; Manchester, 25 m.; Rowsley, 15 m.; Sheffield, 52 m. Stockport, 19¾ m. *** Distances reckoned by 1d. a mile fares.

(*Road*):—Ashbourne, 20 m.; Bakewell, 12 m.; Castleton, 11½ m.; Chatsworth, 16 m.; Dovedale, 18 m.; Haddon Hall, 14 m.; Leek, 12 m.; Macclesfield, 12 m.; Matlock Bath, 21 m.; Sheffield (by Castleton), 28½ m., (by Tideswell and Eyam), 27½ m.; Tideswell, 9½ m., Whaley Bridge, 7½ m.

Carriages. *By distance* :—2-horse, 1s. 6d. *a mile* ; 1-horse, 1s. *a mile.* By *time* :—2-horse, 4s. *an hour, succeeding quarters ,* 1s.; 1-horse, 3s. *an hour, succeeding quarters,* 9d. Mules and Donkey carriages, cheaper. **Bath-chairs :—** *half-hour,* 1s., *hour,* 1s. 3d., *succeeding quarters,* 4d.

Coaches to Castleton, p. 73 ; Bakewell, Haddon, Rowsley, and Matlock, p. 69. Dovedale, p. 76 ; Cat and Fiddle, p. 63.

Pop. 6,000. **Height** above the sea, 1,000 ft.

Buxton ranks amongst the first inland watering-places in the kingdom, owing its reputation to its waters, its dry bracing climate and, in a less degree, to its scenery. It is the highest town in the country and, in respect of climate, may be called the Braemar of England. Its scenery is good, but not of the same class or vying in beauty with that of Matlock, and visitors who arrive with extravagant anticipations on this score will probably be disappointed. The surrounding country, to a great extent limestone, is from a picturesque point of view too much marked by the dulness of outline and bareness of vegetation which characterize the upland districts of that formation. Tree-culture has, to some extent, overcome this drawback, but it is still very noticeable. The hills, which rise to a still greater elevation than the town in almost every direction, though in themselves they have no special beauty of outline or colour, afford opportunities for delightful rambles, and the greater part of the beauties of the Peak are within the scope of a day's excursion.

Besides the fine pure air passing over the limestone formation, visitors have the advantage of a pure and soft water-supply from

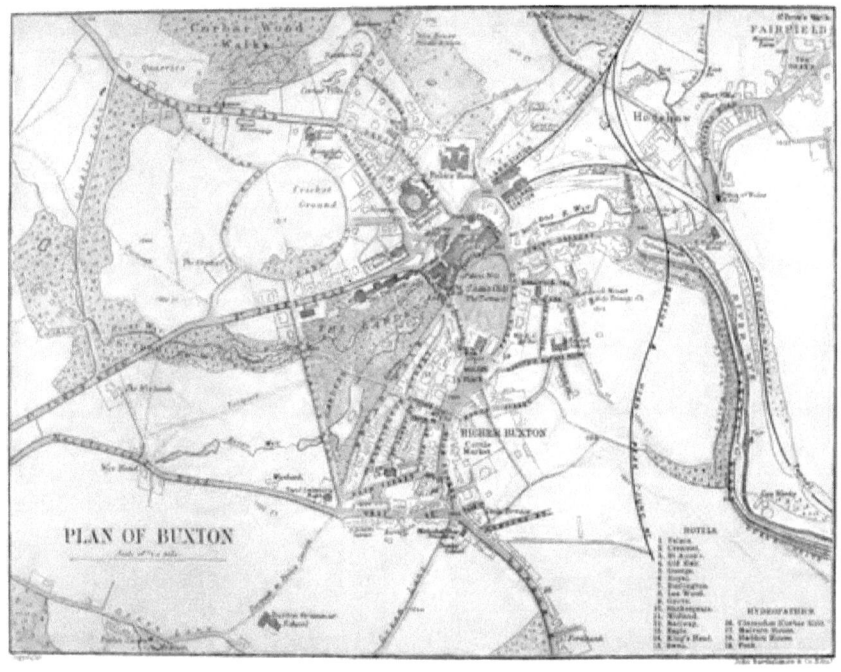

the gritstone of which the hills are mostly composed north and west of the town.

The town may be divided into two portions—the *High* or *Old* and the *Low* or *New*. The latter, which is very little lower than the other, is the fashionable resort. Its finest group of buildings is the *Crescent*, built a century ago, at the same time and in the same style as the famous squares and crescents of Bath. In and adjoining it are the Baths (*see below*.) Opposite the Crescent is *St. Anne's Cliff*, a slight eminence laid out with walks and separating the Low from the High Town. The *Broad Walk* is a fine row of detached buildings, extending southward from the cliff and overlooking the grounds of the Buxton Improvement Society. The town has also extensive Hydropathic establishments.

The Baths are reputed to be, in cases of rheumatic complaints of all kinds, the most efficacious in the kingdom, and have been celebrated since the time of the Roman occupation of Britain; they have been very much extended during the last thirty years and increasingly patronised. The Hot Baths at the east end of the Crescent are supplied with the medicinal water at any temperature, as ordered by the medical men, and consist of 14 private baths for ladies and 10 private baths for gentlemen; with Needle, Russian Vapour, Massage and Sitz baths for both ladies and gentlemen. The *Natural Baths*, at the west end of the Crescent are supplied with the medicinal water at its natural heat of 82 deg. Fahr., direct from the rocks beneath, and consist of one large plunge bath, and five private baths, for ladies; and two large plunge and five private baths, for gentlemen. Each of the baths at both the Hot and Natural wing are supplied with a powerful douche pump, and all the arrangements, including carpeted and furnished dressing rooms, are of the most approved description.

The *scale of charges* is from 1s. for the public plunge to 1s. 6d. and 2s. 6d. for the private baths, including the needle sitz and Russian Vapour baths; and 3s. 6d. for the massage bath.

The following are the analyses of one gallon of the water at 60 degrees, made by Dr. Lyon Playfair, at the request of the Duke of Devonshire in 1852, and by Dr. Muspratt in 1860.

	DR. PLAYFAIR.	DR. MUSPRATT.
Silica	0,666 grains.	1,044 grains.
Oxide of Iron and Aluminia }	0,240 ,,	— ,,
Carbonate of Protoxide of Iron }	— ,,	0,082 ,,
Carbonate of Lime	7,773 ,,	8,541 ,,
Sulphate of Lime	2,323 ,,	0,330 ,,
Carbonate of Magnesia	4,543 ,,	3,741 ,,
Chloride of Calcium	— ,,	1,227 ,,
Chloride of Magnesium	0,114 ,,	0,463 ,,
Chloride of Sodium	2,420 ,,	2,405 ,,
Chloride of Potassium	2,500 ,,	0,260 ,,
Organic matter	— ,,	0,341 ,,
Fluorine (as Fluoride of Calcium) ...	trace ,,	trace ,,
Phosphoric Acid (as Phosphate of Lime)	trace ,,	trace ,,
	20,579 grains.	18,434 grains.

At the far end of the Broad Walk there is a *Swimming Bath* of cold water made tepid by admixture with mineral water.

Churches.—Buxton affords little interest to the ecclesiologist. What it has is pretty equally divided among the different denominations of Christians. The *Old Church* is in High Buxton, almost behind the Swan Inn, and is remarkable as showing what very limited church accommodation the town at one time required. It has lately been refitted for worship. *St. John's*, at the divergence of the Manchester road and behind the Crescent, is of the Tuscan order of architecture, and few who take note of it will regret that that particular style has fallen out of favour. It was built in 1812. *St. James'*, or the *New Church*, is a Gothic building overlooking the gardens. It has an octagonal tower and spire. Amongst other places of worship may be mentioned *Trinity Church*, Hardwick Mount; *St. Anne's Catholic Church*, Terrace Road; the *Unitarian Chapel*, in Hartington Road, and the *Congregational Church*, Hardwick Terrace. At *Burbage*, 1 mile west of the town, there is a modern church, Norman in style; and at Fairfield, half-a-mile east, a plain square-towered fabric completes the ecclesiastical accommodation of the town and neighbourhood.

Amongst the architectural features of Buxton two domes will draw the attention of the visitor. The larger one, close to the Palace Hotel and Railway Stations, crowns the **Devonshire Hospital**, a large building which owes its peculiar shape to the fact that it was once a kind of circus for exercising horses, surrounded by stables. A new wing was opened by the Duke of Devonshire in 1881. The hospital is specially for the benefit of the poor, and is supported by voluntary contributions. The New Wing, by which 100 beds were added to the existing 150, was built by the Governors of the Cotton District Fund.

Pavilion and Grounds. The second and smaller dome is that of the **Pavilion**, a large building erected by the Buxton Improvement Company, a little beyond the Crescent, in the Burbage Road. Herein are a *Concert Hall*, a *Conservatory*, and space for promenading *ad lib.* A band plays for two hours in the morning and for the same time in the evening. Attached to the building are 21 acres of ornamental ground, through which the river Wye, which has only just issued from its cradle in the limestone rocks above, flows in a series of artificial pools and cascades. The grounds are open from 8 a.m. till one hour after sunset. The charge for admission to the Pavilion and Gardens ranges from 4d. and 6d. for a single visit to 15s. for an annual ticket, large reductions being made for families.

A new Town Hall is in course of erection (1887).

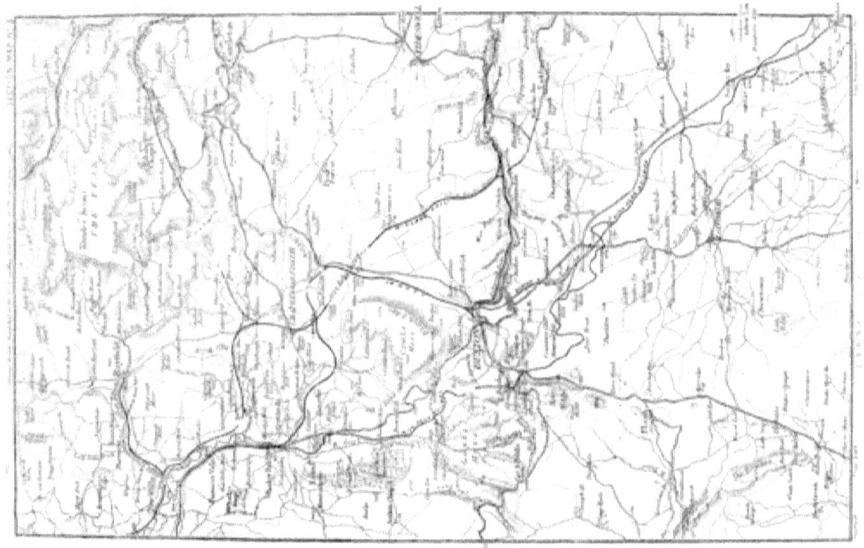

Excursions from Buxton.

We shall divide these into two classes;—the short walks or drives, and the day excursions, arranging both, for convenience of reference, alphabetically.

SHORT WALKS OR DRIVES.

1.—**Axe Edge.** 1810 ft. 800 ft. above Buxton. 2½ m. This is the favourite climb from Buxton. The view from the top is extensive, but lacks character and variety.

Follow the Leek road, through Burbage, as far as the second milestone, exactly opposite which a faint track strikes up the moor to the right and leads to the Ordnance cairn at the top. By carefully following this track, faint as it is, you will minimise the tiresomeness of the ascent, which is caused by the peat bog and rank grass covering the slopes and plateau of the mountain.

By means of powerful instruments the Ordnance Surveyors in 1842 are reported to have seen Snowdon, Lincoln Cathedral, and Bardon Hill in Leicestershire from Axe Edge. With ordinary optics, however, the tourist may congratulate himself if the view reaches as far as Kinder Scout in the north-east, the gritstone edges overhanging the Derwent in the east, the hills about Dovedale and Matlock in the south, and the Cheshire plain with, perhaps, the Mersey estuary in the west. In the last named direction the "Cat and Fiddle" stands "four square to every wind that blows" across a bleak intervening moor and at a scarcely less elevation than Axe Edge itself; indeed, the moorland on the right of it seems to swell upwards to a still greater height than the one we are standing on. An interesting feature in the scene is the group of sharp green peaks which rise from the Dove Valley in the south-east. They include Chrome Hill, Park Hill, and High Wheeldon, and may be identified from the map.

The return journey may be made, for variety's sake, by crossing the moor to the Cat and Fiddle (*about* 3 *m.*) and descending thence to Buxton by the old or new road (5 *m.*).

2.—**Cat and Fiddle.** 5 *m. by the new road*; 1 *mile less by the old. Public conveyance, morning* and *afternoon. Return fare*, 1s. 6d.

The *Cat and Fiddle* is situated on the highest stretch of the Macclesfield road, which diverges from the Leek road a little beyond Burbage (the old road turns off at Burbage), and passing under the High Peak mineral railway, ascends to the lofty plateau stretching north-westwards from Axe Edge. The Cat and Fiddle itself and the view from it are described on page 18. As to the origin of the name, tradition tells of a certain Duke of Devonshire whose constant practice it was to drive up to this lonely habitation in the cheering companionship of his cat and his fiddle.* Pedestrians may ascend by the new and return by the old road, or they may still further vary the excursion by dropping from the latter into the Goyt Valley by a cart-track, and returning to Buxton by the Manchester road (p. 20). This will add an hour to the walk. The cart-track commences 1 mile from the Cat and Fiddle.

Chee Tor and Dale. Railway route: *to Millers Dale*, 6 m. *Thence to Chee Tor, Dale, and back*, 1—2 *hours' walking* ; 3—4 m.
Carriage route: *to Millers Dale or Wormhill about* 6½ m. 1—2 hrs. walking. Pedestrian route: *Chee Dale*, 5 m; *Millers Dale, including ascent of Chee Tor*, 7½ m; *Buxton (by road)*, 14 m. 5—6 hrs. walk.

Chee Dale should be seen by every Buxton visitor. It is amongst the best specimens of limestone scenery in the best county of the kingdom for that class of scenery. The least interesting route is the carriage one to Wormhill. Those tourists, however, who adopt this route, have the advantages of being landed at a very convenient spot for dropping into Chee Dale, and of returning by an entirely different route from Millers Dale. For the two routes to Millers Dale see the rail and road routes to Bakewell and Matlock on pages 70 and 72 respectively. Pedestrians are advised to follow the course of the river and rail through Ashwood Dale to Chee Dale, and after passing through the latter to Millers Dale, to return by the high-road or by rail. There is only a small inn at Millers Dale, and no other house of entertainment on the way, except an inn 2 miles out of Buxton. Wormhill also contains an inn.

Pedestrian Route. Follow the Bakewell road (*p.* 72) for a little more than 3 miles. Then, after passing under the railway, take a track which strikes off to the left along the river-side where the high-road begins to ascend. This track crosses the **river** by a bridge close to the junction of the Buxton branch with the main line, and continues thence between the river and rail to the entrance to **Chee Dale.** The rock scenery on both sides is very fine the whole way. Beyond the second tunnel on the railway the stream sweeps round to the left. The path crosses it, and recrosses it, going under the railway between the two crossings, and entering Chee Dale at the latter. Stream and path are now closely hemmed in by perpendicular masses of rock and steep green slopes abundantly festooned with foliage. The dale is in shape like a horseshoe. **Chee Tor** rises abruptly from the south side of it. Where

* The name is probably a corruption of *chat fidèle.*

the rocks retire, a picturesque dell **descends** from Wormhill. The waters of this dell run underground, **and** only see **the** light of day just before emptying themselves into the Wye, which here bends abruptly to the south. A little further on, the river is spanned by a wooden bridge. To gain Chee Tor, **cross** this bridge and bend back up the hill. The summit is a delightful spot for a mid-day rest. Then, returning to and re-crossing the bridge, you will reach **Millers Dale Station** in about ¼ hour. The road back to Buxton joins the Bakewell road (p. 131) after an ascent of 1¼ miles. A divergence to the left about one-third of a mile from the station will take you to the *Waterloo* Inn.

Those who visit **Chee Dale from Millers Dale Station** pass through a gate between the station and the inn, and proceed along the east side of the Wye as far as the foot-bridge for Chee **Tor** (*see above*). Returning from the Tor to the foot-bridge, they have only to reverse the previously described route all the way to Buxton.

Corbar Wood Walks are entered about half a mile from Lower Buxton on the Manchester Road. They wind through the intricacies of old gritstone quarries which nature and art have combined to render picturesque by covering them with trees, ferns, and undergrowth. They command a fair view.

Diamond Hill and Solomon's Temple. 5 *miles' walking there and back*. The "Temple" is about 450 feet above Buxton and may be reached in half an hour by a direct path commencing behind Poole's Hole. For Diamond Hill direct you follow the Ashbourne road to the far end of High Buxton, and then take a path at the commencement of which a guide-post directs to Brand Side. By this path, passing behind the *Cottage of Content*, a rustic tea-garden, you proceed by a farm called *Fern House*, and up a slight rise from the top of which you will see, to the right of a barren limestone hollow beyond, another house with a few trees about it, on the hill-side. Behind this house is the field where the diamonds are found. To reach it you descend and cross a road, beyond which you cannot go wrong. The so-called diamonds are tiny quartz crystals, and may be found by more or less patient search.

In returning diverge to the left for a quarter of a mile up the road which you crossed in going, and then pass through a stile and climb straight up the hill. On the top is *Solomon's Temple*, a tumble-down heap of stones, which from the isolated character of its position, commands an extensive, though rather a dull panorama. Hence a footpath descends to a farm-shed, where it enters the wood, and drops into the road a few yards beyond Poole's Hole (p. 68).

The Duke's Drive (*a circuit of* 2½ *m.*). In 1795 a carriage way was constructed by the then Duke of Devonshire, leaving the Ashbourne road about half a mile out of Higher Buxton, and joining the Bakewell road a little more than that distance from Lower Buxton. Hence the name. The Drive skirts the perpendicular limestone cliffs of *Sherbrook Dell*, a narrow little ravine which runs at right angles into Ashwood Dale, just one mile from Lower Buxton. The only thing noteworthy in the circuit is the view down Ashwood Dale from a cliff known as the "Lover's Leap," which overhangs the dell and the dale at their convergence. For the rest the map is the best guide. It is better to commence the route at Higher and end it at Lower Buxton than to take it the reverse way.

The Goyt Valley. *Buxton to Whaley Bridge,* 7½ m.

This valley is fully described in the approach from Manchester to Buxton (p. 20). Though lying on the direct route between those towns, it is but little known to tourists generally. Between it and the two railways, by one of which nearly every one reaches Buxton, the high moorland of *Comb's Moss* intervenes. A five-mile walk there and back will introduce the visitor to the best part of the valley. A variation in returning may be made at the expense of an hour's extra walking by ascending a cart-track up *Goyt Clough* to the old Macclesfield and Buxton road, which is entered one mile on the Buxton side of the "Cat and Fiddle."

From Buxton the Manchester road ascends by what is called the *Long Hill* for about 1¼ miles, leaving the *Corbar Woods* on the right hand. From the highest point, where the main road sweeps round to the right to avoid a lateral depression, a rough by-road descends abruptly to the bottom of the *Goyt Valley*, which it reaches near *Errwood House*, a mansion whose striking situation reminds one of a Highland shooting lodge. The grounds are noted for their rhododendra. The bottom of the valley is well filled with trees, chiefly of the fir tribe. A one-arched bridge spans the stream, which here collects its forces from several little tributaries. The public road climbs the opposite moorland. A strictly-speaking private one descends the Goyt Valley to the Whaley Bridge road, which it joins in 2 miles at Fernilee, 5 miles from Buxton.

For the Macclesfield road the way is by a lane alongside the main Goyt Valley, climbing for the first mile through charming woods and high up above the stream, and then passing a quarry which, we are told, once helped to pave Regent Street. Thence the track proceeds up the bare moorland into the road. From the cottages close to the quarry, you may save half-a-mile in returning to Buxton by taking a footpath up the hollow on the left, or by that on the right you may climb straight to the Cat and Fiddle. *Length of round,* 8-10 m.

Lud's Church. *Buxton to Flash (two inns),* 5 m; *Gradbach,* 8 m; *Lud's Church,* 9 m.

Lud's Church, like Dovedale Church and Cucklet Church at Eyam, is a purely fanciful title. It is simply a narrow rock-chasm on the northern slope of the gritstone range of hills between Leek and Buxton, called the "Roches." We have partly described it in the route from Leek to Buxton (p. 14), but it is oftener visited from Buxton than from any other place. Carriages may be taken as far as the Mill at Gradbach, a mile short of the chasm. There are no inns beyond Flash. The locality is private, but tickets of admission may be obtained from Mr. Hill, Quarnford Farm, a little short of Gradbach.

The *Route* is for more than 4 m. along the Leek high-road. After passing Burbage this road makes a long ascent along the eastern slope of Axe Edge. The summit level is nearly, if not quite, as high as that of the Macclesfield-road by the "Cat and Fiddle." Above it, on the right hand, is a group of cottages, which must be amongst the highest, if not actually the highest in the kingdom. On the left is the source of the Dove, whose valley, growing wider and greener as the trickling water collects its tiny tributaries and swells into a streamlet, is the redeeming feature of an otherwise somewhat dreary landscape. The green, isolated peaks of Chrome Hill, Park Hill, and High Wheeldon rise from the bed of the valley. A little beyond a small inn called the "Traveller's Rest" the Flash-road diverges on the right, and in a few hundred yards the village of Flash is reached. Flash has a place in history, but is neglected. Derbyshire guide-books ignore it because it is just outside the county, and probably in its own county, Staffordshire, not one person in a thousand is aware of its existence. Yet it stands godfather to a commodity only too well known, "flash coin," and occupies, if we mistake not, the highest ground of any British village. Further, it is said at one time to have been dear to members of the "P.R.," because if Staffordshire objected to a display of the noble art, the professors had only to move a few yards to get into Derbyshire, and if Derbyshire objected they had still Cheshire open to them at scarcely a greater distance, and *vice versâ*. Beyond its situation and these historic reminiscences Flash has little to individualise it. It is a sombre gray village with the dumpiest of churches and two very fair little inns, the "*New*" and the "*Old Chapel House*."

The ordinary road from Flash descends to the left, but the pedestrian should keep straight on down a long hill, whose steepness the carriage-road modifies by taking a somewhat circuitous course. The two roads unite again in about 1¼ miles. After the junction the stream is crossed, and kept on the right-hand side until *Gradbach Mill* is reached by a drive commencing between two stone gate-posts. From the mill a path traverses the fields alongside of the river Dane, and crosses by a foot-bridge a tributary beck at the foot of the romantic dell on whose wooded slopes *Lud's Church* is situated. Beyond the foot-bridge a track ascends to the right through the wood, passing on the same side a square cottage. Where the cart-track issues from the wood an isolated group of rocks on the right hand is called the *Castle Cliff Rocks*. It is worth while to diverge for a minute to the top of them, for the sake of the view. Returning to the cart-track you take a by-path bending back to the left, and in a few hundred yards enter **Lud's Church**. The entrance has been almost blocked by a fall of one of the natural gate-posts. The so-called church is a rude passage between perpendicular rocks, about two hundred yards in length, and only two or three yards wide. Out of the impending rocks grow stunted ash, and hazel, and oak. A few yards beyond the entrance to the cleft, and lifted out of the profane reach of the visitor, is a mildewed, dilapidated statue of a female—our Lady of Lud, let us call her, for want of better information. The defile ends with a rude flight of steps, which lead on to the open moor. A few yards short of the end, and all but blocked up by fallen rocks, is a deep cavity, which is said to have been a hiding place for hunted down Lollards centuries ago. Robin Hood and Little John are also associated with the history of this singular ravine; but so little historical research has been devoted to it that it is very difficult to separate the wheat of fact from the chaff of fiction.

From the upper end of Lud's Church, the walk may be continued along the ridge of the Roches to *Rock Hall* and *Upper Hulme*, where the Leek road is rejoined nearly 9 miles from Buxton. The walk is fully described the reverse way on page 16. There is a path along the whole length of the ridge, but the right of way may be disputed. In any case, the visitor should climb through the rough and tough heather for a few hundred yards above Lud's Church till he gains the summit of the ridge, for the sake of the view westwards over the hills and fertile plains of Cheshire and North Staffordshire, which contrast strongly with the bare limestone uplands of Derbyshire in the rear. "Unlovely Leek," as our friend Strephon calls that by no means unlovely town, appears in the south, and Congleton Edge forms a bold escarpment to the west.

Poole's Hole. (1 m. *from the Crescent. Admission*, 1s. *Three or more*, 6d. *each.*) This well-known cavern pierces the hill called Grinlow for nearly half a mile. Though inferior in height, depth, and general impressiveness to the vast natural excavations which lure the tourist's feet to Castleton, and in beauty and variety of its incrustations to the unrivalled Cheddar cave in Somersetshire, it is really a fine cavern. Idealists may regret that its ways have been artificially made straight and smooth, and that it is lighted with gas, but it should not be forgotten that an accessible cave left to itself, and free to all comers to grope their way through it at their own sweet will and pleasure, would in a single season lose almost every particle of beauty with which Nature may have endowed it. To rob and mutilate Nature is neither legal crime nor moral guilt, and we tremble to think how many highly respectable and virtuous tourists would without compunction avail themselves of any chance of taking home a beautiful stalactite to their wives and families, just as a "memento" of the place.

The cavern is said to be called after an outlaw named Poole, who made it the storehouse for his plunderings in the reign of Henry IV. It is reached from Lower Buxton by a foot-path which commences at the far end of the Broad Walk, and, after crossing a meadow, enters Green Lane a little to the left of the cottage of the owner, Mr. Redfern, a building "*à la Suisse*" in connection with which there is an interesting museum, containing, amongst other curiosities, a collection of bones and other relics found in the cave itself.

We shall not describe *seriatim* all the various shapes and forms which are to be seen on both sides of the cave as we walk up it, and in which all manner of resemblances—more or less fanciful—to objects of every day notice have been detected to enhance their attractiveness. The continuous dropping of water from the roof has made the stalactites and stalagmites larger on an average than any we remember to have seen elsewhere. The largest stalagmite rises from the water-side to a height of 8 feet, and is broad in proportion. Its creation has been the work of, perhaps, 6000 years. From the roof of the widest opening hangs a huge stalactite, formerly still more huge, a few feet having been wantonly broken off by idiotic "trippers." Of the resemblances perhaps the most perfect is a small *horse-shoe* about half way through the cave, and *Poole's Chair* is in appearance, as well as position, a capital likeness.

The greater part of the cavern is threaded by a stream so thoroughly impregnated with lime as to petrify objects placed in it for the purpose. This is the infant Wye.

The largest opening is called *Poole's Chamber;* the loftiest reaches a hight of 90 feet. Near the latter is *Mary Queen of Scots' Pillar*, a stalactite which is said to mark the limit of the exploration made by that queen when she visited the cave during her stay in Buxton ; in shape it is, to quote our guide, "very like a cocumber." Beyond this point the cavern may be explored for about 150 yards, and still further by those who do not object to make quadrupeds of themselves.

In one of the caves of the Cheddar Cliffs we remember having a pulpit and a man preaching in it pointed out to us. "But how can he preach without his head ?" we asked. We had recognised some slight resemblance to a pulpit in the lower part of the calcareous mass, but though the rest of it might stand for the chest and shoulders of a man, as well as for anything else, the liveliest imagination could not make out a head on the top of them. "Oh!" replied our Cicerone "*that* is a few yards higher up on the other side of the cave."

Buxton to Bakewell, Chatsworth, Haddon Hall and Matlock. Route 16.

By Rail. *Buxton to Hassop*, 11 *m* ; (*Hassop to Edensor Hotel*, 3 *m* ; *Chatsworth*, 3¼ *m.*) ; *Bakewell*, 12 *m* ; (*Bakewell to Haddon Hall*, 2¼ *m.*) ; *Rowsley*, 15¼ *m* ; *Matlock Bridge*, 19¼ *m* ; *Matlock Bath*, 21 *m*. Fares, 1st *cl.*, 1⅜*d.* ; 3rd *cl* , 1*d. a mile.*

By Road. *Buxton to Taddington* (Inns), 6½ *m* ; *Ashford* (Inns), 10½ *m* ; (*Ashford to Hassop Inn*, 2 *m* ; *Edensor Hotel*, 5 *m* ; *Chatsworth*, 5½ *m.*) ; *Bakewell*, 12 *m* ; *Haddon Hall*, 14 *m* ; *Rowsley*, 15½ *m* ; *Matlock Bridge*, 19¼ *m* ; *Matlock Bath*, 21 *m*. Coach* daily to *Bakewell*, *Haddon*, *Rowsley*, and *Matlock* about 10 *a.m.* ;

* Probably during July and first part of August.

returning from **Matlock** about 2.30 p.m. Sing'e fares—Buxton to Bakewell, 5s.; **Haddon,** 5s. 6d.; Rowsley, 6s.; Matlock, 7s. 6d. Return—Bakewell, 8s.; Rowsley, 10s.; Matlock, 12s.

The road and rail between Buxton and Matlock run side by side with the Wye for the first 3½ miles out of Buxton, and nearly all the way from Bakewell to Matlock. For the intervening 8 miles or so the railway follows the course of the Wye, with one little break at Chee Dale, as far as Monsal Dale, between which place and Bakewell it leaves the river considerably on the right; the road climbs out of the Wye Valley to Taddington, one of the highest villages in England, and descends again to the same valley in Monsal Dale, about half a mile after the railway has left it.

Those who wish to see Haddon and Chatsworth, and to return to Buxton in one day, are advised to take a morning train to Bakewell; thence walk or drive to Haddon; cross the hills to Edensor and Chatsworth by a delightful field-route which is fully described in our Matlock Section; and to return from Chatsworth to Bakewell or Hassop station. The walking distance from Bakewell to Haddon, Chatsworth, and back to Bakewell or Hassop by this route is from 9 to 10 miles, which may be reduced to 4 by hiring from Bakewell to Haddon, and from the Edensor Hotel to Bakewell or Hassop.

Railway Route. The railway between Buxton and Matlock affords a succession of the most beautiful *bijou* views to be obtained from any line in the kingdom. First it threads a purely limestone valley, or rather ravine, and then it emerges into a comparatively wide and fertile dale fenced in on one side by the millstone grit, to which Derbyshire is indebted for whatever beauty of mountain scenery it possesses, and on the other by richly-wooded slopes of limestone.

The first 4 miles of the route are down *Ashwood Dale,* the line ever and anon crossing the road and river by handsome iron bridges. One mile from Buxton the narrow opening of *Sherbrook Dell,* with the *Lover's Leap* rock hanging over it, is seen on the right. In about 4 miles the valley opens into a triangular area, and the main Derbyshire line of the Midland Company converges on the left. Lofty limestone rocks, beautifully draped with evergreens and other wood, rise on both sides. Two short tunnels are passed through, and the moment we emerge from the second of them, a charming but momentary glimpse into *Chee Dale* is obtained on the left. Then, after another tunnel, under *Chee Tor,* comes **Millers Dale Station,** where a change is generally necessary. Beyond Millers Dale the left-hand is still the beautiful side. The river, distressingly dammed up for utilitarian purposes, flows far below. There is a pretty peep up the *Tideswell Dell,* and then two lovely bits of river scenery reveal themselves just where the stream makes an "S" curve. Between them, and beyond the latter, the line passes through two more tunnels, emerging from the second into **Monsal Dale,** which yields in beauty to

Dovedale only of all the limestone valleys of Derbyshire. Into it, just beyond the tunnel, drops *Cressbrook Dale* with its steep slopes abundantly wooded from head to foot. **Monsal Dale Station** is quickly passed; the line goes through a short cutting, and then as it crosses the river just before entering *Longstone Tunnel*, affords on the *right-hand*, perhaps the sweetest view of all, **a short vista,** fringed by steep and green copse-covered hills.

Monsal Dale Station to Bakewell, *by road or path*, 3½-5 m. Tourists will be amply rewarded for leaving the train at Monsal Dale Station. From a greensward on the top of **Longstone Tunnel** (1½ m. *distant*) one of the best valley views in Derbyshire may be enjoyed. The view-point is just over a sharp bend of the river, which it commands both upwards and downwards. The little rustic **wooden bridges** which span the stream hereabouts would delight a painter's soul. There is a small wayside inn hard by. A very pleasant walk may also be enjoyed by crossing one of the wooden bridges (¼ *m. south of the station*) and proceeding by a footpath under the railway bridge into the Buxton and Bakewell Road, and so on to Ashford and Bakewell. (*Distance, Monsal Dale to Ashford*, 3½ m ; *Bakewell*, 5 m.). By this route you follow the course of the Wye all the way. Or you may descend from the top of the tunnel by a path along the slope of the hill on the south side of the river and join the same road.

At *Longstone Tunnel* the railway leaves the Wye side, and proceeds through pleasant pastures, with *Longstone Edge* on the left, to **Hassop Station** (*good inn*). Hence the road to Chatsworth rises slightly, and then drops to *Edensor Hotel*. For this village and Chatsworth, see *Matlock Section*.

From **Bakewell Station** (1 m. *beyond Hassop*) pedestrians may make a still shorter cut to Chatsworth. A footpath diverges to the right, 80 yards or so east of the station, and passing an entrenchment on the right, rises steeply through a wood into a road which leads directly through the village of *Edensor* to *Chatsworth*. The distance from Bakewell Station to Edensor Hotel is about 2 miles, and the walk is a more picturesque one than that from Hassop. There is no inn at Bakewell Station.

The **Town of Bakewell** (*see Matlock Section*) is half a mile west of the station. Thence the line descends along the east side of the Wye Valley, which here expands into a fertile dale, whose waters are a veritable Meander. We pass through a tunnel almost underneath Haddon, but the Hall itself is not seen from the railway. At **Rowsley** the Derwent valley converges on the left, and a little beyond the station the rippling waters of the Wye may be seen joining the slower stream of the Derwent on our right hand.

From Rowsley to *Matlock* our route is along the broad and green **Darley Dale**. On the left hand are the grounds of Sir Joseph Whitworth, conspicuous from the adroit manner in which the stones of an old quarry have been utilized to form a huge ornamental rockery. Just beyond it the venerable yew of Darley Dale — accounted some 2000 years old — may be seen behind the church on the right hand. At *Matlock Bridge* the dale again narrows, and passing under the High Tor we enter *Matlock Bath Station*.

Road Route. For the first 3½ miles this runs side by side with the river and railway. For the first mile or two out of Buxton the Wye is woefully discoloured. At the first milestone the narrow defile of *Sherbrook Dell*, with the rock called the *Lover's Leap* hanging over it, is passed on the right. Passing onwards between the limestone cliffs and green slopes of Ashwood Dale with their rich clothing of foliage we commence a little beyond the third milestone a long ascent. The view on the left hand into the open space, where Ashwood Dale becomes Chee Dale, is very fine, though greatly spoilt by railway works, &c. In this space the Buxton branch joins the main line. Surmounting the steep part of the ascent we pass in another mile the *Waterloo Inn*, beyond which we enter the village of **Taddington**, which lays counter-claim to its neighbour Chelmerton for the distinction of being the highest village in England. In the churchyard of this village is one of the oldest, if not the oldest cross in Derbyshire. It is 6 feet high, and Mr. Cox tells us that it is probably the work of the monks of Lindisfarne, who introduced Christianity into Derbyshire.

There is a comfortable inn—the *George*—at the far end of Taddington, as well as several others in the village. Hence the road descends through a picturesque dell into Monsal Dale.

Monsal Dale. Those who wish to explore the upper part of Monsal Dale—one of the most beautiful valleys in the Peak district—from this route, should take a footpath which commences at a gate nearly opposite the 8th milestone from Buxton. This path will lead them by the river-side, to the viewpoint which we have drawn special attention to in our description of the railway route from Buxton to Matlock (p. 71).

The drive through Monsal Dale as far as Ashford is very pleasing. Next to scenery, the chief feature of Monsal Dale is perhaps rabbits. As the summer evening comes on, the river-side meadows simply swarm with them, and the stampede caused by the appearance of a biped on the scene is almost startling. The fisherman, too, delights in Monsal Dale. Here for a few short miles the river escapes from the thraldom of manufacturing industry, and is allowed to linger in deep pools or to rush over gravelly shallows at its own sweet will. Hills and woods flank it on both sides, and form in combination with it a scene of quiet, but at the same time impressive, beauty. It is the Arcady of Derbyshire.

After descending the dale for about 2 miles we reach the large village of **Ashford** (Inns: the *Devonshire Arms* and *Bull's Head*). The situation of the village is remarkably pretty, but suggestive of anything but a bracing air. The inhabitants are to a great extent occupied in the working of the Derbyshire Spar. The nearest station is *Longstone*, $1\frac{1}{4}$ miles distant. The church and churchyard, the latter containing an aged yew tree, will please every passer by. The church was restored in 1870. Amongst other antiquities it contains, over the doorway of the north aisle, what by the uninitiated might be mistaken for five paper flycatchers. In olden days, Mr. Cox tells us, it was the custom to carry these paper garlands at the funerals of maidens, and the custom was not relinquished at Ashford till 1820. The restored church also contains several stained glass windows and a fine oak roof.

In the smoke-room of the Devonshire Arms are a portrait and a biography of a dwarf who died in 1811 at the age of 80. Her sobriquet was Old Molly. She was 3 feet high and hideous to a degree. Her chief exploit seems to have been joining "Sojer John" and "Widow Hales" in holy matrimony over a broomstick. As her end was peace, she presumably only played at witchcraft.

Ashford to Chatsworth. The Chatsworth Road diverges to the left just beyond the village. Beyond its pastoral and umbrageous beauty, it calls for no comment. In 1½ m. it passes under the railway, and half-a-mile further reaches Hassop, whence the route on to Edensor and Chatsworth is notified on page 71.

Quitting Ashford our road crosses the Wye, which hereabouts is once more taken in hand by industrial enterprise. On the left is *Ashford Hall*, a seat of the Cavendish family. We rise and fall again through a country hilly and well wooded, but presenting no special feature, to *Bakewell*. This town is described in the Matlock Section. Beyond it the road proceeds along an almost unbroken level course, hugging the Wye, nearly all the way to *Rowsley*. About 2 miles from Bakewell, Haddon Hall is well seen on the left. It is reached by a drive and a picturesque bridge. For a description of it see p. 117. At *Rowsley* (Hotel, *The Peacock*) our road passes under the railway with which it runs side by side to Matlock. No further description is needed beyond that of the railway route (p. 71).

Buxton to Castleton by Coach Road. Route 17.

Buxton to Dove Holes (*Inns*), 3 m.; *Sparrowpit* (*Inn*), 5¼ m.; *Castleton* (by high road), 11½ m.; by the *Winnats*, 10½ m.

Waggonettes every morning during **the season, returning in the afternoon. Fares: single, 2s.;** return, 4s. About **4 hours is allowed at Castleton.**

The high-road from Buxton to Castleton passes through a bleak and dreary limestone district, affording little or no relief to the eye until the descent is commenced, between 2 and 3 miles short of Castleton. The country has little beauty of shape or colour, and its wildness is not of a picturesque order. Pedestrians should certainly take the rail (L. and N. W.) as far as Dove Holes, or to Chapel-en-le-Frith (L. and N. W. or Midland), whence the road, besides being about four miles shorter, is also more interesting. The two roads—from Buxton and Chapel-en-le-Frith respectively —converge a little beyond their highest point, whence the descent to Castleton, either by the new road or by the old grass-grown one through the Winnats, amply atones for previous shortcomings. The Winnats route is the finer of the two.

⁎⁎ A still better plan for those who wish to make the most of the day, and are not intending to pay another visit to Castleton, is to take the coach as far as the top of the Winnats, and dismounting there, to visit the Blue John Mine (not half-a-mile distant). Thence walk to the top of Mam Tor, or to the *col* a little west of

it, for the view into Edale, which should on no account be missed, and descend to Castleton either by the main road or along the ridge which separates Edale from the Castleton Valley. A mile and a quarter east of Mam Tor this ridge is crossed by a foot-track which takes you into Castleton in another 1½ miles. There you may visit the Castle and either the Peak Cavern or Speedwell Mine, and return to Buxton by coach in the afternoon. The entire walking distance in this excursion is only 5 or 6 miles, and it includes almost everything worth seeing in the neighbourhood of Castleton.

The Route. Quitting Lower Buxton by its main street, Spring Gardens, we turn to the left out of the Bakewell road, and passing under the railway arch, ascend to the suburb of *Fairfield*, whence there is a good retrospect over Buxton. Our road crosses the common, whereon in former days was a race-course, and proceeds in a northerly direction to **Dove Holes** (Inns, *Queen's Hotel*, &c.), which, by the way, has no connection with the River Dove. These "holes," which seem to have originated the name of the village, are called "swallows" from the fact that the running water from above suddenly disappears in them. Leaving the village, we pass on the right a new and very tastefully built little church, beyond which our route continues side by side with the North-Western and above the Dove Holes tunnel of the Midland line. The former is hereabouts upwards of 1,100 feet above sea level, and Dove Holes station is locally accounted the highest in England. Indeed, with the exception of the little station of Barras, on the side of Stainmoor, between Tebay and Darlington, and of Hawes Junction and Dent, between Carlisle and Settle, we cannot think of any worthy competitor for the distinction.

A mile beyond Dove Holes, the Castleton road turns abruptly to the right, opposite a little inn with the strange name of *Bold Hector.* Still more strangely, a sign-post gives the distance to Castleton as 5 miles. This is probably a record of the long past time, when the main road was down the now disused Winnats. Guide-post restoration progresses very slowly in these remote regions. Half-a-mile further a milestone is of equal antiquarian interest. A few yards short of it, on the right of the road, is one of the "Wonders of the Peak," the *Ebbing and Flowing Well.* The passer-by, who cannot spare a few weeks to watch for the event to come off, fails to detect in the so-called well anything but a shallow drinking-pond for cattle.

A mile further, at **Sparrow Pit** (Inn: *The Devonshire Arms*), we gain the brow of a minor ridge, and look forward up a desolate valley, wide, flat, and treeless, to the crest of Mam Tor.

At Sparrowpit a hilly lane from Chapel-en-le Firth (1½ m.) joins our road on the left, and a good road to *Peak Forest* (inn, the *Devonshire Arms*) and Tideswell strikes off to the right. **Peak Forest** was at one time a kind of English Gretna Green, but now its motto in that respect is "Ichabod," and it is a waste of time to visit it for any other purpose.

About a mile beyond Sparrow Pit, and a few hundred yards after passing another by-road to Peak Forest, the tourist who wishes to visit another "Wonder of the Peak"—*Elden Hole*—may do so by crossing a stone step-stile on the right and following the route shown on the map. **Elden Hole** is a vertical fissure in the limestone, once supposed to be fathomless. It lies on the south slope of Elden Hill, nearly a mile from the road. A century ago a Mr. Lloyd found a bottom at 62 yards depth. Further explorations in 1873 revealed at this depth a spacious **cavern, 100 feet across and 70 feet high**, with a "floor sloping at an angle of 45, " whose entire roof and walls were covered with splendid stalac- " tites." We have not ourselves descended to this subterranean " Hall of Delight," and unless the tourist really means business, his only conceivable object in diverging to it would be to wile away the few weeks or so of waiting for the "ebb and flow" of the well we have described above. Since the "hole" has been found to have a bottom, popular interest in it has a good deal subsided. It is walled round at the top.

As we proceed, the line of the Chapel-en-le-Frith road is seen on the left, proceeding straight and level along the dull slope of *Cowburn*. In less than 3 miles from Sparrow Pit we reach the highest point on our road, and the hills which flank the Castleton Valley come into view in front. Prominent amongst them is *Back Tor*, a perpendicular face of gritstone overhanging Edale. To the right of it and in the same range rises the round-topped *Lose Hill*, and still further in the same direction a peak, like a pimple, cresting a long and gently curved ridge, is called, by antithesis, *Win Hill*. For the supposed origin of these names see pp. 43, 90. Win Hill is almost surrounded by Edale, Hope Dale, and Derwent Dale.

The coach will take us on past the convergence of the Chapel-en-le-Frith road to the entrance of the *Blue John Mine*, but it is best to get off at the point where the new road turns to the left out of the old road down the Winnats. Pursuing the latter for a few hundred yards, we reach *Winnats Head*, a little farm-house at which a sign-post directs to the Blue John Mine, by a footpath about 300 yards long. This route gives us the view *down* the Winnats, which the coach-road misses. At the same time do not forget our introductory remarks about the view from Mam Tor, or the *col* a little west of it.

All the "wonders" of this particular route are not yet exhausted, for if we continue down the green road to the foot of the Winnats, we shall pass the entrance to the famous *Speedwell Mine*. The locality is indicated by a sign-board which says, "The Roads into "this **wonderfull place** are particularly good, by which Ladies and "Gentlemen are conducted with the greatest safety." For a description of the Blue John and Speedwell Mines, however, and all the other "wonders" clustering round Castleton, we must refer our readers to the "Castleton Section" of this volume.

Buxton to Dovedale (carriage route there and back, and pedestrian route there). Route 18.

Buxton to Longnor, 7 m ; *Alstonefield*, 14 m ; *Izaak Walton Hotel*, 18 m ; *Newhaven Inn*, 27 m ; *Buxton*, 38 m.

The running of public waggonettes from Buxton to Dovedale and back is entirely dependent on the public demand for them. Such as may, from time to time, be advertised about the town, only run conditionally on there being a certain complement of passengers for them. The minimum number is about 8, and the fare about 7s. 6d. a head. The charge for a private two-horse carriage is 50s., and 5s. for the driver.

Public conveyances leave Buxton about 9 a.m., arriving at Alstonefield about mid-day. Thence passengers descend on foot into the dale and walk through it to the Izaak Walton Hotel. There is no carriage road. Quitting the Izaak Walton, where the conveyance picks them up, about 4 p.m., they reach Buxton between 8 and half-past.

General Remarks. The direct route from Buxton to Dovedale by the Ashbourne road is over a high tableland the greater part of the way, and affords little relief from the general dreariness which pervades the limestone uplands of the Peak district. The route by Longnor, however, whether it be continued thence by road to Alstonefield or by the footpath which follows the course of the stream nearly all the way, presents considerable beauty and variety of scenery, especially in the neighbourhood of Longnor itself. The return journey is made by the aforesaid Ashbourne and Buxton high—very high—road. Such, however, we venture to think, is the absorbing beauty of Dovedale itself, that wise travellers who do not care to have their appetite cloyed by surfeit, will accept with complaisance the scenic dullness of the long and breezy drive home again.

Pedestrians may, with very little increase of distance, descend from Longnor to Crowdecote Bridge, and thence follow a cart-track along the river-side to Hartington (*p.* 55), proceeding onwards by a footpath through Beresford Dale and Mill Dale to Dovedale ; or they may go alongside of the telegraph wire from Longnor to Sheen, by a kind of terrace-road, which commands the best possible views of the green Upper Dove valley, and then reach Hartington by a direct path from Sheen, crossing the river by stepping-stones. Either of these routes is preferable to the carriage one.

Sojourners at Buxton may also make a very interesting round, driving or walking, by pursuing this route as far as Longnor, and thence crossing to Bakewell by Monyash and (for pedestrians only) the Lathkil valley. The return from Bakewell (12 m.) may of course be made by road or rail. The distance between Longnor and Bakewell is 10 miles, and the scenery at both ends very delightful.

The Route. From the railway stations and hotels we start through Higher Buxton, and turning to the left for a few yards, where the Duke's Drive converges, enter a straight reach of road, 2 miles long, broad as a boulevard, and bordered by wide fringes of grass. Far above us on the right, the High Peak railway performs a succession of the most eccentric curves in its efforts to obtain some approach to a regular gradient. In the left front the most prominent object is *Chelmerton Low*, beneath which the octagonal spire of *Chelmerton Church*, old and of varied architecture, is visible. On the Low are two " barrows," in one of which skeletons were found a century ago.

At the end of this straight reach, our route leaves the main road, and climbs a hill to the right, near the top of which it passes underneath the railway. From the summit a rapid descent is made to the Dove Valley. The village of Sterndale (*small inn*) is passed a little way off the road on the left, and on the right, rising from the bottom of the valley, are two remarkably steep and sharply ridged hills, looking like huge natural fortresses, and called respectively *Park Hill* and *Chrome Hill*. To the foot of the former—the smaller of the two—we descend through Glutton Dale, a miniature pass, flanked by steep green slopes from which abut a multitude of limestone crags. Hence we emerge on to the bed of the Dove Valley. The river about here is little more than a well fed brook, but the hill slopes on both sides are steep and graceful in outline. They, as well as the river-sides, are entirely pastoral, green to the verge of monotony. The best views are naturally from the higher ground, and the different roads afford remarkable facilities for enjoying them. Crossing the stream at *Glutton Mill*, we commence at once a steep ascent for *Longnor*, which, strange to say, though less than a mile from the river, is quite invisible, both from the valley and the hills on the other side of it. In fact, it belongs to another valley altogether—that of the Manifold. This singular stream rises side by side with the Dove on Axe Edge, but though throughout its entire course it is never more than a few miles distant from the larger river, the two never form parts of the same prospect. So determined, indeed, is the Manifold to preserve its individuality that before falling into the Dove it plunges into the bowels of the earth, and there continues for several miles until it reappears at Ilam within a mile of its confluence with the larger stream.

Longnor (Inns: *Crewe and Harpur Arms, Grapes, &c.*) is the wee-est of market towns, but its extremely pleasant situation, and the charming character of the surrounding scenery, should make it a much more favourite halting place for tourists than it has hitherto been. When we have said that the only thing uglier than its church is its chapel we have exhausted its æsthetic shortcomings. There is a pleasant old-world flavour about it, and an utter innocence of hurry and time-tables. Traditionally it is one of the oldest market-towns in the country, and there are people in it who still cling to the local conceit that High Wheeldon—a steep green hill on the other side of the Dove—is the highest hill in all England, though it is actually overlooked by the table-land behind it. At any rate, the only other with a chance against it is Axe Edge! and that the latter is the "monarch of mountains" is a widespread belief even within earshot of the railway whistles at Buxton.

Longnor to Monyash (5 m.) and **Bakewell** (10 m.). A few yards east of Longnor the road comes again into full view of the Dove Valley, which, after a steep descent of half-a-mile, it crosses at *Crowdecote Bridge*. Ascending by a couple of zig-zags on the other side it commands a charming general view down the valley. Dullness succeeds as far as *Monyash*, before reaching which village we cross the High Peak Railway at a dismal spot called *Sparklow* (*Public Ho.*), and the Buxton and Ashbourne main road. The appearance of *Monyash* (inns, the *Golden Lion*, &c.) is much more suggestive of the second than of the first syllable of its name. Business, as the people will tell you, is not brisk hereabouts. The church has a cracked tower and a nodding spire. Beyond the village the road continues over the dull upland, broken only by the Lathkil Valley, the whereabouts of which is noticeable on the right, until the descent is commenced about two miles short of Bakewell. Then a beautiful view across the Wye valley reveals itself, fully maintaining its interest until the town is entered. For *Bakewell*, *see Matlock Section*.

The Lathkil. Pedestrians should ask at Monyash to be directed to the source of the *Lathkil*, about 2 miles distant. Like so many of the streams of limestone Derbyshire it spends its early infancy underground, and only emerges into the light of day when it has become a fairly sized stream. There is a track along its north side all the way to *Upper Haddon*, a distance of about 3 miles. The dale is more fully described in our Matlock Section. Suffice it here to say, that soon after its appearance the river enters a narrow, richly wooded glen which is little inferior in picturesqueness to the best of the Derbyshire dales. Emerging thence you follow the stream side for about half-a-mile, and then climb by a steep winding road to the village of *Upper Haddon*, at the further end of which you may enjoy from the *Lathkil View Inn*, a lovely prospect up and down the valley. Hence it is a short two miles over the hill to *Bakewell*.

Pedestrian Routes from Longnor to Dovedale. (1.) *By Crowdecote Bridge*, 1 m; *Hartington*, 5 m; *Beresford Dale*, 6 m; *Mill Dale* **Hamlet**, 10 m; *Izaak Walton Hotel*, 13 m. No inn between Hartington and the "*Izaak Walton.*"

(1.) Descend to *Crowdecote Bridge*, as in the foregoing route, and thence follow the cart-track on the east side of the river to Hartington. (*Charles Cotton Hotel, see p.* 55). The route is between green pastoral hills. From Hartington, the footpath commences at a farm near the hotel, and crosses a level meadow till it reaches the river almost opposite the *Fishing House* at the north end of *Beresford Dale* (p. 55). A little further the path crosses the river only to re-cross it at the other end of the dale. Then it keeps to the left bank of the stream all the way to *Load Mill*, ½ m short of *Mill Dale* hamlet. The route is fully described the reverse way on page 54. At Mill Dale the ordinary route (*see below*) from Buxton is rejoined.

(2.) *By Sheen:*— *Longnor to Hartington*, 4½ m. The road leaves the previous route just outside Longnor, and before the descent to Crowdecote Bridge is commenced. Thence, with the telegraph wire alongside, it proceeds high up above the Dove valley, over which it commands a charming view, enhanced by diverging for a quarter of a mile to the top of *Sheen Hill* which rises to the right of the road, about 2½ miles on the way. Sheen itself is a finely situated village embowered in trees (one or two *Inns*). The church was rebuilt by Mr. Beresford Hope in 1852, and fitted with the internal appointments of Margaret Street Chapel, London. From Sheen to *Hartington*, where we join the last described route, we continue along the road, crossing the Dove half-a-mile short of Hartington.

The carriage road from Longnor follows the line of the **Manifold** which is separated from the Dove by the green hill-range culminating in Sheen Hill. In four miles it crosses the stream, and passes near to *Ecton Hill*, whereon is the famous copper mine which in one year furnished a former Duke of Devonshire with the wherewithal to build the Crescent at Buxton. The mine, whose principal shaft is 1,400 feet deep, is re-opened. There is nothing else noteworthy until we enter **Alstonefield** (Inns, *The George*, &c.). Here we may take a peep into the church, a building of mixed style, wherein is an ancient pew, erected by Charles Cotton, and, if we remember rightly, a huge pulpit.

Thor's Cave. An active pedestrian may make a détour through Wetton to Thor's Cave before descending into Dovedale. The distance to the cave and back to Mill Dale hamlet is about 5 m., and those who wish to fully appreciate Dovedale and to return by coach to Buxton, will have little time to spare. The cave is described on page 54. It overlooks the Manifold, whose stream, a little lower down, gradually dwindles away in its limestone bed till it vanishes altogether, only to re-appear at Ilam, after running underground for 3 miles. The gradual disappearance of this stream has sorely tried the neighbouring farmers.

From Alstonefield a footpath descends directly to **Mill Dale** hamlet, where the exploration of Dovedale commences. All this region is so fully described in our Dovedale section, that we shall only give an abstract of its chief features taken in this direction.

The beauty of the valley commences a mile south of Mill Dale hamlet, where the river bends to the right underneath the huge-mouthed caves called *Dove Holes*, and enters Dovedale proper between two sheer limestone crags. The view here is very striking. On the top of a cliff on the Derbyshire side is a square block called the *Watch Box*. Then the dale grows still narrower, and the path has only just room to thread the "*Straits*." As the defile slightly expands again, we pass underneath *Reynard's Cave*, a wide opening, behind a natural archway, on the top of a steep slope of shingle. Then come, on the Derbyshire side, the exquisitely beautiful rocks called *Tissington Spires*; on the Staffordshire, the smaller isolated ones, to which the names *Dovedale Church* and the *Twelve Apostles* have been given. *Sharplow Point* succeeds, from which a lovely view up and down the dale is obtained, the southern vista being blocked by the pyramid of *Thorpe Cloud*. Underneath this hill we may cross either the stepping-stones or, a little way further, a foot-bridge to the foot of the grassy slope on which the *Izaak Walton* stands. Any further spare time is best given to a visit to *Ilam*, a short mile distant. For details, as well as for the return to Buxton, we must again refer our readers to the Ashbourne and Dovedale Section. (p. 51.)

Buxton to Tideswell, Eyam, Hathersage, Baslow, &c.
Route 19.

Buxton to Millers Dale Station (rail or road), 6½ m; Tideswell (road), 9½ m; Eyam, 14½ m; Stoney Middleton, 16; Baslow, 18¾ m; Edensor, 20¼ m; Rowsley Station, 24 m.
— Eyam to Hathersage, 5 m; Castleton, 11 m.
— Eyam to Sheffield (by Grindleford Bridge and Fox House), 13 m; (by Froggatt Edge and Fox House), 14 m. Coach from Froggatt Edge (2 m. partly footpath, beyond Eyam), daily at 7 p.m. Fare, 1s. 6d.

This is a pleasant excursion, the only dull part of it being that between Tideswell and Eyam. Carriages should either be taken the whole way from Buxton or written for to the George Hotel, Tideswell, to meet the train at Millers Dale Station. A halt of two hours at Edensor will enable tourists to include Chatsworth in the day's excursion.

The Route. From Buxton to Millers Dale Station, both rail and road are the same as to Bakewell, the former (p. 70) throughout, and the latter (p. 71) for nearly 5 miles, the remaining 1¾ miles being by a sharp and interesting descent through *Sandy Dale.* An alternate and equally short route for pedestrians is to follow the course of the Wye the whole distance, through Ashwood Dale and Chee Dale, as described on page 64—a very beautiful valley walk.

From Millers Dale, where there is a small inn, the ascent by the old road, which saves half a mile, is steep. It commands a good view down Millers Dale, but the stream has been sadly spoilt about here by the restrictions placed upon its free course for industrial purposes. Low down on our right hand is a small tributary valley called **Tideswell Dale**. Threaded by a sparkling streamlet which descends from Tideswell itself, carpeted with the brightest verdure and flanked by perpendicular limestone crags, it forms the first part of a very pleasant up and down hill walk from Tideswell to Monsal Dale (4 m.), Ashford (6 m.), and Bakewell (7½ m).

Tideswell (pop., about 2,000. Inns—*George, Cross Daggers, King's Head,* &c.) has nothing noteworthy but its **Church**, which is perhaps the finest in the Peak district. Its style is Decorated 14th century, and its shape cruciform. The *restoration* of this church was taken in hand some time ago, but the outside of the tower and one or two parts of the interior are not yet done. The *tower,* plain in itself, is surmounted by massive turrets and crocketed pinnacles. The *East* and *transept windows* are very beautiful; the *side* ones of the *chancel* are square-headed—an almost unique feature. Inside, the most interesting objects are :—the original *stone reredos* in the chancel, wherein have been added an oak *reredos* and oak *choir-stalls*; a fine new *screen,* also of oak, in the S. transept, and a new *eagle lectern.* Among the *Monuments* are a fine brass of Bishop Pursglove (1579), founder of the Tideswell Gram. School; the Foljambe (1358) and Meverill (1462) brasses, in the chancel; the Lytton brass (1458), and the fine marble tomb and recumbent figures of Sir Thurston de Bower and his wife Margaret, in chapels of the S. transept.

At Wheston, 1½ m. west by north of Tideswell, there is an interesting *old cross*.

The direct route from Tideswell to Stoney Middleton runs nearly a mile south of our present road, but its adoption involves the loss of Eyam,—a thing not to be thought of. Half a mile beyond the **town** we reach *Tideswell Lanes End* (public ho.), whence roads **diverge** in every direction. Ours continues **straight** on for another half mile, and then bends to the right, soon passing—¼ m. on the left hand—the *village* and *edge* of *Great Hucklow*. At **Foolow** (3 *m. beyond Tideswell*) there is a modern Cross, and a small inn or two. The heights of *Eyam Moor* now rise on the left, and on the same side, ½ m. beyond Foolow, we **pass close to a curious scene**. Into a deep hollow compassed by limestone crags and without any outlet, a streamlet descends over the three perpendicular ledges, after which the water, when there is any, at once vanishes underground. This is called, emphatically, *The Waterfall*. In another 1½ miles we enter the celebrated village of

Eyam, pronounced, be it noted, Eem, and not Eyam (principal inn, the *Bull's Head*, opposite the Church). This village, straggling and untidy, rather than picturesque in itself, is beautifully situated high up above, and more than a mile distant from the Derwent valley. Two circumstances have made it notorious from one end of the country to the other:—the fearful calamity which overtook it two centuries ago, and the self-denying heroism which the inhabitants displayed under the visitation. It is this remarkable combination of natural and historic interest which draws so many visitors to it now-a-days. The plague broke out in the summer of 1665 and is supposed to have been imported in some goods sent by a tailor from London. It raged through the autumn of 1665; then there was a lull, till the dog-days of 1666 brought it back with redoubled virulence. The most terrible time was the August of the latter year, during which month 79 villagers fell victims to the pestilence. In several instances whole families were swept away. To avoid the contagion spreading, a *cordon* was drawn round the village within which strangers were forbidden to enter, and inhabitants were bound to remain. To the credit of the latter, we are told that there were not more than two instances of the prohibition being disregarded. Food was brought every morning to appointed places on the *cordon*, and fetched by the villagers during the day, the Duke of Devonshire taking the lead in arranging for a sufficient supply. The hero of the time was the clergyman, Mompesson by name, who, by authority, entreaty, and encouragement, induced his people to imitate his extraordinary example of self-denial and to abide the issue. His wife, who also stuck to her post and her husband, succumbed in the second year. When the plague ceased in October, 1666, there were but 91 survivors out of a population of 350. Amongst these survivors was, strange to say, one Marshall Howe, described as a man of immense strength and stature, whose ghastly occupation, undertaken, it is said, from by no means unselfish motives, was that of burying the bodies of such as had none of their own family left to perform the office.

For a full and well-written account of this fearful event consult Wood's History of Eyam, which may be obtained in the village.

The only building of any note in Eyam is the *church*, which is pleasantly situated in the higher part of the village. It dates from the early part of the seventeenth century, and consists of a pinnacled tower, chancel, and nave. Over the south doorway is a sun-dial, which will deeply interest the meteorologist, however much it may puzzle ordinary people. The churchyard, though many of its trees have of late years been cut down, is still pleasantly embowered in foliage, chiefly that of lime trees. It contains two objects which cannot fail to interest the tourist—an old Saxon Cross about eight feet high, embossed, like the one at Bakewell, with circles curiously working into each other, and with figures of the Virgin and Child and angels, and the tomb of Catherine Mompesson, the devoted and ill-fated wife of the clergyman whose heroism we have already recorded. Both these memorials are near the south-east angle of the church—the latter almost under a small yew tree. Epitaph collectors will thoroughly enjoy an hour's loitering in the churchyard, though the oft-quoted

" Here lie my two children dear,
The one's at Stoney Middleton, the t'other here,"

is not to be found. Was it not once at Blyth, in North Notts?

The visitor should by all means take a peep at *Cucklet Church*, as a perforated limestone rock, close to the village, is called, from the fact that its arched recess served Mr. Mompesson for a pulpit, whence he could address his parishioners during the continuance of the plague, without aggravating the risks of infection. It is reached through the iron gates on the left hand, a few yards west of the church. The key is kept at the hall opposite. The "church" overlooks a grassy dell, which descends to the upper part of Middleton Dale. At the head of the dell is a narrow chasm called the *Salt Pan*.

The *Riley Graves*, as the tombstones of the Hancock family—seven in number, who died within seven days—are called, lie on the hill-side to the left of the Hathersage road, a good half mile from the church. They are reached by a cart-track commencing just beyond the village with a gate and a stile, where the road bends slightly to the right. The house of the Hancocks was a few yards south of an ash-tree north-east of the gravestones. The victims of the plague were buried close to the spot where they were stricken, as is testified by the sad memorials scattered here and there over the now pleasant and healthful fields around.

Eyam to Hathersage by Eyam Moor—*pedestrian route*, 4 m. On this track the Ordnance Map marks and Guide Books describe a Druidical Circle of about a dozen stones " none of them more than 3 feet high." We confess that neither by careful searching on our own part nor by the aid of local information have we been able to identify the spot. The tourist may be more clever or more **fortunate**. We have marked the locality on the **map**. Circle or no circle, however, the walk over Eyam Moor to Hathersage is a very beautiful one.

Route." Take the footpath through the churchyard and at its end turn **to the right** along the **road** which in **a** few yards bends abruptly to the left **and climbs** to the top of the moor. A long mile from Eyam **you** cross Sir William **Road on** to the open moor. For the Druidical **Stones** (?) follow the track which proceeds most nearly in a straight line with your previous course; for Hathersage direct, the one that bends slightly to the right. From the Moor the rich Derwent valley and the rocky edges **to the** right of Hathersage, compose **a** charming landscape. After passing through **a** wall, the track descends to **a** by-road which joins the main road 1¼ miles south **of** Hathersage. On the way the little *Highlow Valley* rich in wood and **pasturage, looks** its best.

Eyam to Hathersage by high road (5 m.), or **to** *Froggatt Edge and Sheffield* (13 m.). The first mile out of Eyam is along the southern slope of *Eyam Moor* and commands a beautiful view on the right hand over that part of the Derwent valley in which Middleton Dale joins it. The eight-sided tower of Stoney Middleton church is its architectural feature. For Sheffield take the field-track straight a-head where the road bends abruptly to the left (1 m. *from Eyam*). The track descends through two fields and then enters the main road of the Derwent Valley opposite the by-road to Froggatt. Continue the descent **by** this by-road, cross the Derwent by the Froggatt Bridge and ascend to the **Sheffield road** which **you reach a short** distance **left of the** *Chequer's Inn*. **Hence** the distances are—Chequer's Inn to Fox House Inn, 3½ m; Whirlow Bridge **Inn,** 7 m; Sheffield, 11 m. The **view in ascending Froggatt Edge** between the Chequers and Fox House is one of the finest in Derbyshire (*see p.* 35).

The Hathersage **road** joins **the** main **road of the** Derwent **Valley** nearly a mile **after** the divergence of the footpath mentioned above. For a description of the **rest of** the route, see Matlock Station (**p.** 133).

The road between Eyam and Stoney Middleton passes down a narrow ravine into the centre of Middleton Dale. There is an alternative footpath, to which the map will be the best guide. For Stoney Middleton see *Matlock Section*, **and for** the route thence to Baslow and Rowsley, **p.** 97.

Castleton Section.

Castleton (Inns: *Castle, Bull's Head, Nag's Head*).

Distances: *Chapel-en-le-Frith Stations, (Midland,* 7¼ *m. L.&N.W.* 8 *m.). Millers Dale Station (viá Tideswell),* 8½ *m. Hathersage,* 6 *m. Sheffield,* 17 *m. Baslow* (*for Chatsworth*), 13 *m.*

Mail-cart leaves for Sheffield 5.30 *p.m. This has ceased to carry passengers.*

Four-Horse Coach to Sheffield (Mon., Wed., Fri.), 6 *p.m.*, Fare, 2*s.* 6*d.*

Return Conveyances to Buxton about 4 *p.m.* Fare, 2*s.* 6*d.*

The village of Castleton is the tourist centre for the most mountainous part of the Peak district. It is situated at the head of Hope Dale, a wide and pastoral valley, which contributes several streamlets to the Derwent, and almost under the crumbling screes of Mam Tor. Castleton in itself is void of artificial interest, except in its museum, which is rich in the beautiful varieties of Derbyshire spar, of ferns, mosses, and fossils found in the district. There are several other spar shops. The Fluor, or "Blue John" spar, as it is called, is a speciality, having lately become very rare. The *Church* has a good Norman archway, but little else to claim attention, except a library of 600 volumes, including a "Cranmer's" and a "Breeches'" Bible, bequeathed to it 60 years ago. Those who prefer good and reasonable inns to bad and expensive hotels will find the accommodation at Castleton to their liking.

Peveril Castle. The village derives its name from an ancient stronghold perched high above it, on a narrow spur between the entrance to the Peak Cavern and Cave Dale. William Peveril, natural son of the Conqueror, received from his father a grant of land hereabouts, and was, as Sir Walter Scott tells us, the builder of this structure. After several changes of ownership it passed during the reign of Edward III. into the possession of the Duchy of Lancaster, in whose hands it has continued ever since. Nothing now remains to attest its by-gone importance except a square keep and so much of the encircling wall as serves to mark out the extent of ground originally covered by it. Tradition has adorned it with the usual stories of tournaments and pageantry, one writer styling it "Peveril's Palace in the Peke," but it is difficult for the matter-of-fact observer to realise that it can ever have been anything but a massive and well-nigh impregnable stronghold. Sir Walter Scott, by the way, can hardly be accepted as an authority on Derbyshire scenery. It is as hard to identify any of the localities described in the Peveril of the Peak as to realise that the "rugged halls" of Ardtornish on the Sound of Mull were once the Parliament House and festive court of the Lords of **the Isles.**

The position of the Castle is strong **to defiance. On the south** the rocks descend sheer into Cave Dale and **are** only separated **by** a narrow *col* from the still deeper precipices which overhang **the** Peak Cavern on the north-west, while from **the** village side **the** approach is made by a zigzag walk, for the maintenance of **which** a toll of 1d. a head is levied from visitors.

The *keep* itself shows **alarming** symptoms **of** decay. The stone facing has been almost **entirely** stripped from two of its sides, and a third has required the support of a stone buttress, which **necessarily detracts a** good deal **from its** venerable appearance **as a whole. The ruins** of a round staircase, which used to ascend in one **of** its angles, **have** been railed off.

From the *courtyard* there is a **fine view** of the dale of Castleton, **the** Kinder Scout ridge peering **over** the depression between Mam Tor and Lose Hill in the north.

Cave Dale. It is worth while to walk half a mile up this secluded little valley with its floor of short and soft turf and its bulwarks of limestone crag, crowned by the keep and enclosure of the Castle. The entrance is through **a narrow** lane which strikes to the right from the Tideswell road at the south end of the Square.

The Caverns. Hard by Castleton are three of the most remarkable caverns in the country:—the **Peak Cavern**, the Speedwell Mine, and the Blue John Mine. Of these **the Peak Cavern** is, except for the enlargement of one or two **passages,** natural throughout. The Speedwell and Blue John Mines **consist** of huge underground chambers connected by artificial passages. None of them are equal in beauty **to** the famous Cheddar **Cave in** Somersetshire, but **all** are worthy of being visited by **lovers of subterranean** mystery. The Peak Cavern is the grandest **of the** three, the Speedwell the most sensational, and the Blue John displays the finest incrustations.

The Peak Cavern (*Minimum charge for admission*, **2s.** *For a party*, 1s. *a head*) **is at the west end** of the village. A narrow lane, passing several little spar shops, and skirting the stream which issues from the cavern, leads to it. The entrance **has a** very imposing appearance. An immense archway extends **for** a considerable distance under a perpendicular mass of limestone rock, crowned on the left hand by the square keep which constitutes the Castle, and partly clothed with ivy and shrubs. The wide rock-paved vestibule thus formed is utilized as a rope-walk. At the end of it the opening narrows, and free progress is barred by a small door, whereat the candles are lighted. A narrow and low passage, about 30 **yards** long, succeeds. This leads into the first chamber, called the *Bell House*, from the number of bell-shaped perforations in the roof, beyond which another passage is cut near a gloomy little stream, which takes this cavern on its way from the Speedwell mine to the main waters of the Derwent. Beside it the decaying ribs of an old ferry-boat show how visitors used formerly to accomplish this part of their journey. We next come to the *Grand Saloon* or *Pluto's Hall*, about 200 feet square, and 100 feet high. At its further end is a group of broken rocks called *Roger Rain's House*. After continuous rain the interior of the Peak Cavern is a torrent fed by furious cataracts. Our next halting place is the *Chancel* or *Orchestra*, an elevated chamber which, as seen from below, by no means belies its name. From it we descend again to the *Devil's Cellar*. The Devil, by the way, lays claim to the whole cavern, calling it his 'Hole.' There are no special indications of appropriate nomenclature in this apartment, but a loud rumbling sound convinces us that there is plenty of Adam's, we mean the Devil's, ale about. Our next halting place is the *Half-Way House*, which is gained after a rough walk of about 50 yards. Beyond this we pass beneath a huge arcade, in which the effect of the natural arches revealing themselves one after another is very striking, and enter a bell-shaped chamber called *Great Tom of Lincoln* or *Victoria Hall*, the latter name being due to a visit of Her Majesty in 1842. Soon after this the cavern comes to an end. In retracing our steps the first effect of restored daylight is not a little curious. It is somewhat similar to that produced by looking at natural objects through yellow glass. Everything has a bright glow upon it, be the day ever so dull.

Castleton to the Speedwell Mine, the Winnats, the Blue John Mine, and back.

Castleton to the Speedwell Mine, $\frac{3}{4}$ m; *Winnats Head*, $1\frac{1}{4}$ m; *Blue John Mine*, $1\frac{1}{2}$ m; *Castleton*, $3\frac{1}{2}$ m.

Admission for a party, 1s. a head; *minimum charge*, **2s**.

This is a charming little round for the subterraneously-inclined. It may easily and profitably be extended so as to include Mam Tor and the ridge extending thence to Lose Hill, a return being made to Castleton either from the dip in the range about half-way between the two heights, or from Lose Hill to Hope, $1\frac{1}{2}$ m. east of Castleton. *See below*.

The Route. Proceed out of Castleton for a-third of a mile along the Chapel-en-le-Frith road. Then continue straight on along the old Buxton road, which passes through the Winnats. At the foot of the pass you reach the cottage that commands the entrance to the Speedwell Mine, of which we may say at once that it is, without exaggeration, described on the sign-board as a " wonderful place " (see p. 75). The entrance is through a most prosaic doorway—the very antithesis of the magnificent portal of the Peak Cavern. Once inside, you go down a rock-staircase of more than

100 steps, at the foot of which you enter a canal boat, and—with "Charon" plying his pole or hands from side to side—proceed for nearly half-a-mile along a water-way just wide enough for the boat, just high enough for you to sit upright in, and not deep enough to drown you. As you proceed, Charon places candles at short intervals along the sides; and so straight is this artificial passage, that when you reach the end of it, a vista is obtained of the whole. Here and there along the sides veins of lead are seen, and Nature's cavities, caused presumably by the cooling process which the rocks underwent in the pre-Adamite days, are from time to time encountered. At the *Half-way House* another passage branches off to the right.

The end of the passage opens into the *Grand Cavern*, as the one absorbing object of interest in the mine, is called. Here we moor our boat, and stepping out of it look down over a railing into a pit which, for all we can see, is bottomless. Then climbing some way up the steep rock-pavement we turn our gaze upwards, without being able to detect a top. Rockets, as we are told by "Murray," have been sent up 450 feet without reaching the roof. The impressiveness of this vast and dismal chamber is really very great. Around hang rocks torn and fissured into all manner of shapes and below is the ceaseless thud of the falling water. The actual depth from the railings to the surface of the stream flowing below is something less than 100 feet. Here in fact we have one of the very few glimpses which Nature allows us to obtain into the dark infancy of the limestone streams of Derbyshire. The history of the Speedwell Mine is briefly this:—it was excavated during the last century by an enterprising company in search of lead, who spent £14,000 upon it, and then from want of success abandoned it. As a show-place at a shilling a head it is at the present time worth something, though the receipts must fall considerably short of a satisfactory dividend on £14,000.

Returning to the doubly welcome light of day we enter at once the celebrated **Winnat's Pass**. The name is a corruption of *Wind Gates*, and is another sample of the expressive nomenclature of semi-barbarous days. With a strong sou'wester blowing it is often as difficult to crawl up the pass as it is to avoid flying down it. Those who are familiar with the similarly formed Cheddar Cliffs of Somersetshire will probably think the scenery of the Winnats overrated. The ravine is flanked by steep green slopes overhung in many places by sheer masses of limestone rock. The old road which winds up the bottom of it, has been overgrown with short grass, and affords delightful walking. The sudden bend half-way up, just where the impending rocks are most massive, gives a distinctive character to the pass, but pleasant and picturesque as it is, there is no sufficient perpendicular height, or piling up of rock about the scene as a whole to justify the catalogue of big epithets which has been lavished upon it by different writers. To speak of its "limestone cliffs rising in fantastic forms to a height of 400 feet" is to encourage a very erroneous anticipation in the mind of the visitor. The cliffs may be in places 400 feet above the bottom of the valley, but nowhere do they rise a fourth of that height above the green slope in which their feet are imbedded. In parts of the Cheddar Cliffs, on the contrary, the summit actually overhangs the base at a height of nearly, if not quite, 400 feet.

From the top of the Winnats, whence, perhaps, the best view of them is obtained, a guide-post, standing close to *Winnats Head Farm*, places you on a footpath to the *Blue John Mine*, a few hundred yards distant, on the other side of Tray Cliff, the grassy hill which lies between the Winnats and the modern road to Buxton and Castleton.

The **Blue John Mine** is a few yards from this road. As with the Speedwell, there is no natural external sign of its existence. Passing through a doorway in the hill-side, we descend a flight of steps to a narrow but lofty corridor roofed with stalactite, and walled with fossils and carbonate of lime crystals. This corridor leads into a spacious chamber, 50 yards high and 50 feet wide, called *Lord Mulgrave's Dining Room*, from the fact that his lordship, during a three days' exploration of the mine for the purpose of finding another outlet, entertained his miners in this part of it. Another succession of passages conducts us to the most beautiful part of the mine, the *Variegated* or *Crystallized Cavern*. To see this chamber properly Bengal lights are required, by the aid of which we have an obstructed view upwards of nearly 100 feet. The roof and the sides of the chamber are covered with stalactites and beautifully crystallized. Regarded from a sensational point of view, it cannot compete with the grand cavern of the "Speedwell," but from a picturesque, it is the finest example of Nature's Gothic in the neighbourhood of Castleton.

Further progress through the many ramifying passages of the mine is railed off. In returning, the guide will point out a set of pipe-like columns, formed by the contact of the stalactites above with their corresponding stalagmites below, and called the *Organ* —a somewhat fanciful resemblance, and now spoiled.

The Blue John Mine is still worked, but the "Blue John," or Fluor Spar, is got in decreasing quantities, and is becoming very rare. The finest specimen of its artificial use is a vase at Chatsworth. The blue vein, to which it owes its unique appearance, is oxide of manganese.

In returning to Castleton, a footpath along the west slope of Tray Cliff lessens the road-distance by about half a mile. Pedestrians with a couple of hours to spare are advised to join the following route:—

Castleton to **Mam Tor**, 3 *m*; **Back Tor**, 4½ *m*; **Lose Hill**, 5¼ *m*; **Hope** (*Inn*), 7½ *m*; **Castleton**, 9 *m*. *Blue John Mine to Mam Tor*, 1 *m*.

From the Blue John Mine continue along the Chapel-en-le-Frith road for about half a mile, passing the divergence of the Buxton road on the way. Then cross a field on the right to the slight depression on the west side of Mam Tor. The road to this depression or *col* quits the Chapel-en-le-Frith route a little further on, and makes an acute angle. From the *col* thus gained, almost the whole length of Edale, backed by the lofty Kinder Scout ridge, bursts suddenly on the eye. As seen from this view-point, Edale has a more severe appearance than any valley in Peakland, an effect which it owes in some measure to the dark green colour which pervades it. Its strath is dotted with farmsteads, and intersected by hedges and stone walls. Along it runs the little River Noe. Towards the head of the dale, which is fully exposed to view, cultivation ceases, and the steep, crag-crested slopes of Kinder rise to the unbroken line which forms its ridge, and extends behind the entire length of the valley. Numerous little lateral gullies, or *cloughs* as they are locally called, give variety and picturesqueness to a panorama which, if it depended on outline only, would be monotonous. Near the chapel is a small inn, the *Nag's Head*.

The summit of Mam Tor is less than a quarter of a mile from the view-point on which we are standing, and not more than 150 feet higher. The way to it is plain enough and just as steep as you like to make it. The name "Shivering Mountain" applied to this hill arises from the disintegration which it undergoes under the influence of frost on the south or Castleton side, due to the fact that it consists of alternate layers of hard gritstone and friable shale.

The crest of the hill is surrounded by an old British entrenchment, the interruption in which on the Castleton side shows how great the above described disintegration has been since the Celtic period.

Besides the different objects of interest above described as visible from the *col*, Mam Tor commands a full-length view of Hope Dale, with its hateful chimney, and of the moors beyond Hathersage and Derwent Dale, as well as of Eyam Moor and the wooded hills descending thence to Hathersage. Buxtonwards the limestone uplands present their usual dull outlines and bare surfaces. Castleton, with its keep and rocky gorge, lies mapped out almost immediately beneath the gazer's eye.

The writer once pursued the ridge all the way from Mam Tor to Kinder Scout, a route so heavy and wearisome that he specially wishes to warn others against it.

The ridge walk from Mam Tor to *Back Tor* and *Lose Hill* is perhaps the pleasantest hill excursion in Derbyshire, for the simple reason that it is a real ridge — in places almost meriting the term razor-edge — and on that account commands an extensive prospect on both sides, — of Edale on the left and Hope Dale on the right, two of the finest of the Derbyshire valleys. A striking feature upon it is Back Tor, an almost perpendicular face of gritstone, overlooking Edale and rising from a delightful copse-wood of hazel, birch and other trees. The hollow of the ridge beneath it is crossed by a footpath leading from Edale to Castleton, by which the latter may be reached in half an hour. The walk, however, may be very pleasantly extended over Lose Hill, which is close at hand and only a little higher than Back Tor. This hill is separated from its neighbour and rival Win Hill, which oddly enough, it exceeds in height by 40 feet, by the narrow entrance to Edale, through which flows the River Noe. As to the popularly ascribed origin of the names **"Lose" and** "Win", see page 43. Another explanation is that they are **corruptions of** " Laws," **from an** Anglo-Saxon word meaning **hill, and** " **whin,**" a word which is north-country for furze or gorse. **The word Laws, written 'law' in Scotland —** " **Berwick Law** " to wit—is generally written ' Low ' in Derbyshire, **in recognition,** doubtless, **of its** invariably being applied to something high.

Looked at from Lose Hill, the truncated top of **Win Hill just cuts the line** of the wide moorland between Hathersage **and Sheffield. Over the** depression to the left of it we mark the line of the **old Roman road and the** position, though **not the** depths, of the beautiful Ashop **Dale.**

In descending, keep along the shoulder of **the** hill in the direction of Hope, recognizable by the abnormal thickness of its church spire. You will enter the Edale-road nearly a mile north of the **village, which, as well as** the road **from** it to Castleton, is described **on page 40.**

Castleton to Ashopton, over Win Hill. Pedestrian route (No. 20).

Castleton to Hope, 1½ m ; *Top of Win Hill*, 3½ m ; *Ashopton*, 5 *m. Height of Win Hill*, 1,532 *feet.*

A very pleasant two hours' walk, and **much to be** preferred to **the road route by** Aston or Mytham Bridge, which **is** 2 miles **longer.**

Between Castleton and Hope there is nothing noteworthy beyond **what we have already** become familiar with from the neighbourhood **of Castleton.** At Hope turn **to** the left, opposite the church **and by the side of the** *Hall Inn*, so called from its **having been once Hope Hall.** Follow the road thus **entered for a third of a mile, and then cross the** stream at **the first bridge over it. A few yards beyond the bridge** the lane forks right and left. **Mount a flight of** steps between the two **branches,** and ascend the **hill** to a new farm-house a few fields ahead. Here, turning slightly **to the** right, and avoiding a cart-road which ascends by the side of **some iron** railings **on** the left, you enter a footpath which climbs **through a** succession of stiles to the brow of the hill, whence the peak is five minutes' **walk** to the right. The view thence **and the** descent **to Ashopton are described** on **pages 43 and 40.**

Castleton to Bradwell and Eyam or Hathersage. **Pedestrian** Route (No. 21).

Castleton to **Bradwell** *(Inns),* **2** *m;* ***Abney,*** **4** *m;* *(**Hathersage,** 7¼ m.)* *Eyam,* **8** *m.*

A very delightful and little known walk either to one place or the other. Little that is seen from the high-road is missed, and a great deal is added.
Diverge to the left from the Tideswell road at a sign-post a few hundred yards out of Castleton. A by-**lane** leads to *Pindale*, a group of houses on a cross-road from Hope into the Castleton and Tideswell road. From Pindale a footpath, succeeded by a narrow lane, leads direct into **Bradwell**, a large village, whose inhabitants find employment in the mines and quarries. Here is a cave, *Bagshaw Cavern*, accounted by some more interesting than any of the Castleton ones. We have not explored it, but the natives tell us it is so extensive that a party failed to find the end of it in twelve hours, and that the consumption of a pound of "dips" left them "nowhere" in it.
The only part of the route in which the pedestrian is likely to go astray is that between Bradwell and Abney. Before entering the former place he may have noticed a footpath climbing the opposite hill by the side of a wall. The by-ways of Bradwell are so intricate, as to defy all directions to the commencement of this path, but there are plenty of people to inquire of. Leaving a narrow limestone defile on the right, it climbs the hill called *Bradwell Edge* very steeply. From the top there is a fine retrospect across Hope Dale to Mam Tor and Lose Hill, backed by the Kinder Scout ridge. The prospect in other directions is very dull. Southwards it extends to Longstone Edge. After crossing a couple of fields beyond the top of the Edge, the path enters an almost disused road close to a gate. Pass through this gate, and leave the road a few yards beyond by a stone step-stile opposite a trespass board. The path thus entered crosses an expanse of heather and rushes, till it re-enters the road by an opening in the wall opposite a gate leading into a narrow lane. This lane takes you direct to **Abney**, a neat and clean little hamlet, as remote from the ordinary thoroughfares of mankind as any we have ever visited. Placed on a slight depression of the moor, it sees nothing around but the fields which its own industry has reclaimed and swelling uplands of sable heather.

Abney to Eyam (over *Eyam Moor*). Enter a cart-track which strikes to the right from the dip in the road, just opposite *Heather Lodge*. Do not cross the stream, but keep it on the right hand until another has joined it, nearly a mile down. Then, in a few hundred yards, cross and leave it, continuing very much in your previous course, and gradually climbing *Eyam Moor*. If you can find the *Druidical Circle* marked on the map—and the existence of which we should be the last to dispute—you are cleverer than we. Near it, or its reputed position, the track turns south, and crossing *Sir William Road* in less than a mile, enters a road which passes near two prominent chimneys, and soon descends abruptly upon Eyam, the last corner being cut off by an obvious footpath. The part of the route between the Druidical Circle and Eyam is described the reverse way on page 82. It is a very pleasant walk.

Abney to Hathersage. This route is by an unmistakeable road all the way. In about a mile a glorious view across the Derwent Valley opens out. Hathersage lies below; behind it, Stanage Edge. Northwards the river comes down between Win Hill on the left, and Bamford Edge on the right. Close at hand is a deep fir-clad glade; on the right of the road the old Elizabethan-looking farm, called *Highlow Hall*, behind which is a green knoll, ascended in a few minutes and commanding a lovely panorama. Eyam Moor, heathery from head to foot, rises beyond the stream on the right.

From Highlow Hall a continuous descent takes us into the main road of the Derwent Valley, close to the bridge at *Low Mill*; whence to **Hathersage** (*p.* 40) the distance is a short mile.

Castleton to Bakewell by Tideswell, and (1) Millers Dale Station; (2) Litton, Monsal Dale and Ashford; (3) Wardlow and Ashford.

Castleton to Tideswell (road), 5½ m.
(1) Tideswell to Millers Dale Station (road), 3 m; Bakewell (rail), 9 m.
(2) Tideswell to Litton (road), 1 m; Monsal Dale Station, 3½ m.—(Monsal Dale to Bakewell by rail 3½ m.)—Top of Longstone Tunnel, 4 m; Ashford, 5¼ m; Bakewell Town, 7 m; Station 7½ m.
(3) Tideswell to Litton (road), 1 m; Wardlow Mires, 2½ m; Wardlow, 3 m; Top of Longstone Tunnel, 5 m; Ashford, 6¼ m; Bakewell Town, 8 m; Station, 8½ m.

Hotel and Inns at Bakewell: Inns at Tideswell and Ashford; Road-side houses at Tideswell Lane Ends (5 m.), Millers Dale, Litton, Wardlow Mires, Wardlow, and top of Longstone Tunnel.

Millers Dale is, as far as concerns the Midland line, a more convenient station than Chapel-en-le-Frith to make for from Castleton because, being the junction for Buxton, nearly all the day-expresses stop at it.

Of the two carriage routes to Bakewell the one through Monsal Dale is much the more picturesque. That by Wardlow is only to be commended for the opportunity it affords of diverging to Wardlow Hay Cop and looking down thence into Cressbrook and Monsal Dales. Pedestrians may see Cressbrook Dale by taking either the footpath on its west side from Litton, or a rough one on the east side from Wardlow Mires; both enter Monsal Dale at Cressbrook Mill.

The scenery between Castleton and Tideswell is, except for the first mile or so, during which it overlooks Hope Dale, uniformly dull.

The Route. The Tideswell road quits Castleton by the south end of the square, passing on the right the narrow entrance to *Cave Dale*. The ascent begins at once, and is made by one acute zigzag. Pedestrians gain little by taking an obvious footpath which avoids the **corner**. The back view over Hope Dale during the ascent is very fine, **but when** once the summit-level is reached the scenery becomes **very monotonous**. Proceeding due south we reach the hamlet of *Little Hucklow* (3½ m.), and *Tideswell Lane Ends* (5m.). From the latter spot roads diverge in every direction. For Litton we keep straight on, for Tideswell we **turn to the right, and for** Wardlow to the left.

(1) *By Tideswell.* **From the** Lane Ends **to** Tideswell the distance is a long half mile. The town and church are described on page 80.

Tideswell to Millers Dale Station (3 m). The road goes the length of the town, and then keeps along the hill-side for some distance. A full mile from the church a by-road on the left drops through an avenue to the bottom of Millers Dale (*not the station*) and **to** *Litton Mill* where further progress is barred, except to such as like to climb a cart-track and join the direct road from Tideswell to Monsal Dale. Nothing particular is gained by following this route throughout, but that part of it which **lies between** the fork and Litton Mill passes through a very pleasant little valley—**Tideswell Dell** by name —characteristically green in its lower parts, and fenced in by sheer limestone cliffs.

The road to Millers Dale station continues for some distance above this valley and then drops abruptly to the railway. The old road is half-a-mile shorter.

Tideswell to Bakewell. (1.) *Carriage route through Monsal Dale* (7 m.). This route commences **over the high ground between** Cressbrook Dale and Monsal Dale. **In less** than **two miles it overlooks** that beautiful part of the Wye Valley **of which such** delightful but tantalizing glimpses are obtained from the railway **on the other** side between Monsal Dale **and** Millers **Dale** Station (*p.* 11)—a kind of debateable **ground between the** two dales. Except perhaps one bit **of Chee Dale there** is nothing so fine along **the whole course of the Wye; nothing in fact except that** and **Dovedale in all the limestone scenery of Derbyshire. The** river forms two S curves, the lower part of one being the upper part of the other. Sheer cliffs rise from the water's edge, their summits on the **north-east** side **surmounted by towering** groves of varied foliage—to a great **extent evergreen—which**, however, greatly obstruct the view from the road we **are travelling along.**

From this scene a steep descent brings **us to the** bottom of *Monsal Dale*, at the point where **Cressbrook Dale** converges. The latter is one **of** the narrowest valleys **in** the county, and, like all those hereabouts, is richly diversified with rock and wood. The Cressbrook mill at the foot **of it is a huge** affair. Those who wish to examine the dale more **closely must travel on foot by** one of the routes described below.

Our road continues along Monsal Dale for about a mile with the river, spanned by two rustic foot-bridges,—the first leading **to the** station,—on the right hand, and beautifully wooded hills on the left. Then we rise sharply to a point almost over the top of the **Longstone** tunnel, whence the sudden bend of the river admits of a **view both up** and down it. Here **is a** small road-side public-house, and **we** could wish that native enterprise had bethought itself of the opportunities offered for **a comfortable inn, for a more charming spot** to spend a few hours or **a** few days at we cannot **well imagine.** *For the view see p.* 71.

All the possible routes from Castleton and Tideswell to Bakewell converge here.

The **road onwards to** Ashford and Bakewell calls for no description. It gradually descends to the former place, branching in **about a mile into** two roads, both of which pass through Ashford, and beyond Ashford being identical with the Buxton and Bakewell **road.** *For Ashford, see p.* 72, **and for** *Bakewell*, p. 128.

⁎ From the top of Longstone Tunnel pedestrians may proceed by the Wye-side all the way to Ashford by more than one route. A footpath descends to the river, crosses it, and comes out on the Buxton and Bakewell high-road opposite the eighth milestone from Buxton, 2 m. short of Ashford, and 3½ m. short of Bakewell. For this part of Monsal Dale see p. 72. This route involves about 2 miles' extra walking.

(2) *Carriage Route by Litton and Wardlow.* Beyond Litton **this road passes above the head of** *Cressbrook Dale*, but does not **show the best part of it.** Pedestrians, however, may follow the dale **the whole way down,** striking out of the road at *Wardlow Mires*, **2 miles on the** way, **where it is as well** to satisfy one's self **as to** the practicability of the route at the little inn (*Three Stags*). **From** this, the **east** side of Cressbrook Dale, the view is less obstructed by wood than **from the west** side. The track joins the **road** described in the last paragraph **at the** north end of Monsal Dale.

The carriage-road proceeds **from** Wardlow Mires through the hamlet of *Wardlow* to the junction of the roads above Longstone **tunnel (p. 71).** To see Cressbrook Dale, **a** divergence of half **a mile must be** made on foot **to** *Wardlow Hay Cop*, from the **other side of which,** nearly half **a mile** beyond the top, the cliffs **descend** abruptly into the dale. From this "Cop" *Monsal Dale* **Station** may be reached in 1½ miles, by a lane descending steeply through **a narrow valley.**

(3) *Footpath from Litton to* Monsal **Dale.** **Monsal** *Dale Station*, 2½ *m*; *Top of the Tunnel*, 3 *m*. Take the lane that turns southwards from the east end of the open green at Litton. In 300 yards this **lane turns** at right angles both ways. A few yards to the left the **footpath** commences, crossing two or three fields to a wood which drops abruptly to the bed of *Cressbrook Dale*. About half a mile after entering the wood, the path becomes a lane again close to a spring. Avoid a branch up the hill to the right, and you will reach **in another half** mile *Cressbrook* **Mill and** the direct carriage road from **Litton** to Monsal Dale (p. 93). The view down into, and across Cressbrook Dale by this route is **a** good deal hidden by trees

Castleton to Buxton, by coach-road. Route 23.

Castleton to Sparrowpit (Inn), 6 m; Dove Holes (Inns), 8½ m; Buxton, 11½ m.—Pedestrian route through the Winnats, 1 m. less 3 miles saved, and nothing lost, by taking the train at Dove Holes.

Waggonettes (return to Buxton) about 4 p.m. Fare, 2s. 6d.

Route fully described the reverse way on p. **73.**

The pedestrian route proceeds in a straight line from Castleton to the foot of the Winnats, the high-road diverging from it to the right in a third of a mile. It passes close to the Speedwell Mine (p. 87), and within a quarter of a mile of the Blue John Mine, rejoining the carriage route a quarter of a mile beyond the head of the Winnats. To visit *Elden Hole* (p. 75) on the way, take the lane on the left, 1¼ miles beyond the junction, and work round *Elden Hill,* again entering the main road by a step-stile half-a-mile beyond the point at which you left it. The *détour* is about 1½ miles. Nearly a mile beyond *Sparrow Pit* is the *Ebbing* and *Flowing Well* (p. 74) on the left of the road, half-a-mile beyond which, opposite the *Bold Hector Inn,* turn to the left. *Dove Holes* is one mile further, and *Fairfield* half-a-mile short of *Buxton.*

Castleton to Chapel-en-le-Frith, by high-road. Route 24.

Castleton to Slack Hall Inn, 5¼ m; *Chapel-en-le-Frith (Midland station),* 7¼ m; *(L. and N.-W. station),* 8 m.

Route fully described the reverse way on p. 22.

**** The milestones on this route reckon from a point **half-a-mile** short of the town, and 1 mile short of the Midland station.*

Two miles from Castleton by high-road, one and a-half by footpath, which leaves the road about a mile on the way and climbs the side of Tray Cliff, is the Blue John Mine (p. 88). Half-a-mile further, and a few hundred yards beyond the divergence of the Buxton road, it is worth while to cross a field on the right to the slight depression west of Mam Tor for the view of Edale (p. 89). The main road is regained a quarter of a mile beyond the point at which you left it, the *détour* having involved only a few hundred yards' extra walking. Two miles of high-level country succeed, after which the descent to Chapel-en-le-Frith commands an interesting view in front and on the right hand. The centre of Chapel-en-le-Frith is a quarter of a mile short of the Midland, and 1 mile short of the L. and N.-W. station.

Castleton to Hayfield by Upper Edale and Edale Cross.
Pedestrian Route (No. 25).

Castleton to Barber Booth (Edale), 4¼ m; *Edale Cross*, 7½ m; *Hayfield*, 11 m. *No inn on the way. A small one at Edale Chapel.*

Route fully described the reverse way on page 25.

This is a delightful walk, and should be taken by every one who may be returning in the direction of Cheshire and Lancashire without having previously seen Edale. It is much to be preferred to the direct routes to Buxton or Chapel-en-le-Frith.

Follow the Chapel-en-le-Frith road (*p.* 95) as far as the diverging point therein mentioned, half a mile beyond the Blue John Mine. Thence cross the field to the depression west of Mam Tor, where you will re-enter a road after cutting off an acute angle. For the view from this point see page 89. A winding road commanding a beautiful prospect up and down *Edale*, descends to *Barber Booth* at the bottom of the valley. Thence follow the dale upwards as far as the road will take you. At the last group of cottages called *Lees*, a charming spot, it becomes a mere bridle path, and then, after crossing a little stone bridge, commences the steep climb to *Edale Cross*, p. 25. The bridle-path doubles round to the left and makes an acute angle, which an obvious foot track, called *Jacob's Ladder*, cuts off, re-entering the authorised path by a stone step-stile. At the highest point of the pass, and hidden by a wall on the right hand of it, is the *Cross*, whence to the top of Kinderscout is only about 20 minutes' walk. The descent from the Cross to Hayfield needs no further description than that given of the reverse route.

Castleton to Hathersage, Eyam, Stoney Middleton, Baslow, Rowsley, and Matlock. Route 26.

Castleton to Hope, 1½ m; Hathersage, 6 m; Grindleford Bridge, 9 m;—(Eyam, 11¼ m.) Calver 11½ m; Baslow, 13 m; Edensor (Chatsworth Park), 14¼ m; Rowsley Station, 18¼ m; Matlock (by train), 24 m.

This is deservedly one of the most popular driving routes in Derbyshire, but it is much oftener commenced at Matlock or Rowsley than at Castleton. The part of it between Castleton and Hathersage has been fully described the reverse way in the Sheffield and Castleton coach route (*p.* 40), and the remaining portion we shall describe in detail in the Matlock Section. We shall, therefore, in this section give a bare outline of the route.

The "lions" of Hope Dale, which extends as far as Hathersage, have already been seen by every traveller who has entered Castleton, no matter by what route. On the left, the valley is flanked by Back Tor and Lose Hill; on the right, the hills retire behind Bradwell Dale. Half-way to Hope we pass the never-to-be-sufficiently-execrated chimney, to which we have so often, alas!

Rte. 26.] CASTLETON TO MATLOCK. 97

felt bound to draw attention (it has been our "pet" nightmare for years). A **cupola** smelting furnace is, **we** believe, responsible for it. At Hope **(p. 40), the** waters descending from Castleton **are** quadrupled by **the contri**bution of Edale, and **at** *Mytham Bridge*, 2½ miles further, the **Derwent** swallows both **up in its abundant** stream. As **we** approach Hathersage, **a** modern building crowning the hill above Bamford is a prominent object; **it is called** *The Tower.* At *Hathersage* **(p. 40)** we diverge to the **right from** the coach-road to Sheffield. Those who have no other **opportunity** of travelling this road, should **certainly** make time to ascend **by it as far as** the view-point called **the** "Surprise" (1½ **m. from Hathersage**), although the prospect, gradually worked up to as it is by those who **travel** in this direction, loses that part of its effect which it derives **from** the suddenness of its appearance in the other. The ascent may be continued **to** *Fox House Inn* (p. 38), 1½ miles further, whence the Derwent **valley** may be **again** reached by good roads either **at** *Grindleford Bridge* (2½ m.) **or at** *New Bridge*, beyond *Froggatt Edge* (p. 35, **4 m.).** The **descent by** Froggatt Edge is very fine.*

Continuing **along the valley from** Hathersage, **we** pass through beautifully **wooded scenery with the** river, alternately still and restless, by our side, to *Grindleford Bridge* (Inn). Half a mile further the Eyam road **(p.** 38**) climbs to the** right. *For a description of the village see p.* 81. Then **we pass on** the left **the** square mansion of *Stoke Hall*, **and soon join the** Froggatt Edge road from Sheffield a little short **of the divergence to** *Stoney Middleton*, whose strange, **not** to say ugly octagonal church, is visible on the right hand. At **Calver** (Inn), we recross the Derwent close to **a huge mill, and after** passing on **the left the** *Hulme Cliff College*, **a large new building, erected for missionary purposes, very soon reach the** village and charmingly **placed little church of** *Baslow* (p. 132). The principal inns **are** nearly **half a mile to the left of our route, on the** Sheffield road, and close to **the northern entrance to Chatsworth** Park. Chatsworth House is 1½ miles distant from this part of Baslow, but proceeding **along our present route, we only enter the park at** *Edensor*, 1¾ miles beyond Baslow village. *For Edensor and Chatsworth see p*. 110-115. The Rowsley route continues for more than a mile through the park, **and then crosses the river** for the fifth time. Just beyond **the bridge the pedestrian may cut off a corner** by taking a wide **footpath on the right hand which** rejoins **the road at the** little **village of** *Beeley*, 1½ miles short of Rowsley station. **For** *Rowsley see p.* **127, and for the route on to** *Matlock p*. 71.

---

* From the "Surprise," or *Millstone Nick*, **as it is properly called, you may** continue across the moor pretty much in the same **direction as you have been** ascending, and in about half-a-mile drop into and **cross by a footbridge the** *Burbage Brook* (p. 38), at its most beautiful part. **On the other** ide is the road to Grindleford Bridge.

Guide, IV. H

MATLOCK SECTION.

Matlock.

Hotels: MATLOCK BATH; *New Bath, Royal, Temple, Bath Terrace*; on the hill-side to the right of the terrace, ¼ to ½ m. from the station. *Hodgkinson's, Devonshire, Rutland Arms*; comfortable inns between the station and the hotels. *Midland, Station*, close to the station, frequented by excursionists.

MATLOCK BRIDGE. *Old English*, by the river-side. Chief Hydropathic Establishments: *Smedley's, Matlock House, Rockside House*, &c.

Distances. *Ashbourne*, 12 m. *Bakewell*, 10 m. *Buxton*, 22 m. *Castleton*, 24 m. *Chatsworth*, 10 m. *Chesterfield*, 11 m. *Derby*, 16 m. *Haddon Hall*, 7½ m. *Sheffield* (rail), 32 m. (road), 23 m. *N.B.*—Reckoned from hotels at *Matlock Bath*.

Post Office, in the Terrace; *Arr.* 7 a.m., *dep.* 7.45 p.m.

The district which goes by the name of Matlock consists of Matlock Bath, Matlock Bridge, and Matlock Bank, and extends along the valley of the Derwent for upwards of two miles. The scenery of this part of the valley is perhaps the most romantic in Derbyshire. All the hills which contribute to the beauty of Matlock are over-topped by others within a very short distance, but they drop so abruptly into the valleys as to gain an impressiveness out of all proportion to their height. The river flows through a narrow gorge which begins at Matlock Bridge and ends at Cromford, a mile south of the centre of Matlock Bath. Both Matlock Bridge and Matlock Bank lie a little to the north of this gorge, at the southern end of the strath of Darley Dale, but Matlock Bath is in its very centre, just where the river suddenly sweeps round to the right, and the surrounding hills shut out all the world beside. On the right bank, as you descend the stream, the slopes rise green and steep and sylvan, and it is on this side that nearly all the village is built; on the left bank, except for a break of a few hundred yards, sheer precipices of limestone variegated with ivy and yew and such other trees and plants as find a genial soil in that kind of rock, rise almost from the water's edge. Scotch tourists may be reminded of Dunkeld, though the cruel treatment which the Derwent has suffered from the weirs and dams which obstruct its course has quite spoilt whatever chance it might otherwise have had of holding its own against the lordly Tay, and the precipices of the High Tor cannot vie in grandeur with the fir-clad heights of Craig-y-Barns.

That Matlock should be overrun with trippers during the holiday season is the inevitable penalty of its beauty and accessibility, and it is idle to deny that on bank-holidays and such-like occasions the ordinary tourist requires a philosophic spirit. The place, however, contains abundant accommodation for all classes of visitors, and those whose purses or legs are long enough to carry them to the various spots of interest in the neighbourhood may always escape from the periodical incursions of the *profanum vulgus*.

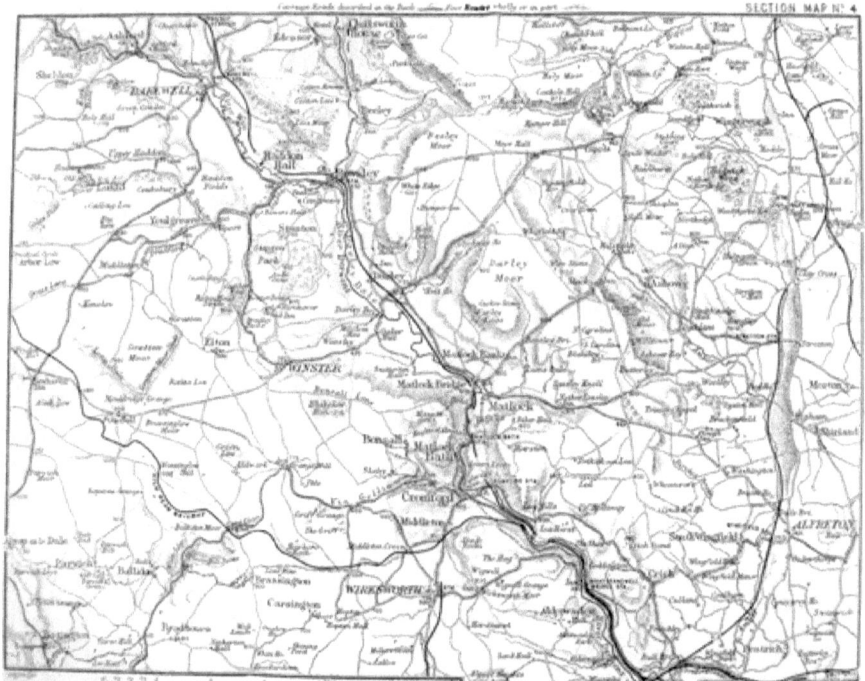

SECTION MAP Nº 4

holly or in part

SECTION MAP Nº 4

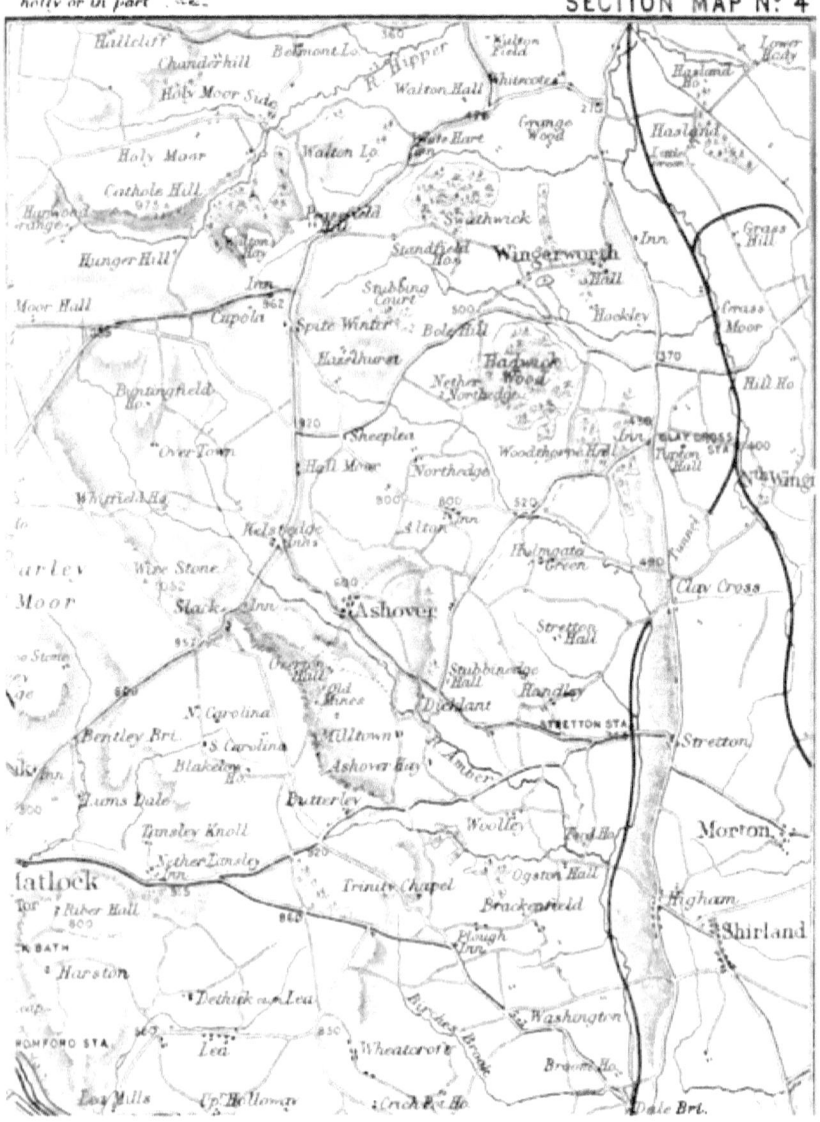

Pavilion and Gardens.
This latest addition to the attractions of Matlock covers an area of about 15 acres, and extends upwards from the New Bath, Terrace, and the Royal Hotels, almost to the Bonsall footpath. The whole overlooks the valley, and the views, especially from the higher parts, are very fine, the chief feature being the richly-wooded limestone cliffs which beetle over the Lovers' Walks and the Derwent. The *Pavilion* itself is a fine building, with a spacious central saloon, adapted for concerts, promenading, &c., and with wings on each side. It also contains, in the way of apartments and appliances, whatever may be needed for indoor recreation when outdoor is denied. In front of it is the *Terrace*, extending the length of the building, and fronted by a handsome balustrade. The gardens are laid out with a maze of winding walks, planned so as to change the steepest of slopes into a gently rising promenade. The difficulty has been—not to produce picturesqueness—rock, wood, and rugged unevenness of surface already provided that; but to avoid destroying it; and how far success has been attained the visitor must judge for himself. High up, in the north-east corner of the grounds, are the *Romantic Rocks*, a strange group of huge isolated fragments, which have been torn away from the adjacent hill-side without losing their equilibrium. Walks wind between them. In this part of the grounds, too, is an old excavation called the *Victoria Cavern*. It is about 250 yards long and almost straight. Though possessed of no unique attractions, it has a special interest for the geologist.

The Baths.—The *Fountain Baths*, on the main road in the centre of the village, include a large Swimming Bath in a lofty and cheerful room; also Hot Baths, Shower Baths, and Douche Baths. There are also *Swimming Baths* at the New Bath and Royal Hotels. In the gardens of the "New Bath" is a fine old lime-tree.

The **Petrifying Wells.** These abound in and about the Museum Parade. As the admission is only 1d. most visitors will like to witness an operation of Nature which can only be seen in this and a few other places. To be thoroughly petrified requires, we believe, about two years. In this street there are also a large number of museums, or shops, for the sale of the spar ornaments and articles of use made in the locality.

The Caves. These are to a great extent old mining excavations, though some part of nearly every one is the result either of violent natural disruption or of the characteristic wearing away of limestone rock by water. Those whose standard of subterranean impressiveness has been fixed by the Castleton caverns, or of beauty by the famous one at Cheddar, will probably think lightly of these hybrid Matlock ones, but caverns, after all, are rare in tourist districts, and whatever motive may prompt you to go in, there is always a certain pleasure in getting out again. If it is not a "trip" day you should decidedly make at least one underground excursion. To geologists these caverns are specially interesting, and the comparative absence of stalactitic formations is often atoned for by the abundance of dog-tooth crystallizations and the frequent outcrop therein of the precious metal in search of which the openings were originally made. The minimum charge for admission is 1s. or 6d., parties being charged at a reduced scale according to their number. It is well to strike a bargain before entering. As to position, four of them, the Cumberland, the Speedwell, the Fluor Spar, and the Devonshire are on the hill-side, behind the Pavilion grounds; two, the Rutland and the Great Masson, on the Heights of Abraham, near the Victoria Tower, and one, the Grotto Cavern, underneath the High Tor. There is also the Victoria Cavern in the Pavilion grounds.

(1) **The Cumberland Cavern** (*minimum charge*, 1s.). This is the longest and least artificial of all. The shortest way to it from the Parade is by a steep foot-path, commencing with some steps adjacent to the Bath Terrace Hotel and skirting the far side of the Pavilion grounds. Another route is to ascend at once after crossing the bridge from the station, and to take the Cromford foot-path, between which and the Pavilion grounds the cavern is entered. It consists of a labyrinth of artificial passages, with many steps connecting several natural chambers fairly extensive but deficient in height. The first of these chambers has its roof as flat and horizontal as the floor is the reverse. The end of the cavern displays a chaotic collection of rocks of all shapes and sizes. The total length is 600 yards. Fossils abound.

(2) The **Speedwell Cavern** (*minimum charge*, 6d.). This is a few yards beyond the divergence of the lower Bonsall and Cromford foot-paths, close to which is the cottage of the proprietress. It may be approached by the same route as the Cumberland. It is upwards of 400 yards long, entered by many steps, and chiefly remarkable for the quantity of calc or cubic spar—called also dog-tooth. A few small stalactites are pointed out, some effective transparencies, and a little well.

(3) The **Fluor Spar Cavern** (*minimum charge*, 6d.). This, also on the lower Bonsall foot-path, may be reached either from the station by the same route as that already described to the Cumberland Cavern, or by the zig-zag path leading up from the near (east) entrance to the Pavilion grounds. It is entered from an artificially formed level called "*Jacob's Hillock*" at the top of this path. The area, like the foot-path behind it, commands a very fine view across the valley. It is in the same proprietorship as the cave, but the only charge is for visiting the cave, which, as usual, is entered by many steps. The length of the excavation is about 40 yards. It contains barytes, veins of lead ore, fluor spar, and calc spar. As a feature a little gallery is shown, a copy in miniature of the one in the Peak Cavern at Castleton.

(4) The **Devonshire Cavern** is on the direct Bonsall path, a few yards beyond the point at which it strikes up the hill from the more circuitous one. Its most remarkable feature is the immense slab of rock, quite flat, which forms its roof and slopes at a considerable angle. It contains a large quantity of stalagmite, also fluor spar and calc spar. The floor is a débris of rock and boulder.

(5) The **Rutland Cavern** (*admission*, 6d.). This is the largest of the Matlock caverns. It is approached either by the Holme Road from the station, or from the Waterloo Road, near Hodgkinson's Hotel. The guide's cottage is at the east entrance to the heights of Abraham, in Masson Road. There is a very pretty bird's-eye view of the valley between Matlock and Cromford from the roadway opposite the entrance to the cavern, which begins with an artificial passage nearly 80 yards in length. Then comes a chamber about 100 yards long and reaching in one place a height of 120 feet, and branching into two towards its end. On the sides there is a fair quantity of fluor spar and carbonate of lime spar. Perhaps the most striking object in the cave is a pillar which with the ribs of the arches it supports resembles the gnarled trunk of an oak tree. The cave is lighted with gas.

(6) The **Old Roman Lead Mine and Great Masson Cavern** is just above the Heights of Abraham, on the way to Masson. Its entrance is reached by a passage between two rocks, and visitors may pass through it on to the upper part of Masson. The cavern is about 70 yards long and attains a height of 90 feet. It contains fluor spa and dog-tooth crystals.

(7) The **High Tor Grotto** (*admission*, 6d.). This cavern, though small, is the best for crystalisation in Matlock. It is under the High Tor, ¼ m. north of the station, and is entered from the main road by a foot-bridge across the Derwent.

MATLOCK.

A passage of 12 yards or so leads to the natural cave, which has been lo vered in the first part, and raised in the last, to admit a walk through it. The limestone strata, resting on clay, dip inwards from above the entrance till they sink below the level of the river outside. The dog-tooth cry-tals are very abundant, some parts of the surface being entirely made up of them; about 12 feet above the roof is one of the High Tor tunnels, and the trains, as they pass through, produce a sound like thunder. At the further end the opening becomes lower than the level of the river, which the water inside always maintains. This cave was discovered by an old man tracking a rabbit in 1820.

The Heights of Abraham. *Admission* 6d. This steep acclivity rises directly from the north side of the Museum Parade, and is reached by several narrow roads—one striking up from the station. Broad zigzag walks lead to the top of it, whereon is the *Victoria Tower*, more conspicuous than graceful. Near to the Tower are the *Rutland Cavern* and the *Old Roman Cave*. Visitors should extend their walk from the tower to the top of *Masson*, about half-a-mile distant, and recognizable by its clump of trees. Its height is 1,076 feet, and it commands a wide and beautiful all-round view, including the valley of the Derwent north and south of Matlock, and the smaller dales which strike up westwards to the high ground between it and Dovedale. A path connects Masson with the highest part of the Bonsall track (p. 102).

The High Tor, 400 feet. Admission 4d. This rock dominates the gorge between Matlock Bridge and Cromford, and perhaps contributes more than any other object to the romantic character of the Matlock scenery. Its upper part is quite perpendicular, and the lower consists of screes overgrown with scrub and timber of larger dimensions. The approach to it is across the river by the bridge leading to the station, and under the line between the station and the first northward tunnel.* A good walk skirts first the edge of the cliff, and then the face of it a little below its crest.

Through the green slope a little behind the scarped front of the tor, runs a deep fissure only a few feet wide, and so narrow at the top as only to admit a streak of daylight. It is needless to say that the rough parts of this fissure have been smoothed over so as to make it passable throughout. The walk should be taken.

The Lovers' Walks. Along the east side of the Derwent, opposite Matlock Bath, a line of cliff extends, considerably lower than the High Tor, but similar in character. The picturesque effect of these cliffs is greatly enhanced by the ivy which spreads itself all over them, the yews which grow out of their crannies, and the wood which covers the scree at their feet. There is an upper and lower walk along them—the latter by the river-side. These walks can only be reached by crossing the river at the ferry opposite the bend of the road at the Royal Hotel, and about a third of a mile from the station. Otherwise either the cliffs themselves or high walls and trespass boards forbid both entrance and exit.

* Or by a footbridge ½ m. nearer Matlock Bridge, whence also there is a drive.

WALKS FROM MATLOCK BATH.

(1) Bonsall, 1½ m; Cromford, 3 m; Matlock Bath, 4 m.

A more delightful ramble than this can hardly be imagined. In less than two hours it brings before the eye every beautiful object that is typical of Matlock scenery. The view is only curtailed northwards, in which direction Masson interposes its superior height, hiding Darley Dale and the Chatsworth and Haddon country, a district which, with all its attractiveness, is as essentially distinct in character from Matlock as the sudden change from the limestone to the gritstone formation can render it.

There are two footpaths from Matlock Bath to Bonsall. One may be seen climbing the hill westwards from all parts of the village; the other, the longer and prettier of the two, diverges to the left half way up the hill and passes above the Cumberland Cavern and the Pavilion Gardens. A little way up the latter path is a stage on the left hand called "Jacob's Hillock," and affording access to the "Fluor Spar Cavern" (p. 100). The view from this part of our walk is very charming, and must have been much more so before the valley below was so filled with houses and the free course of the stream held back by weirs. The "Lovers' Walk" cliffs look their best.

Beyond the "Hillock" the footpath reaches the brow of the hill, and a view of the valleys which converge upon the Derwent at Cromford, opens up in front. Chief amongst them is the *Via Gellia* (p. 122), a winding V shaped glen with finely wooded sides and here and there a limestone cliff cropping out above them. This valley in contrast and combination with that of the Derwent, stretching southwards to Ambergate, and the charming retrospect over Matlock itself, makes up a prospect of a high order of beauty. Riber Castle crowns the hill behind us; south of it is Crich Stand.

Our route now joins the lane leading up from Cromford, and in a few hundred yards enters Bonsall, a quaint and sweetly placed little village with a very picturesque little church, an inn of the seventeenth century (*The King's Head*), a Cross still more ancient on a pedestal of some twenty steps, and drinking fountains innumerable. We may go far before we find a village combining so picturesque a situation with so much that is interesting in itself. The spire of the church is octagonal, and belted in two places with ornamental carving, which gives it a very pleasing appearance.

Dropping into the valley from the village, we pass an elegant fountain opposite the entrance gates to *Bonsall Manor House*, and descend at once to the lower part of the Via Gellia (p. 122), entering in a short time Cromford, which we shall describe in our next excursion.

This walk may be very pleasantly prolonged by taking a footpath close to the entrance to Bonsall Manor House and crossing by it into the Via Gellia, or by climbing from the latter to the Black Rocks, which are the subject of our next description.

(2) **Cromford**, 1 m; **Black Rocks**, 2½ m. The Black Rocks command the best view of Matlock from the south, and should either be made the object of a special excursion, or **taken in combination with the** above described walk to Bonsall Dale.

The village of **Cromford** (Inn: *The Greyhound*) lies 1 mile south of Matlock Bath, and is entered by a narrow opening in the rock, just beyond the point at which the river turns away to the left through the grounds of Willersley Castle. From this opening a narrow isolated limestone ridge extends about half a mile eastwards. The most picturesque part of Cromford lies at the east end of this ridge, where the church, whose architectural blemishes are concealed by a complete covering of ivy, and the three-arched bridge, with round arches on one side and pointed ones on the other, materially assist Nature in producing a picture. The grounds of **Willersley Castle**, which rise from the north bank of the river hereabouts, are open to visitors by ticket on Mondays.

The *Cotton Mills* here only call for notice by reason of their size, and the fact that they were the first built in Derbyshire. (p. 10.)

From the open square in the centre of Cromford village, we ascend by the Wirksworth road till we have left the last row of houses a few hundred yards behind us. Then turning through a gate on the left we follow a cart-track with a plantation on the right, and cross the High Peak railway. The Black Rocks, or Stonnis, as they are sometimes called, rise directly from the other side of the line. The path works round them to the right, and on reaching the edge brings us face to face with the view.

Wherever the millstone grit crops out it affords favourable opportunities for obtaining views, and this peculiarity is nowhere better exemplified than by the **Black Rocks**. Behind them the ground rises to a somewhat greater elevation, and is covered with evergreen wood, but in front the entire geography of the Matlock district is seen at a glance. The rocks standing boldly out from the surrounding slopes, and often projecting in a way which suggests field-guns, afford a natural platform which no human contrivance could excel.

The great charm of the view centres in Matlock Bath, and the course of the Derwent above and below it. Where the river first appears, we have the High Tor rising almost sheer from its banks on the right, and the green, sylvan Heights of Abraham sloping more gently, but still steeply, on the left. Above the latter is the beech-crested Masson. Then we trace the river-course through the bowl in which Matlock lies, hemmed in by limestone crags on one side, and separated from Bonsall Dale and the Via Gellia by a lofty green ridge on the other. At Cromford, which is mapped out just under our eyes, the stream escapes from its gorge and flows through the rich park-like scenery of Willersley Castle, which is the most beautiful, if not the most conspicuous, architectural adornment of the scene. Riber Castle, whenever it forms part of a view, is perhaps the most conspicuous building in the country. Its square towers and solid walls rear themselves on the summit of a hill perfectly destitute of foliage, their size and massiveness making them more prominent than even Crich Stand, which occupies a similar but somewhat higher **plateau** a few miles further south.

By strolling through the **wood behind the** rocks for a short distance you will obtain a **comprehensive view** of the **Derwent valley between Ambergate and Cromford, and** quite as pleasing an impression of Wirksworth as is likely to result from a closer inspection of it (*but see p.* 139).

The return route may be varied in more ways than one: firstly, you may pass through the large mining village of *Middleton*, more conspicuous than inviting as seen from the rocks, and descend by road or path into the *Via Gellia*, whence Matlock is reached by road through Cromford or by footpath through *Bonsall*—the latter a delightful route (p. 59); secondly, you may drop into the Wirksworth valley, and after visiting the town cross the hill to the Derwent again, reaching Matlock either on foot through *Cromford* or by rail from *Whatstandwell Bridge* (**p.** 139). *Distances:* Black Rocks to Middleton, 1¼ m; Via Gellia, 2 m; Bonsall, 3½ m; Matlock Bath, 5 m. Black Rocks to Wirksworth, 1½ m; Whatstandwell Bridge Station, 4¾ m.

Crich Stand. 6 m. *by road.* A thoroughly pleasant **walk or drive from** end to end. Those who wish to shorten it may take the train to Whatstandwell Bridge (3½ m., p. 9), **and** thence reach Crich in about 1¼ m. by road or path. A path which begins ⅙ mile north of the station is the pleasantest route. In either case the return may be agreeably varied by descending from Crich village (*small inns*) to Ambergate station. Crich village is half-a-mile south of the Stand, and Ambergate 2¼ miles further. About half way enter a by-road through a gateway opposite **the hamlet of Fritchley.**

Route. This passes through Cromford village (p. 103), and thence to the south of the singular ridge of limestone separating it from the river to the church and bridge. The scenery about here is very charming. Willersley Castle has been already mentioned (p. 103). After passing under the line at Cromford Station, we continue for a long mile side by side with the river, and then leave it to climb the hill on which stands **Lea Hurst**, the occasional residence of Florence Nightingale. The house, Elizabethan in character, is beautifully placed on the brow of the hill and to the right of our road. Beyond it we keep high up along the hill-side, and enjoy a charming view across the Derwent valley. **The tower called Crich Stand** crowns the hill on our left. Its base is 955 feet above sea-level, and higher than anything else within a circuit of several miles. In fact, except in the north and north-west, **where** the higher uplands of the Peak rise more or less near at hand, it commands an unobstructed view in every direction, the possibilities including Lincoln Cathedral and Belvoir Castle.

In the summer of 1882 a tremendous land-slip occurred **here,** breaking up the brow of the hill into a confused tract of ridges and chasms, removing a portion of the Cromford road many yards, as well as utterly destroying a house upon it, and even threatening the existence of the Stand itself.

Geologically speaking, **Crich Hill**, on which the tower stands, is one of the most interesting in the country. The highest part consists of limestone, which has been forced up from below through a later formation of millstone grit. A shaft sunk through the limestone, in search of lead ore, revealed the volcanic agency which caused this singular upheaval, a bed of lava being found in the middle of the hill. The quarry is extensively worked.

From the Stand we may devise a variety of routes. (1.) Descend by footpath to Whatstandwell Station (*Inn*), $1\frac{1}{2}$ m. distant. (2.) Continue through the village of Crich (*inns*) to Ambergate (3 m.), taking in the last mile a foot-road to the right which leads past the lime-kilns to the station. (3.) Follow the Alfreton road as far as Wingfield Manor ($2\frac{1}{2}$ m.) and Station ($4\frac{1}{2}$ m.) whence you may return to Matlock by rail. There is a delightful view from the footpath along the edge of the gritstone rocks at the highest part of the ridge which descends from Crich to Ambergate.

Wingfield Manor is both in appearance and situation a most attractive ruin. It occupies the brow of a green hill abundantly wooded, to a great extent with evergreens, and overlooking the valley of the Amber. It dates from the reign of Henry VI., and shares the stereotyped history of the residential ruins of the country:—it was a prison-house of Mary queen of Scots, and Cromwell dismantled it. Within its walls the futile Babington conspiracy for the liberation of the Scottish Queen was hatched.

The ruins, which are extensive, consist of two enclosed courts, entered by a fine gateway. Perhaps the most striking feature in connection with them is the diversified sky-line which they present, produced by the lofty tower, the gable ends of the banqueting hall, and the outside walls. Queen Mary is said to have occupied rooms on the west side of the inner court, which contains, amongst other good features, a fine octagonal window. Part of the interior has been converted into a farm-house, from which permission is easily obtained to explore the ruins.

There are village inns at Crich, Whatstandwell, and Wingfield, as well as a larger one with very fair accommodation at Ambergate Station. Crich also contains an ancient Market Cross recently restored, and some interesting features in its church.

(4.) Matlock Bath to Chesterfield and back. *To Chesterfield by road*, 12 m ; *by rail*, 20 m.

The most easterly ridge of the Peak country extends in a direction generally north and south between Matlock and Chesterfield, dwindling away to its end in the little angle formed by the union of the Derwent and Amber at Ambergate. Except for the part which we have described in the foregoing excursion—to Crich Stand— this district is hardly of sufficient picturesque interest to require detailed description in a tourist's guide book. The uplands are bleak and monotonous, and it is only along the course of the Amber, which in its upper part breaks the ridge into two, that real beauty of scenery is to be found. We shall, therefore, confine ourselves to a brief account of the special objects of interest, and a few hints as to the best way of getting at them.

The pedestrian's best plan is, perhaps, to take the train to one of the stations between Ambergate and Chesterfield, and to walk back. By so doing he keeps the best of the scenery before him. The half-way house of the walking part should, in any case, be Ashover, one of the pleasantest villages in the country. It is distant from Stretton Station 3 miles, from Clay Cross, 4½, and from Chesterfield, 7½. The last named has the advantage in the number of trains stopping at it, and some public interest attaches to its corkscrew spire. Otherwise, it is as uninteresting a town as can well be imagined. The Matlock road, however, commands fine and extensive views during the first four miles, which are almost entirely on the rise.

The road from Clay Cross has no special interest till it crests the hill a little south of Ashover. Then a scene of great beauty bursts suddenly on the eye. From Stretton a pretty country road follows the valley of the Amber.

The Route. The six miles between Matlock Bath and Ambergate are described the reverse way on page 9. Quitting Matlock the train enters a tunnel, from which it emerges into *Cromford* Station. Then, after running side by side with the river for a long mile, it goes by another tunnel underneath the hill on which stands Lea Hurst, and passes the terminus of the High Peak mineral line on the right hand. A good view of Crich Hill and Stand (*p.* 104), rising above a semi-circular combe, is then obtained on the left hand, and after passing *Whatstandwell* Station, rail, road, river, and canal run side by side all the way to *Ambergate*. At Alderwasley the scenery is greatly spoilt by a huge chimney rising from the centre of the valley.

Half an hour's waiting at Ambergate (*Inn:* The Hurt Arms) may enjoyably be spent in taking a little walk up the hill. From the inn pass under the two most westerly of the station bridges, and a few yards short of a third bridge turn up the lane on the left, which goes past the lime-kilns. After crossing the river and canal you will come to a footpath which takes you behind the lime-kilns and across the canal again into the Matlock road, a little north of the station. During the walk you cross an inclined plane leading from the top of the hill to the lime-kiln. The ingenious plan on which the trucks are moved up and down this plane is worthy of passing notice.

From Ambergate the Chesterfield line turns to the north-east, and after passing through a short tunnel, affords a view of Crich Church and Stand on the left hand, succeeded in a very short distance by Wingfield Manor (*p.* 105), which shows its tower and gable ends, rising from a grove of evergreens on a gentle slope, to great advantage. Beyond it is the village of *South Wingfield*, a full mile from the station, close to which, however, is the church. Nothing noteworthy now presents itself until we reach Stretton, the **nearest** station for Ashover (p. 108). The road thither, a very pretty one, needs no description. Between this and the next station is the well-known *Clay Cross Tunnel*, one mile long. At the station of Clay **Cross** the main Midland line from London converges. Considering the immense quantity of coal which the Clay Cross district produces, the usual unsightly indications of **such a** district are wonderfully few and far between. The **" black** country " element only shows itself intermittently. The **town** itself is more than a mile away, over the **tunnel.**

To reach **Ashover** (4½ m.) from Clay Cross you **strike** westwards from the station, and in about 10 minutes take a path in front **of** *Tupton Hall*, which brings you out at a junction of the roads, where there is an inn. Thence follow the Ashover high-road for about 2½ miles, at which distance take a lane to the right. By so doing you get **the** beautiful view over the Amber Valley referred to in **our** introductory **remarks to** this **route.**

Between Clay Cross and Chesterfield the only noteworthy objects visible **from the line are** *Wingerworth Hall* and *Church* situated on the slope **of** the **hill to the left.** The former is a large white **mansion** in the Italian **style. It was** garrisoned for the Parliament in 1643.

Before entering the station **at Chesterfield** we obtain a full **view** of the extraordinarily **twisted** spire of the Parish Church. **" Looks as if it had a** spinal **complaint,"** a fellow passenger once **remarked to us.** To travellers **it** is the most unfailing source of conversation we know. At a rough guess 40 through trains a day will pass Chesterfield between sunrise and **sunset,** and **it is** seldom that a fairly filled compartment **gets** past without one **of its occupants** hazarding a guess as to how the deformity arose. **There can be little** doubt that **the** woodwork underneath the outer case **of** lead **was** put in before **it was properly** dried, and that consequently it warped. Setting **apart the** ' wonderful,' **few people** will deny that the spire is about as unsightly an object as the eye can rest upon, and nothing, probably, but association prevents **it being** rebuilt. In other respects the church is interesting.

The chief hotel—and a very good one—at Chesterfield **is** the *Angel*, in the Market Place, half **a** mile from the station. A local feud with the gas company led to Chesterfield being the first town **in England to** adopt the electric **light for its** street illumination.

Chesterfield to Ashover, 7½ m ; **Matlock Bath,** 13 m.

The long line **of hills** between Chesterfield and the **Derwent** valley is crossed by roads which **reach** the latter at Baslow (8½ **m.**), Rowsley (9¾ m.), Darley Dale **(10 m.),** and Matlock Bridge (10 **m.**). The introduction of railways **into the** district **has** reduced **the** second and third of these almost **to the condition** of grass-roads in their highest parts, about **1,**000 feet above sea-level, but the other two,—to Baslow and Matlock respectively,—**are** still **good carriage** roads. To the tourist in search of **scenery they are none** of them to be recommended throughout, but the route which we are going to describe—by road as far as Ashover and thence by a cross-country track, is really interesting. The milestones, as usual, misrepresent the distance. Reckoning from the centre of the town half a mile should be added to the number given on each, and from the railway station, 1 mile.

All these roads are identical to begin with, taking a direction due west out of Chesterfield. One mile from the Market Place that to Matlock, Rowsley and Darley Dale, strikes out of the Baslow one at right angles, and for the next $3\frac{1}{2}$ miles is mostly on the rise. Then, a short distance from a road-side inn, called the Red Lion, the Darley Dale and Rowsley road strikes off to the right. The Matlock one goes straight on, and in another 2 miles drops to the little hamlet of Kelstedge (2 *small inns*) in the Amber valley. Hence we see the church of Ashover about a mile away on the left. A road diverging in the same direction leads directly to it.

Ashover (Inns: *The Red Lion*, &c., &c., all small, but comfortable) is delightfully placed in the best part of the Amber valley, but except its church, which is very pleasing in situation and outward appearance, it contains nothing calling for special remark. Inside the church is an old font adorned with leaden figures, and seven centuries old. Outside, the visitor may remark a stone coffin. Above the village is a comfortable and well situated Hydropathic establishment.

In walking from Ashover to Matlock you may either rejoin in a mile the high-road which you left at Kelstedge, or you may cross the moor to *Tansley*, and thence continue over the high ground past *Riber Castle*, whence you will drop into Matlock Bath by the path which passes south of the High Tor, and goes under the railway a little north of the Station. In either case, start from Ashover by a stone footpath, which you may see from the churchyard climbing the green hill opposite. From the top of this path the high-road is easily regained. For Tansley (*inn*) the pleasantest route is by a narrow lane, a little to the right of Overton Hall, and on by a footpath which climbs obliquely over the refuse of an old mine to the top of the ridge and there enters another lane, reaching in another mile the high-road from Matlock Bridge to Stretton Station, at a point 3 miles from the former, and $1\frac{1}{4}$ miles short of Tansley.

Chatsworth House and Haddon Hall.

Among all the artificial adornments of the Peak of Derbyshire, these two places rank immeasurably first in popular regard. Their proximity to each other brings them within easy scope of one excursion. We include them in this particular section of our volume, because Matlock is the nearest to them of the centres which we have chosen, and because a larger number of tourists visit them from Matlock than from any other of those centres. As, however, there are many smaller places at which good tourist accommodation is obtainable, within a shorter distance of one or both of them, we append a distance table.

	CHATSWORTH.		HADDON.	
	By carriage.	On foot.	By carriage.	On foot.
Bakewell	4	3	2	2
Baslow	2½	1¾	6¼	5
Edensor	—	⅓	5½	5¼
Matlock Bath	10	9½	7¾	7½
Rowsley	4	3½	1¾	1½

All the carriage routes to Chatsworth reach it from the west side of the river, whereon, half a mile from the House, and close to the village of Edensor, is the Chatsworth Hotel, a large and favourite hostelry. No one is allowed on the direct drive which passes between the Baslow and Rowsley ends of the Park, along the east side of the river, close to the House. The gain which pedestrians obtain in several instances arises from their being able to use a direct footpath leading from Baslow to the House, and running parallel with the drive; from their avoiding the winding road between the bridge at the Rowsley end and that opposite the house, and from the convenience afforded by the footpath across the hill between Chatsworth and Haddon. We have been at special pains to describe this path in both directions, because it is as great a pity to miss it as it is a difficulty to find it. The walk is a charming one, affording lovely views over the richest portions of the valleys of the Derwent and the Wye, and to many tourists it will bequeath the happiest reminiscence of their day's excursion. It is, perhaps, easier to follow from Haddon to Chatsworth than in the reverse direction, the difficulty in going from Chatsworth being to get out of the park at the right point.

The road from Matlock needs little description beyond what we give in other routes. As far as *Rowsley* (6 m.) you may "go as you like"—rail, carriage, or foot. During the season public conveyances make the round at very moderate fares—about 3s.—every day. They leave Matlock Bath about 10 a.m. and return from Edensor Hotel about 5 p.m. *For the rail to Rowsley, see p. 10; for the road p. 127.*

Pedestrians who visit Haddon first should not forget the footpath which starts at the Wye Bridge, one mile beyond Rowsley, and leads directly to the Hall.

Rowsley to Chatsworth. Omnibuses from the Edensor Hotel meet several trains at Rowsley. **These are the** only conveyances privileged **to use the** direct drive. Pedestrians may take **either** side of the **river from** Rowsley. The footpath along the west side is rather the shorter, and in dusty weather the pleasanter **of the two routes. By the road route** on the east side you obtain **a beautiful** view up the **river**, including Chatsworth itself, very soon after **leaving** Rowsley. Then just opposite the little *Church** of **Beeley (***Inn***),** which half a century ago was re-naved in the **most knavish fashion,** take a wide footpath to the left. This cuts **off a corner, and ends at** the bridge at the south end of the park, **after crossing which** you join the footpath along the west side of **the river and may** proceed by the water's edge to the bridge opposite the House.

For **the** approaches to Chatsworth from Bakewell, **see p. 71**; from Haddon (direct), p. 120. The footpath from Baslow **starts** either **from** the main road near the "Peacock," **or** from a **by-road behind the** other inns.

* Now prettily restored.

Chatsworth House.

Open *from* 11 *a.m. till* 4 *p.m. Saturdays till* 1 *p.m. No charge is exacted from visitors.*

Of the appropriateness of this palatial mansion to the natural **features** of the ground on which it is built, it is hardly our pro**vince to speak.** Those who accept a Palladian style of architecture **as suitable to** any and every kind of scenery will go on piling up **their favourite** epithets as long as the building exists and they are **alive to see it,** while others will gratefully recognize the liberality **which throws the** house and **its** artistic treasures open to all comers, **and the privilege** of being allowed to wander at their pleasure through **the glades of its really** beautiful park. The only demurrer which **we would venture to put in, is** against the artificial treatment which **the Derwent has undergone in** its course through the grounds, **whereby its channel has** been converted **into a** series of fishponds. **In this** respect it offers a strange contrast with the neighbouring Wye. **The latter** stream left to **its** own devices between **Bakewell and Rowsley winds** and sparkles past the leafy glades of **Haddon with a** joyousness which can hardly fail to communicate **itself to** the heart of every passer-by.

It is, perhaps, hardly fair to compare, **without reservation,** Chatsworth with Haddon,—a comparatively modern inhabited **building** with an old uninhabited one. *Quæque antiquissima optima*—**"the** oldest the best"—is a widely accepted motto, and **to** no **art is it** more applicable than to architecture, as well domestic as ecclesiastical.

History. The last thing that Chatsworth, the first that Haddon suggests is history. The glamour of newness about the former is almost painful. Under its spell even the grand works of the old masters which it contains look as if they were scarcely a hundred years old, and the rosary of King Henry VIII. is as bright and fresh in its appearance as if it had been made yesterday. Yet Chatsworth has a history, and one by no means devoid of interest. It formed part of that wide domain, including also Haddon and Castleton, which the semi-royal William Peveril received from his father, William the Conqueror. Then it passed through two families whose names are not sufficiently suggestive to modern ears to be worth mentioning, into the possession of the Cavendish family. The first representative of that name to hold it was Sir William Cavendish, second husband of the famous "Bess of Hardwick," whose passion for building was attributed to a superstitious belief on her part that she would never die as long as she continued doing so. She finished the building which last occupied the site of the present one, and then married her fourth and last husband, the Earl of Shrewsbury. It was at this time that Mary Queen of Scots occasionally resided at Chatsworth, and the reason ascribed for her being so often brought here would still hold good under similar circumstances, viz.: the remoteness of the locality from large towns where conspiracies might be conveniently hatched. After this Chatsworth was held alternately for King and Parliament during the Civil War. The present building was begun in 1687 by the fourth Earl of Devonshire and finished in 1706. Here again the quasi-newness of Chatsworth strikes us forcibly. Few people could imagine from its present appearance that it was anterior to the crescents of Bath and Buxton.

Description. Almost everything pertaining to Chatsworth, both inside and outside, is splendid and magnificent, and it will save visitors the vexation of having these words constantly before their eyes, if they will kindly realise this fact to begin with, and excuse us for not repeating them with each work of art to which we shall draw passing attention. They apply to every square yard of the outside of the mansion, and the only part of the inside which does not merit them, even to a still greater degree, would seem to be the passages and staircases connecting the different suites of rooms. These hardly consist with the style of the rooms themselves. One thoroughly beautiful and distinguishing characteristic of the interior is the exquisite *wood-carving* found in the Chapel and the suite of State Rooms. Whether this carving is to be ascribed, according to popular tradition, to Grinling Gibbons, or, according to "accounts rendered," to the Derbyshire-born-and-bred Samuel Watson, we must leave abler authorities than ourselves to settle. Of parallel interest with the wood-carving are the *frescoes* which adorn the walls and ceilings of the principal rooms. Here we must again turn 'heretic' for a moment, and with the remembrance even of the Doge's Palace at Venice, as well as the Duke's at Chatsworth venture upon a humble opinion that the painting of ceilings is a mistake, implying a wanton disregard of Nature's "honest rule" that a man should stand upright and look straight before him.

Obliterate intervening history, and fancy an observant critic a century hence visiting Chatsworth. He would write somewhat as follows:—" The customary attitude of the higher classes of European Society during these centuries of refinement was a supine one; their chief paintings were executed on the ceilings of their mansions, and they lay on their backs to admire them." Those who have ricked their necks at Chatsworth will understand what we mean.

As to the *Paintings* on canvas, and *Sketches in Sepia* at Chatsworth, we content ourselves with enumerating the chief masters who executed them—to offer the slightest criticism would be an impertinence. They include Titian, Giorgioni, Tintoretto; Leonardo da Vinci, Michael Angelo, Andrea del Sarto; Raffaelle; Albert Dürer; Correggio; Paul Veronese; the Caracci, Guido Reni, Domenichino, Guercino; Holbein, Rubens, Teniers, Van Dyck, Rembrandt; Claude Lorraine, Salvator Rosa; Poussin; Murillo; Sir Joshua Reynolds, and Sir Edwin Landseer.

Sculpture is another of the features of Chatsworth. In this department of art we meet with the master-pieces of Canova and Thorwaldsen.

The **Exterior** consists of one large rectangular block erected by the first Duke of Devonshire, and a long wing of one storey rising to three at its end, added by the last. Its style is Classical throughout, Ionic pillars rising between each set of gilt-framed windows, and a pediment, adorned with the Cavendish arms, crowning the central ones. On both sides of the pediment extends an open balustrade, surmounted by statues and urns. The words of *Cibber*, which we quote from " Murray," are very amusing with regard to this part of the ornamentation. He says, " For two statues, as big as life, I had £35 apiece, and all charges borne; and at this rate I shall endeavour to serve a nobleman in freestone." The identification of all these figures we must really leave to the visitor and the guide between them.

The Interior. Entering at the north end of the modern wing, through iron gilded gates, we obtain our guide at the Porter's Lodge and cross the courtyard to the Sub-Hall, a small apartment with a tesselated pavement, and a ceiling adorned with a copy of Guido's " Aurora," by Miss Curzon. Here, too, are several busts and a statue of Domitian.

From the sub-hall we pass through the *North Corridor* to the **Great Hall**. This room is 60 feet long, and nearly half that width. The floor is of black and white marble mosaic. Round three sides runs a gallery, above which the walls are frescoed with scenes from the life of Julius Cæsar, by Verrio and Laguerre, culminating in a representation of his apotheosis on the ceiling. In the centre is a large table, the top of which consists of one slab of Derbyshire marble, and in the way of curiosities we have a long *Turkish canoe* presented by the then Sultan.

Hence passing through the *South Corridor*, in which we may

notice the "English Club Room," said to be by Hogarth, and a *sarcophagus*, we enter the

Chapel. This apartment is wainscoted with cedar, carvings of flowers, fruit, foliage, and corn depending between the panels and over the upper doors. The floor is of black and white marble in mosaic. The *altar*, which is at the west end, is of Derbyshire spars, and on it are sculptured figures of "Faith" and "Hope" by Cibber. The painting above it is the "Incredulity of Thomas," by Verrio. Those round the room, above the panelling, represent various scenes in the life of Christ, the "Ascension" being depicted on the ceiling.

From the chapel we are conducted up two narrow flights of stairs through the *Etching Gallery*, noticing as we pass a fragment of the foot of Hercules, about two feet long in itself, into the State Apartments, which occupy the third storey, and have a south aspect over the garden. In the view thus gained the beauty of the valley and the formality of the gardens are equally noticeable. From the second doorway of this suite a full length view of the whole of it is obtained, doubled by a mirror at the farther end. The floors are of oak parquetry throughout, and the *wood carvings* are a special feature. The association of the Queen of Scots with these apartments it is surely unnecessary to refute. The first of them which we enter is the State Dressing Room. Herein is a master-piece of wood carving, with which Gibbons is still accredited by our conductress. It represents a cravat of point-lace, amid other objects as beautifully executed as they are inappropriate. The "China-maniac" will find much to interest him in this room. The principal subject of the ceiling is the "Flight of Mercury on his mission to Paris." That of the next apartment, the Old State Bedroom, is "Aurora chasing away the night." Herein is the canopy of the bed in which George II. died, and on either side of it the *coronation chairs* of George III. and Queen Charlotte; also one of Louis the Fourteenth's wardrobes. The walls of this and the next room are hung with leather relieved with rich gilding.

The State Music Room is the next in the suite. The *fresco* on the ceiling represents the story of Mars and Venus. Here, too, are the *coronation chairs* of William IV. and Queen Adelaide. A *cabinet* of precious stones contains, among countless other beautiful ones, a piece of emerald which, we are told, is the largest in the world. Behind a door, kept artistically half open, hangs a *fiddle* by which Verrio, it is said, successfully played off on his rival Gibbons the very trick which Parrhasius played on Zeuxis 2,300 years ago. The thing is as real as if it were seen through a stereoscope. Hence we pass to the State Drawing-room, the walls of which are hung with *Gobelin tapestry*, representing Raffaelle's cartoons. The ceiling shows "Phaethon driving the horses of the Sun."

In the State Dining Room, which we next enter, the *wood-carving* attains its climax in strings of game hanging down on each side of the fireplace. On the ceiling are the "Fates cutting the thread of life." The central table has on it, among other treasures, the *rosary* of Henry VIII. and its case. At the side is a *malachite clock* presented by the Emperor of Russia.

Amongst the other ornaments of this suite we may mention full-length portraits of the first Duke of Devonshire and others of royal or noble blood, in the full pomp of their robes of office; innumerable tables and cabinets, inlaid or enamelled; a set of ivory chess-men; a model of a Russian farm-house; and amongst the curiosities a gentle reminder of the "bag and baggage" policy, which in its time found favour with the house of Cavendish, in the shape of a *Turkish portmanteau*.

We now descend again, and pass through the **Picture Gallery**, in which will be found works by the old and modern masters we have already enumerated, and by many others of almost equal repute. One picture which attracts a good deal of attention, chiefly from its strong distinctions of light and shade, is the "Monks at Prayer." In the so-called Billiard Room, just beyond, are Landseer's "Bolton Abbey in the Olden Time" and the same artist's "Laying down the Law;" also an unfinished sketch by Sir Joshua Reynolds, representing the "beautiful duchess" as a baby. The baby hardly does justice to its after-self.

In traversing the passages from the picture gallery we may notice a large picture of the celebrated race-horse "Flying Childers" an equine "Colossus" under whose "huge legs" his pigmy rivals almost look as if they might literally "walk."—Then we enter the

Sculpture Gallery. Here amongst a host of figures between which only the critical eye will distinguish anything beyond the nicest shades of merit, we may, perhaps, draw attention to the "Endymion" and "Mother of Napoleon" of Canova; Thorwaldsen's "Venus;" Schadow's "Spinning Girl," and "A wounded Achilles" by Abricini. In the centre of the room is a huge *Mecklenburg vase* by Canteen, and in one corner a real Derbyshire gem,—a *vase*, which, though comparatively small, is the largest sample of "*Blue John*" handiwork in existence.

We now enter the **Orangery**, the transition room from in-door to out-door Chatsworth. In it, besides what its name implies and many other specimens of choice exotics, are beautiful sculptures, and a huge quartz crystal. Then, issuing into the open air we are placed under the conduct of a gardener, who with characteristic politeness introduces us to the wonders of the

Garden. If we once admit that Art does not out-step its province in entering into direct competition with Nature in Nature's own department; that there is nothing impertinent in the cockney pleasantry that a beautiful landscape is *almost equal* to the transformation scene in a pantomime—we may derive unmixed pleasure from the Chatsworth gardens. Indeed, in some parts of them Art has almost become second Nature, so forgiving a spirit has the latter manifested in over-growing hand-built rockeries with her own green livery, and effacing the signs of artificial treatment. In others, however, she has been openly defied. You cannot make a flooded stone staircase—the *Grand Cascade*, to wit—kept constantly swept and garnished, anything but a travestie on a natural cascade, nor a copper **willow tree** that squirts water on refractory visitors, anything but **an artificial** shower-bath. But the chief object of attraction in the gardens is the **Grand Conservatory**, a glass building erected by Sir Joseph Paxton, and which was the original of the Great **Exhibition** building of 1851. It is nearly 300 feet long, 120 wide, and 65 feet high. In it the rarest exotics, from the fan-palm, gaunt and heavy-topped, to the maiden-hair **fern**, the most beautiful thing in the building, find a congenial home. There is one cactus-like **plant—the American** aloe—which is **fabled to take** a hundred years to flower, and then to die.

Of the many **fountains** in the gardens the chief is the *Emperor Fountain*, named **in honour of the Czar** of Russia, who visited Chatsworth in 1844. When it plays, which it only does on special occasions, it shoots up water to a height of 267 feet—higher, we believe, than any other fountain in Europe.

High up on the hill-side, behind the house, is the **Hunting Tower**, a square turreted tower commanding a splendid prospect, and surmounted with flying colours when the Duke is at home.

Behind the House is the *French Garden*, and in front of it the *Italian*—both all a-glow with flowers in their proper season. Between the latter and the house we make our exit, the last things specially pointed out to us being a trio of fairly grown trees planted by various members of the Royal Family.

On our way to Edensor, for which take the broad footpath on the far side of the bridge, to the right of the carriage drive, we notice on our right hand, close to the river, a relic of old Chatsworth,—a low square-walled enclosure, surrounded by a moat, and called **Queen Mary's Bower** from its having been a favourite place of resort with that ill-fated lady during her sojourn at Chatsworth. Upon it grow several trees—amongst them a fine yew.

Edensor. This 'model' village, locally called 'Ensor,' lies on the opposite side of the river to Chatsworth, on the road to Bakewell, and just outside the park. The church, built from the designs of Sir Gilbert Scott, supersedes an old one taken down in 1867. It has a fine spire and is well proportioned throughout. The village displays all sorts of architecture from the Norman to the Swiss "cottage ornée," and basks under the gentle feudal sway of the lords of Chatsworth. To realise that its elegant villas are the residences of people of the "butcher and baker and candlestickmaker" order is a difficult matter.

A stained window in memory of the late Lord Frederick Cavendish has lately been placed in the church. The chief figure is that of Christ as the "Man of Sorrows."

Edensor to Bakewell Station, 2 *m*; **Town**, 2½ *m*. A beautiful walk. The carriage route is a mile longer, and far inferior in interest.
Take the road through Edensor village, passing to the right of the Church. A continuous ascent of more than a mile begins at once. From the hill thus gained both the Wye and the Derwent valleys appear to great advantage. A little beyond the crest of the hill the road splits, turning abruptly both right and left. From this point an obvious footpath descends steeply through a wood to Bakewell station and town.

Chatsworth to Haddon Hall (3¼ *m*.). *Pedestrian Route.*
For general remarks see p. 109.

From Chatsworth cross the river by the stone bridge opposite the house to Edensor (*p.* 115), which you should certainly take a peep at on the way. The hotel lies to the right of the village, just outside the park. From it or from the village, keep along the main drive southwards for a quarter of a mile, and then, just beyond a slight depression, cross the park to the belt of wood opposite. Enter the wood by a wooden step-stile, whence a plain path climbs through it, and emerges by a similar stile on to open ground. Looking ahead from this second stile, you will notice a clump of beech trees on the top of the hill beyond an intermediate valley, and slightly to the left of your previous direction. This clump you must make for. Your way to it is by an obvious cart-track to the bottom of the valley, just short of which you pass through a gate and over a stile on the right. Thence, leaving the farm called *Calton Houses* on the left, you pass along the dam of a little pool and ascend to the clump through a pasture dotted with numerous thorn trees. The beech-clump is on the highest ridge of the hill which separates the Derwent from the Wye. Beyond it you enter a field with a wall on the right hand. Cross the field diagonally, and pass through the wall at the first gate. A beautiful view over the Wye valley now discloses itself in front. From the gate continue along the ridge, with the wall on your left for about 200 yards, and then descend through the wood by a steep but evident track, which brings you out through a gate on to an old grass-road from Rowsley to Bakewell. In front of you as you pass through the gate is a narrow little ridge, with a grass-road across it, separating two opposite valleys, both of which must be avoided. Cross the ridge, and on the far side of it turn to the right, along a grass-road, between two stone gate-posts. This road passes in succession on the left hand a plantation, a farm, and the old bowling green of Haddon, and comes out close to Haddon Hall.

Haddon Hall.

However many and strong conflicting opinions may be formed about Chatsworth, there can be no question as to the claims of Haddon. Unless it be Raglan Castle, in Monmouthshire, we can bethink ourselves of no unmonastic building in the country which takes so firm a hold on our admiration. It has all that retirement and coyness of situation which Chatsworth lacks. Trees partially hide it from every point of the compass, and in conjunction with its own broken architectural outline divest it of all that formality of aspect which might appear incongruous with the diversified character of its natural surroundings.

History. William Peveril, natural son of the Conqueror, whom we have already mentioned in connection with Castleton, received also from his royal father the Manor of Bakewell, wherein lies Haddon. From his descendants the Ville of Haddon, as it was called, passed during the reign of Henry II. into the family of Avenell, which had already held it for some time as a fief. About the time of Richard I. the male line of the Avenells became extinct by the death of William Avenell, who, however, left two daughters. One of these presented a moiety of the Manor, as her marriage portion, to Richard de Vernon. The Vernons continued to hold high festival at Haddon for four centuries. During that time the other moiety of the Manor reverted to them. In the middle of the sixteenth century Dorothy Vernon, daughter of Sir George Vernon, who was dubbed from his magnificent hospitality, "King of the Peak," married John, afterwards " Sir" John Manners. Into the authenticity of the story of the elopement of this couple it is no part of our duty to enquire. True or false, as long as the door is there, and the steps with the darkling grove of yew at their foot—the tale will live and visitors will cherish it as devotedly or obstinately—which you will—as they cherish the romances of the faithful hounds of Beddgelert and Helvellyn.

Sir John Manners was a son of the Earl of Rutland, and by the decease of the seventh Earl without issue, his grandson succeeded to the title. The "Lords" of Rutland occupied Haddon as a residence till the beginning of the eighteenth century. Then they gradually forsook it for the more princely castle of Belvoir. Since then, though strictly speaking, as much private property as ever, it has practically become a possession of the people, who justly regard it as one of the most precious heir-looms of mediæval England. This, of course, by favour of its present owner!

As to the dates of the various parts of the building—the entrance tower and the nave and aisles of the chapel exhibit late Norman details. Then comes the central block, consisting of the banqueting hall and the culinary offices, all of which, as well as fragments of other parts are of the fourteenth century, and a hundred years in **advance** of the extreme eastern and western ranges. The mixed house and garden architecture which, from a picturesque point of view, constitutes the chief artificial charm of Haddon—the south façade, the terraces, the steps and balustrade—belong to the late Tudor period and **are** not quite 300 years old.

A noticeable point about Haddon, and one which removes it still further from all suspicion of formality, is the admirably chosen **site on** the *slope* of the **hill, the west** range of the building sinking some 20 or 30 feet lower than the east.

Description. The drives from the Bakewell road, the footpath from Rowsley way, and the route across the hills from Chatsworth, all meet on the east side of the bridge close to the Guide's, or rather the *Custodian's Cottage*, a house in thorough keeping with the characteristic style of the hall itself. On the trimly kept grass-plot in front of it are the only two "Chatsworthy" objects which we shall meet with in the whole course of our explorations, a couple of small yews clipped into the shape of the Manners and Vernon crests,—a peacock and a boar's head. From this garden we pass to the main gateway under the Norman Tower. A trio of gargoyle heads projecting from the upper part of this tower are called the *Three (!) Muses.* Beneath them are a number of *carved shields* containing the bearings of the Vernon family. Inside the gateway the immense hoop of an old *brewing tub* hangs from the wall. Then, after peeping into a gloomy little chamber, which served as the *porter's lodge*, and which contains a very uncomfortable looking bedstead, we enter the lower courtyard, the first door on the right of which leads into an apartment called by misnomer the **Chaplain's Room.** The contents are by no means ecclesiastical according to modern ideas,—jackboots, pewter plates, a matchlock, a holster, a leather doublet, to wit. The real chaplain's rooms were above; they are not now shown. Passing onwards through the court we enter the **Chapel.** The *bell-turret* rising above the entrance is singularly chaste and beautiful. The chapel itself has a nave and aisle in the late Norman **style,** and a perpendicular chancel. Its noteworthy contents are a *Norman font*, an old *vestment chest*, some *family pews* of characteristic discomfort, and a *window* in memory of Sir Richard Vernon, who lived four and a half centuries ago. The stained glass was nearly all stolen many years ago. In the side-wall is a *squint*, in alluding to which we catch Sir Walter Scott again tripping. From it, he says, the lady of the house, who like John Gilpin's wife, "had a frugal mind," could attend to religious and culinary matters at the same time. Now, unless the good lady was gifted with that "patent hextra double million magnifyin' glass microscopic" power of vision which, in Sam Weller's opinion, would have enabled her to see across the courtyard through a couple of eighteen inch stone walls, this must have been impossible. The lords and ladies of Haddon had not, comparatively, a large space of their establishment set apart for religious exercises, but while engaged in them, we doubt not that they gave them their undivided attention.

Crossing the courtyard to the central portion of the building we enter a passage separating the kitchen from the banqueting hall. In the vestibule is an old **Roman Altar** dug up in the neighbourhood some centuries ago. In the **Kitchen** two huge *fire-places* suggest quite a **Saxon** prodigality of good fare. Next to them the salt-box, the *chopping block*, and the *mincing bowls* are the most noticeable cooking utensils. Opening out of the kitchen are three larders, in one of which is a *salting trough* made of one block of wood.

The **Banqueting Hall**, into which we now pass, measures 35 by 25 feet. Round two sides of it runs the *Minstrels' Gallery*, with a panelling of oak to which several antlers are attached. At the far end of the room is a *daïs*, like that of a college hall, whereon is a worm-eaten table at which the "quality" feasted while the humbler members of the household occupied the lower floor. On the walls are two old *paintings*, one of Martin Middleton, a forester of the Vernons, and the other, restored, of a race-horse. There are pictures too, of the first Earl of Rutland's game-keeper, and the keeper of the wine-cellar. On one side of the doorway through which we entered, an *iron ring* bears witness to the penalty inflicted on a guest who failed to take his proper *quantum* of liquor in the old days of rude hospitality. To it his wrist was fastened while the *arbiter bibendi*,—the toast-master—and other guests poured the "precious liquor" down his doublet.

Contiguous to the banqueting hall is the more modern **Dining Room**, oak-panelled and containing an *oriel window* which looks out on to the garden. The ceiling of this room, originally frescoed, has been plastered over. In the window-recess are carvings of Henry VII. and his wife, and Will Somers, the jester. The upper part of the panels is ornamented with *boars' heads* and *shields of arms*, and over the fire-place the motto "Drede God and honor the kyng" is inscribed. On the window-sill opposite the door is an ancient *wine cooler*.

In the landing at the head of the steps leading from the dining room to the drawing room, three time-worn *paintings* represent "Abraham offering up Isaac," the "Reproof of Peter," and "Time devouring his children."

The **Drawing Room**, which is above the dining room, is surrounded by *tapestry* from three to four centuries old, above which is a stucco cornice in four tiers. Notice also the *fire dogs*. The recessed window commands a lovely view.

The **Earl's Bedchamber**, which is entered from the drawing room, is tapestried with scenes from the hunting field. Beyond it is the **Page's Bedchamber** chiefly remarkable for the view from its window.

Returning through the drawing room on to the landing, we mount by a flight of solid oak steps, made from the root of one tree, into the

Ball Room or **Long Gallery**, the largest and most pleasing apartment of all. It measures more than 100 feet by 18, and has a recess half way up it 12 feet deep, with a glorious window. This room, too, is wainscoted with oak. Over the fire-place is a large picture, copied from Rubens, of the "Presentation of the head of Cyrus to Tomyris," the Scythian queen. At the far end of this room is a cast of the face of *Lady Grace Manners*, who died at the age of 93 —a most determined asserter of "woman's rights" if looks go for anything. The floor of this room was made from the trunk and branches of the tree whose roots supplied the steps leading up to it.

In the **Ante Room**, next entered, we find a painting of "Queen Elizabeth," and one of "Wild Fowl," copied from Schnyder.

Hence we pass to the **State Bed Room**, in which a lofty four-poster is shown as the bed of *Queen Elizabeth*, and afterwards, during its temporary removal to Belvoir, of *George IV*. By the side of it is the first Duke of Rutland's *cradle*. The walls are hung with *tapestry* from the *Gobelin* manufactory at Paris. Their subjects are taken from Æsop's Fables. Over the fire-place is a most grotesque *bas-relief* of "Orpheus charming the beasts." In the window-recess stand the *dressing-table* and a *looking glass* of the "Virgin Queen."

The last room of any interest which is shown, is the **Old State Room**, in which is an old *rack* for stringing bows. Thence we climb by a cork-screw staircase to the **Eagle**, or **Peveril's Tower**. The prospect from this pinnacle is lovely in the extreme. Below us we have a bird's-eye view of the courts and ranges of the Hall itself, beyond which we trace the windings of the Wye, backed by the richly-wooded eminences extending from Stanton Moor to Longstone Edge. The panorama is rich rather than grand.

Descending again, we are admitted by Dorothy Vernon's steps to the **Garden**. In the upper part of this is an avenue formed by noble elm and sycamore trees, and floored with aconite. Below this is a second terrace, called the *Winter Garden*, crowded with ancient yews. Hence we obtain by far the most beautiful and lasting impression of the exterior of Haddon. The south façade, partly overgrown with ivy, is seen at full length. A beautiful open *balustrade* separates this from the *Lower Garden*, which lies immediately under the Long Gallery and the Dining and Drawing Rooms. Hence, making our exit through a door and down a flight of steps, we may either take the river-side route (p. 109) to Rowsley, or return to the custodian's cottage.

Haddon Hall to Edensor (3¼ m.) and Chatsworth (3½ m.).
Direct Pedestrian Route.

The wood-crowned hill-range separating the Wye from the Derwent between **Haddon** and Chatsworth, is broken by two or three lateral valleys which have the effect of making this route very difficult to find, and missing it involves a good deal of vexatious labour. It is, however, an exceedingly pleasant and remunerative walk, and much to be preferred to the round-about road-routes either by Bakewell or Rowsley. We have marked the track carefully on our map, and with the following directions no one can well miss it.

From Haddon climb the hill by a cart-track which passes to the left of the old *Bowling Green*, beyond which pass through a gateway, leaving a farm-house on the right. Hence continue the ascent along a green lane, working round a fir plantation on the right. This brings you to another gateway, beyond which is a little ridge separating two opposite valleys, one of which looks towards Bakewell, the other towards Rowsley. Cross this ridge, and on the other side of it enter the wood through a gate. Then climb by a green cart-track as directly as it will take you to the top of the higher ridge before you, avoiding all level or less steep paths, and turning right near the top, up a track with a drain by the side of it. This ridge is the main one between the Wye and the Derwent, and the highest point on your way. It is wooded to the summit, along which runs a stone wall. Follow this wall northwards for about 200 yards till you come to a gate in it. The views southwards and westwards from about here are very charming. Pass through this gate, and cross the field diagonally by a faint cart-track to another gate at the far corner of it. This opens into a beech plantation, through which there is a cart-road for a few yards. Emerging from the trees you look down a lateral valley into the main Derwent valley on the right hand. In front and below you, in the lateral valley, is a farm called *Calton Houses*. Your path, now very indistinct, drops into the valley, at the bottom of which it passes through a little wood, and over the dam of a small pool to the *left* of the farm, ascending again at once, and joining a cart-road from the farm. Climbing this road, you cross a broad green drive, at the end of which, a few hundred yards to your right, is a modern lodge, the "Russian Cottage." Beyond the drive you come to a belt of wood which the cart-road enters by a gate, and the path by a *wooden step-stile*, a few yards right of the gate. Cross the stile and descend by a plain and direct footpath, which enters Chatsworth Park by another *wooden step-stile*. Chatsworth House presents a very imposing appearance at the bottom of the valley straight before you; the handsome spire of Edensor Church lies a little to the left. Crossing the park for some distance, you enter the main drive and in five minutes more reach Edensor village (*p.* 115). The hotel is beyond the village, just outside the park. The direct public drive to the House leaves Edensor a little on the left.

Haddon to Rowsley, 1½ m. Pedestrians should take the footpath along the east of the Wye. It enters the high-road at the Wye bridge, 1 mile short of Rowsley Station.

Matlock Bath to Dovedale or Ashbourne. Route 27.

Carriage route. *Matlock Bath to Cromford*, 1 m ; *Grange Mill*, 5 m—(*Ashbourne*, 14½ m.) *Tissington*, 12 m ; *Dovedale* (*Thorpe*), 14 m. Public conveyance about 10 a.m. Return fare, 5s.

Pedestrian route. *Matlock Bath to Bonsall*, 1½ m ; *Grange Mill*, 4½ m ; *Ballidon Moor*, 7½ m ; *Parwich*, 9½ m ; *Tissington*, 11½ m ; *Thorpe*, 13¼ m.

Reverse route described on page 58.

Nearly the whole of this route has been so fully described the reverse way that we shall confine ourselves in this Section to a brief repetition of its main features.

The carriage road bends sharply to the right at Cromford (*p.* 103), and enters the Via Gellia.

Pedestrian Routes :—(1), *By Bonsall.* On reaching Bonsall (*p.* 102), turn down the hill to the left at the King's Head Inn, and take a footpath which goes almost straight on from the fountain at the bottom of the hill. This path joins a road on the top of the hill near some cottages, after passing which, all but the last two or three, you will notice a gravelly track on the left, commencing with a stile. Follow this path, keeping along the side of the hill which overlooks the Via Gellia, till you come to a little wooden gate in the wall. Hence the path drops steeply through the wood to the bottom of the valley.

(2) *By the Black Rocks.* Shorter but rather less interesting. Underneath the Black Rocks (*p.* 103) you leave the Wirksworth Road, and follow that which crosses the south end of Middleton Village, and for the next two miles proceeds as near as may be to the side of the High Peak Railway, crossing it a long half mile beyond Middleton. A little beyond the crossing the line goes through a short tunnel. The pedestrian's nearest way is also through the tunnel, which is wide enough for two lines of rail, although there is only one. A mile beyond the tunnel the line strikes away to the right from the top of the Hopton Moor Plane, and the road continues straight on to Brassington (6 m. *from Matlock*). From the small inn in this village we turn to the right along a lane which almost skirts the south side of Brassington Rocks (*p.* 58), and in 1½ miles reach the high-road as described below.

The **Via Gellia**, locally known as the "Via Jelly," is a deep, winding valley bordered by wood, overhung in places by limestone cliffs, and a good deal spoilt in its lower parts by industrial works. It forms a favorite drive out of Matlock, "a big road for t' quality i' t' summer time," as we once heard it described in Bonsall. The name, a misleading and unfortunate one for a Derbyshire dale, is due to its constructors, the Gell family of Hopton Hall, near Wirksworth. It is famous for its lilies of the valley. Four miles from Cromford the dale reaches the upland plateau of the High Peak at *Grange Mill*, where is a small inn, the *Holly Bush*. Here the Ashbourne and Dovedale road turns to the left, and in 1½ miles passes under the High Peak Railway, where it commences a long winding descent, passing between the Brassington Rocks (*p.* 58) and White Edge. The carriage road on to Tissington or Ashbourne needs no description. Pedestrians should take a cart-track to the right, 1½ miles beyond the railway, and just opposite the by-lane from Brassington mentioned in the *détour* above described. This track crosses the south end of White Edge to the tiny village of *Ballidon*, whence a footpath (*p. 58*) leads to Parwich (*inn*) and on to *Tissington*. For Tissington and the routes on to Dovedale, see pp. 49 and 50.

Matlock Bath to Winster, Rowsley, Bakewell, &c.
Route 28.

Matlock Bath to Winster, by road all the way, (or by rail to Darley Dale Station, 3 m., and thence by road) 6 m; Rowtor Rocks, 8 m; Robin Hood's Stride, 9½ m; Alport, 11½ m; Upper Haddon, 13½ m; Bakewell, 15½ m.

There is a great deal of beautiful scenery to be met with by those who devote a day to this route with its many ramifications. Carriages may be taken by Winster to either Rowsley or Bakewell, and by getting out and walking a mile or two here and there, their occupants may include in the day's excursion the greater number of the special objects of interest,—Rowtor Rocks, Robin Hood's Stride, Cratcliff Tor, to wit; but only the pedestrian can gain all the possible enjoyment from the day's excursion. In describing the most remunerative route for him to take, we shall at the same time accommodate ourselves to the requirements of carriage people.

First, the carriage route from Matlock Bath to Winster is 6 miles. The pedestrian will save three of these and lose nothing by taking train to *Darley Dale Station*. Quitting the train here, and turning to the right from the Winster road in about 200 yards, he may reach in a third of a mile the patriarchal yew of Darley Dale. This tree we have already described on page 10. It has two trunks, and, considering its age, shows remarkable vigour and vitality. The churchyard which contains it is one of the most pleasantly characteristic in the country. Then, retracing your steps to the Winster road, you cross the Derwent by a four-arched bridge, and ascend through the village of *Wensley*. Here is a modern church built on Norman lines. On the left rises the grassy isolated hill of **Oaker**, an eminence which calls for passing remark not only from its singular position—isolated and volcanic in appearance—but also from the history or fable which attaches to it. The name, it is said, is a corruption of the Latin *occursus*, signifying "conflict," and is due to the former existence of a fort built upon the summit by the Romans to intimidate the Britons. On the top, far away from all their fellows, are two sycamore trees, looking from a distance like one only. With regard to these twin trees, Wordsworth, in a graceful sonnet, akin in language and sentiment to Coleridge's beautiful lines about "Severed

Friendship," in *Christabel*, **accepts the tradition that** they were planted by two brothers, who **parted on this** spot never to meet again,

> " **Until** their spirits mingled **in the sea,**
> That to itself takes all—Eternity."

At the foot of this hill the carriage-road from Matlock converges with our route. The rest of the way to Winster is along the side of a pleasantly wooded valley. Several chimneys on the other side indicate the position of lead mines. One of these, called *Mill Close*, was once described to us as the " wonderfullest mine as ever was." It has been known to produce ore at the rate of £800 worth a week, and still continues its prosperous **career.** Before hitting the lode, the first proprietor of it was so **nearly ruined that his friends had to** subscribe for tallow **candles** in order to enable him to continue his explorations.

Winster is a large village, once a town with a considerable market, consisting of one wide street and two or three smaller ones climbing the hill on the left. There are two comfortable inns, the *Angel* and the *Crown*. Opposite the former is the *Old Market Hall*, whose bricked-up windows testify to the decadence of country life in England and the popular preference for carbonic acid gas to pure air.

Direct Route from Winster to Robin Hood's Stride, 1¾m. Follow the Bakewell Road for nearly 1½ miles, **and** then take a path **to the left, which climbs** by **a hill past a** small farmstead **on the right, and then doubles round the north side of the "**stride**" to the table of rock which forms the summit.** The two tower-shaped rocks which mark the extent of the "stride" are conspicuous all the way.

The carriage-road **from** Winster to the Druid Inn, at **the entrance to** the Rowtor **Rocks, is** very devious. Pedestrians should follow a footpath which commences with a short lane a few yards west of the Angel Inn, and crosses the valley to the village of *Birchover*. In the only place where it forks, take the **left** hand branch over the flags. In ¾ m. it enters **a lane which climbs a steep pitch to Birchover. From** the top of **this lane turn to the left, and in a few** hundred **yards** you will **reach** the *Druid Inn*, through which **Rowtor Rocks** are entered. There is nothing Druidical about them, but in shape and disposition they **are even more eccentric than the average** curiosities **of the gritstone formation.** There are well worn passages **up and** down and through the midst of them, and the inevitable " **rocking stone," and what is more, they command a** beautiful **view. Just** opposite and **across the valley are the twin** turrets of **Robin** Hood's Stride, and **Cratcliff Tor. A yew tree at the** foot of the precipice of the latter marks the position of the Hermit's Cell. **Then** over the lower **line** of hill **northwards** we see Youlgreave **with its fine** church tower, **Upper Haddon, and the** spire of Bakewell **Church.** In the northwest **the dull** outline of Axe Edge cuts the horizon, and due north **Longstone Edge** bounds the prospect. Less than half **a mile south-**

west the **Bradley Rocks** present almost equal irregularities of shape.

Over Stanton Moor to Rowsley, 4 m. Instead of following up our present main route you may return up the hill through Birchover village, and taking a sharp turn to the left in half a mile, make your way by a fair road across *Stanton Moor*, a plateau which contains several isolated blocks of gritstone. The most remarkable is one in a field on the left hand, a little distance from the road, and about a mile from Birchover. The proper name is the **Andle Stone**, but it is locally, and not inappropriately dubbed the *Twopenny Loaf*. Steps and iron handles worked into the rock enable you to reach the commanding view-point afforded by its level top. Returning to the road you reach in another mile the picturesque little village of **Stanton**, which in addition to the charm of its situation on the slope of a densely wooded hill, boasts a Gothic church with a spire, a fine hall and a small inn, named after the celebrated race-horse, Flying Childers. Of the equine wonder last named there is a local tradition that in his advanced years he would never rest without a cat on his back.

The view from Stanton over the valley, and up the Bradford stream to Youlgreave and Middleton is delightful, and those who continue their walk to Rowsley will obtain during the steep descent to that village, a still finer, if not so charmingly rustic a prospect, over that portion of the Derwent valley where the Wye joins the main stream.

From the "Druid" our road drops again to the valley through which runs the Bakewell road. Crossing this and its tiny stream we at once attack **Cratcliff Tor** and Robin Hood's Stride. The former consists of huge masses of disrupted gritstone, of which its summit forms quite a Cyclopean table. At the foot of its sheer part and just above a rustic farmstead is the *Hermit's Cell*, a shallow cave, walled in and guarded by a larger and a smaller yew. Inside is a notched crucifix, the figure showing no great dilapidation. On a bright day the spot is a charming one, and suggests that hermits as well as monks had a decided eye for the picturesque.

From Cratcliff Tor to **Robin Hood's Stride** is scarcely a stone's-throw. The latter extraordinary arrangement of rock is also called *Mock Beggars Hall*, and indeed one may, with very little strain, imagine the Autolycuses of past years being taken in by the artificial appearance of its façade and turrets when they first saw them from the valley below. The stride which Robin Hood must have taken to get the place named after him—*i.e.* the distance from turret to turret—is perhaps 10 to 15 yards. We have already seen that "Little" John, by the measurement of his grave at Hathersage, was 10 feet high—so putting the two facts together, we have incontestable evidence that "there were giants in those days." One of the turrets is quite unscaleable, and the other equally so except to weasels and the small boys of the neighbourhood.

The view from the "Stride" covers very much the same ground as that from Rowtor Rocks (*see above*) except that it is more extensive towards the west. The village on the high ground to the south is Elton.

From the "Stride" the pedestrian should make for a road descending to Alport along the ridge separating the valley through which the Bakewell road passes from the ramification of the Bradford river on the other side. By so doing he enjoys a view all the way, of which a direct descent into the valley involves the loss. About half way to this road and only a few hundreds yards from the "Stride" he will notice four stones standing on their beam-ends in a field. These are called on the Ordnance Survey "Nine Stones," but three full-sized ones and a 'cub' are all that is left to represent the nine.

The road lies between these stones and a farm-house to the west of them. Once in it, there is no mistaking the way to Alport. It commands an interesting view over the Bradford valley on the left. The hamlet of **Alport** is at the junction of the Bradford and Lathkil rivers. It contains a fair-sized inn, the *Boarding House Hotel*, principally occupied by visitors on boarding terms. The village of Youlgreave (*p.* 57) conspicuous by its handsome church-tower, is on rising ground half a mile to the left. Both the Lathkil and the Bradford are famous for trout, but are strictly preserved by their ducal owners, and only that enterprising class of sportsmen who "fish till they are 'themselves' catched" as we had it put to us by a local authority, will think of disregarding the prohibition.

From Alport to Upper Haddon the way is either by road through Youlgreave, or by a direct footpath along the river-side. Pedestrians, who are not anxious to see Youlgreave church, should adopt the latter. The pleasantest route is by a private green drive on the east side of the river, but the authorized one is on the west. It passes through a succession of distressingly narrow stiles and enters in a mile the high-road from Ashbourne to Bakewell. This part of the Lathkil is prettily diversified with wood and limestone cliffs, and contains a long, picturesque 'rapid,' partly natural and partly artificial, about half way between Alport and Upper Haddon.

Crossing the stream by the road we have just mentioned, the pedestrian will find a footpath on the left hand a few yards beyond the bridge. This path ascends through two or three fields to the *Lathkil View Inn*, one of the most pleasantly situated little hostelries in Derbyshire and possessing a very fair amount of accommodation. It stands on comparatively high ground and, as one may guess from its name, commands a lovely view up and down the Lathkil. Those who do not intend visiting Upper Haddon on another occasion should certainly make a *détour* of about 5 miles, there and back, up the Lathkil valley from this inn. The way is described on p. 129. This portion of the Lathkil valley almost reaches the Dovedale standard of beauty for about half a mile.*

Hence the road is direct and needs no description. It crosses a slight ridge, and during the descent to Bakewell affords a fine view across the Wye valley. *For Bakewell, see p.* 128.

---

* There is a direct footpath from the inn to Haddon Hall, distant 2 miles—a charming walk in dry weather.

Matlock Bath to Bakewell and Buxton. Route 29.

By Road. *Matlock Bath to Matlock Bridge,* 1½ m; *Rowsley,* 5½ m; *Bakewell,* 9 m; *Ashford,* 10½ m; *Taddington,* 14½ m; *Buxton,* 21 m. *Reverse route described on p.* 71.

By Rail, *see p.* 10.

The Buxton road passes out of Matlock through the gorge between the High Tor and the Heights of Abraham, continuing side by side with the rail and river to **Matlock Bridge** (Hotel: *the Old English*), and then passing between the river and Matlock Bank along the level strath of *Darley Dale.* On the hill which rises behind the High Tor, the huge fortress-like mansion of *Riber Castle* presents a most formidable appearance, while across the river and rail, on the left hand, the remarkable isolated hill called *Oaker* is made very conspicuous by the lonely pair of trees which crown it (*see p.* 123). Beyond *Darley Dale Station,* near which is a good inn, the *Grouse,* we should diverge to the left by a footpath across the line, for the sake of visiting *Darley* Churchyard and its venerable *yew* (p. 123), beyond which we rejoin the main road and passing the meeting of the Derwent and the Wye, reach **Rowsley.** Here is the *Peacock Hotel,* a fine old Elizabethan hostelry with a lawn sloping to the Derwent. Some years ago the writer, staying at this inn with a party of ladies and gentlemen, asked for the day's paper in the smoke room. The reply was that the papers were not allowed to be taken out of the bar-parlour. Next morning a little after 8 o'clock, two of the party, being about to bathe in the Wye, asked for glasses of rum and milk. "The bar" was "not open," the servant said: a polite message was sent up-stairs to the landlady whose answer, as reported, was that the bar was "never opened till 9 o'clock."—The same name still appears on the signboard.

Rowsley to Bakewell by the old road. 3½ m. This is the pleasantest variation on the modern high-road, especially in hot or dusty weather. The track, in its higher parts a grass one, strikes northwards close to the 'Peacock,' and going under the railway, passes the **new** and prettily placed little church, Norman in character. Then it winds upwards and reaches 3 gates, beyond which, after passing through one on the left hand, it continues through a wood on a comparative level to the *col* which is crossed by the pedestrian route between Haddon and Chatsworth. For the way to Haddon see p. 116; to Chatsworth, p. 120.

From this point there is a beautiful view both in front and behind. The *col* separates two short valleys, one opening on to Rowsley, the other on to Bakewell. Our road does not cross the *col,* but drops along the right-hand side of the latter valley, and the rest of the way is quite plain.

One mile beyond Rowsley we **cross the Wye** by a neat bridge, on the near side of which the river-side path to Haddon (½ m. distant) strikes off. The course of the Wye between Bakewell and Rowsley is singularly tortuous and picturesque. To travel the distance along its banks would be half-a-day's journey. It is the "brimming river" all over, and both in respect of its many windings and bright rippling surface, contrasts strikingly with its neighbour over the hill—the Derwent, which is about to swallow it up at Rowsley.

Beyond the bridge the road from Yonlgreave and Winster joins ours on the left, and then we pass the drive to Haddon on the right. The turrets of the hall rise above and between their sylvan surroundings in the most seductive fashion. Nothing more is specially noteworthy till we enter

Bakewell.

Hotel: Rutland Arms. **Inns**: Castle and Commercial, Red Lion, &c., all from ¼ to ½ m. from the Station. *Pop.* 2,500.

Distances. Ashbourne, 16 m. Buxton, 12 m. Castleton, 12½ m. Chatsworth (carriage) 4 m. *foot*, 3 m. Dovedale (*Thorpe*) 15 m. Haddon Hall, 2 m; Matlock Bath, 9 m.

Post: Box closes at 8 p.m.

Bakewell, as we have before hinted, is, perhaps, the most pleasantly situated town in Derbyshire—just the kind of one to which a tourist, after exploring during the day the hills and dales around, likes to return for his night's repose. There is nothing either wild or grand about the immediate vicinity. Swelling uplands, hills draped to their summits with wood, and rich meadows with a sparkling stream winding through their midst, are its constituent parts. The inn accommodation of Bakewell is comfortable. There is fishing in the Wye at 2s. 6d. a day for such as make the Rutland Arms their head quarters.

The only architectural object of interest in Bakewell is its fine **Church**. We were going to add "old," but the reconstruction—in 1841—of its most prominent part, the spire, has robbed it as a whole of that appearance of antiquity which many of the other parts possess. The site, almost outside the town, and a few yards up the long slope which culminates in the wide uplands of the High Peak, was well chosen.

The building is cruciform, and has, besides its octagonal spire, a tower of the same shape. It is of various styles. The oldest portion is the west doorway, Norman in style, and one of the few Norman features allowed to remain by the restorers. The original nave dates from early in the twelfth century, but its Norman arches have been supplanted by Gothic ones. The restoration also included the renewal of both transepts, the tower, and the Vernon Chapel, and the insertion of four stained-glass windows at the west end. During the alterations a large number of Saxon remains were discovered, including some incised slabs, and fragments of stone carved after the curious interlacing scroll fashion of the one which still stands outside the south-east angle of the church. Many of these remains are to be seen in the porch on the **south** side of the nave. A curious and by no means graceful peculiarity is the way in which one of the transepts starts from the centre of a window. The chancel has two east windows.

The most interesting objects in the **interior** are the old *font* in the south aisle, **octagonal in shape, and** showing traces of elaborate sculpture; the *monument* to Sir **John** Manners and his wife, the celebrated Dorothy **Vernon, in the** Vernon Chapel; and a number of other memorials **of the lords of** Haddon, including one in the south **transept to the prodigal " King of** the Peak," Sir George Vernon, and **his two wives. The** quaint epitaph in **the** churchyard, ending

"A period's come to all their toylsome lives,
"The good man's quiet,—still are both **his wives**,"

does not refer to this illustrions trio.

The Cross in the churchyard to which we have above referred is, Mr. Cox tells us, more than 1,000 years old.

The *Baths*, to which Bakewell is supposed to owe its name, are not now of much public account. They are in the centre of the town; the principal one about 30 feet by 16, and is kept supplied by a flowing stream at a temperature of 60 degrees.

Excursions from Bakewell.

(1) **To Upper Haddon and the Lathkil.** A beautiful stroll of from 7 to 8 miles there and back; a very prettily situated village, and one of the finest samples of glen scenery in Derbyshire. Tourists proceeding to Dovedale or Hartington from Bakewell, are advised to adopt this route, following the Lathkil to its source, a natural well in the limestone, and thence joining the main road at Monyash (*see page* 78). The roads about Monyash, Newhaven and Hartington, are described in the Ashbourne and Buxton section.

Route. For Upper Haddon climb the hill from Bakewell on the left of the church. In about a mile a guide-post puts you right for the rest of the way. A little short of the village you come suddenly on the *Lathkil View Inn*, which, as well as the view from it, we have described on page 126. Then passing through the village and by the new and charmingly placed little church, you reach by a zigzag road the bottom of the valley, from which take the path along the north side of the stream. At first the glen is horribly blotched and blurred by the remains of some mines, but beyond them it takes a sudden turn; the path enters a wood, and you are in the best part of **Lathkil Dale.** The dale, or rather glen—for its north side is wooded from top to bottom, gains its impressiveness more from its exceeding narrowness, and the abrupt slope of its flanking hills than from any particular size or grandeur of detail. The strong part of it lasts from half a mile to a mile, and ends at an old mill, beyond which the slopes become more gradual, the wood ceases, and the only variety is caused by an occasional outcrop of limestone. Just above the mill and beetling over a fine side-ravine is a grand facing of that rock, but altogether the rock scenery, even in the best part of the dale, is far inferior to that of Dovedale.

From the mill you may ascend to the road by a winding lane, and so reach Upper Haddon or Monyash, or you may continue along the side of the stream to its source and thence to the latter village; but Monyash has no charm of its own to offer.

Those who wish to extend their walk may with great reward do so by following a path *down* the Lathkil from Haddon, as far as *Alport* (inn) whence is a delightful walk, either over *Robin Hood's Stride* (2 m.) to *Winster* (4 m.) and *Darley Dale Station* (7 m.) by a route described the reverse way on page 123; or to *Rowsley Station* by the village and moor of *Stanton* (p. 125).

Guide, IV. E

(2) **To Edensor and Chatsworth**, 4 m. *by carriage*, 3 m. *by foot-road*. *See* p. 71. Pedestrians should on all accounts take the short cut.

(3) **To Ashford, Monsal Dale, Tideswell, and Castleton.** *See below.*

(4) **To Stoney Middleton** (6 m.) **and Eyam** (7½ m.). The road passes by Hassop Station 1½ m. *Inn*), and then climbs the beautiful little green col between Longstone Edge and Bubnell Cliff, near the top of which is *Hassop Village* and *Hall* (p. 36). Then doubling round the east-end of Longstone Edge it passes *Calver* (small inn) and joins the route from Sheffield and Baslow. For *Stoney Middleton* see p.133; for *Eyam*, p. 81. The return may be made by *Foolow* and *Tideswell* (p. 81).

The Buxton road strikes northwards from Bakewell, and as far as Ashford passes through a richly-wooded country more or less near the Wye, which is hereabouts utilized in all manner of ways, reservoirs and mill-races abounding. Close to its banks, on the right hand of our route, is *Ashford Hall*, a seat of the Cavendish family.

Ashford is fully described in the reverse route on page 72.

Ashford to Monsal Dale Station (over the hill), 2m; *Tideswell*, 5½ m; *and Castleton*, 11 m. *All routes described the reverse way on* pp. 92-94. The road to Monsal Dale Station by the point from which there is such a lovely view of the valley cannot be mistaken (avoid the turning to Longstone Station). From Monsal Dale if you want to see down into the "S" winding of the Wye between it and Millers Dale, take the left hand route near *Cressbrook Mills*, if *Cressbrook Dale*, the right hand. The latter route soon becomes a mere path climbing through the wood, on emerging from which you will see the village of *Litton* before you, and need no further direction.

Quitting Ashford we find the Wye valley still more contracted and the hills on each side steeper and higher, those on the left and in front being covered with wood from head to foot.

The road follows the windings of the river, crossing it in about a mile, and affording glimpses up one or two most tempting little lateral valleys on the left. It is quite worth while to turn aside and explore for half an hour the second one, *Dimon's or Demon's Dale*, a recess as dark and shadowy as the second name implies. Monsal Dale, as the first of the valleys which we are now entering is called, is one of the prettiest of Derbyshire valleys, but it hardly shows as effectively from our present route as from the railway (p. 11). It abounds in fishermen and rabbits.

Opposite the fourth milestone from Bakewell (3½ m. Bakewell, 8 m. Buxton) a footpath strikes away to the right through a gateway. This path commands the best part of the valley, and by it *Monsal Dale Station* may be reached in half an hour, or the *little inn* at the view-point on the top of the tunnel. For the station, you may take which side of the river you like, the left side is the shortest.

Our road now leaves the large valley and ascends a narrow and picturesque but streamless dingle to the long mining village of **Taddington** (inns, *the George*, &c.). The churchyard contains a cross which Mr. Cox tells us is "probably the work of the monks from **Lindisfarne**."

From Taddington, *Millers Dale Station* is distant 2 miles by the second turn to the right from our present route. The road is down hill nearly all the way, and commands good views.

Continuing Buxton-wards, we pass on the left the little *Waterloo* Inn and one or two grass-lanes which bear witness to the declining prosperity of rural districts. Then for nearly two miles our road maintains a high level, affording a wide prospect eastward over Longstone Edge and the hills between the Wye and the Derwent, and northwards to Kinder Scout and the Castleton heights, while on the left the high ground beyond Buxton gradually comes into view. Then with striking suddenness the depths of the Wye valley appear beneath us on the right just at that break in the limestone cliffs where the Buxton branch diverges from the main line (p. 12). A sharp descent into the valley follows, and the rest of our journey is beneath the crags, the steep green slopes and beetling woods of *Ashwood Dale*. This valley is more fully described in the Buxton Section (p. 72.)

Matlock Bath to Baslow, Stoney Middleton, Eyam, Hathersage, and Castleton. Route 30.

Matlock Bath to Rowsley (rail or road), 6 m; *Edensor Hotel (Chatsworth)*, 9½ m; *Baslow Village (inn)*, 11¼ m; *Calver (inn)* 12¾;— *(Stoney Middleton,* 14 m; *Eyam,* 15½ m.)—*Grindleford Bridge,* 15¼ m; *Hathersage,* 18¼ m; *Hope,* 22½ m; *Castleton,* 24 m.

By the side of the Derwent and its tributaries from Matlock to Castleton we have the longest stretch of comparatively level road in the Peak. This fact, added to the interest of the scenery, which seldom flags all the way, makes the drive an extremely popular one. We strongly advise pedestrians to give themselves an extra half-day, and to vary the monotony of travelling so many miles along or near to the bottom of the same valley by ascending here and there to the hills or moors which flank it. The best way to get variety is to diverge at Calver by Stoney Middleton and Eyam; thence to cross the valley and ascend to Fox House either by Grindleford Bridge or Froggatt Edge; then drop to Hathersage by the famous "Surprise" view, and from Hathersage follow the route which we shall describe by Abney Moor and Bradwell.

For the route as far as *Rowsley* (by rail or road) and *Chatsworth* we must refer our readers to pages 10 and 127. Pedestrians who wish to see Edensor, as well as Chatsworth, should take the carriage route to that village, cutting off a corner by the footpath from Beeley Church to the bridge over the Derwent, as before described, and avoiding the footpath beyond that bridge. Then after visiting Chatsworth from Edensor, continue along the north drive, or the footpath which commences between the bridge and Queen Mary's Bower, to the east end of Baslow, where the principal inns are situated. In either case they leave the park by a wooden step-stile about half way between the kitchen gardens and the village. Beyond the step-stile the track branches, the right hand branch leading to the *Royal* and other inns, and the left hand one to the *Peacock* and the main part of the village. The latter is the shortest route for tourists proceeding Eyam and Castleton way.

Baslow. (Inns: *Peacock, Royal, Devonshire Arms, Wheat Sheaf,* near the north entrance to Chatsworth; *Green Man, Prince of Wales,* in the village. *Hydropathic Establishment,* good and finely situated on the brow of the hill north-east of the village). *Post Town, Chesterfield. Mail Cart leaves 9 p.m.*

Baslow in itself has no special feature of interest to the tourist, though its situation is very pleasing. The church, noticeable for its short stumpy spire, is charmingly placed in a grove of lime trees by the river-side. The number of well-to-do, fair-sized inns which the village possesses is due to its position at a main entrance to Chatsworth from Sheffield and other places in that direction. During the season two or more coaches or omnibuses leave for Sheffield every evening; one at 7 o'clock by the direct route (12½ m.) through Owler Bar (p. 33), and one at 6 by the roundabout, but more picturesque, Froggatt Edge route (16 m. p. 35). *Fares by either route,* 1s. 6d. Good public communication is also kept up between the Hydropathic Establishment and Sheffield, there being on several days in the week a morning coach to the latter place. An omnibus, too, from the same establishment meets morning and afternoon up and down trains at Rowsley Station, passing through Chatsworth Park on its way. Hitherto the trains have been between 11 and 12 a.m., and 4 and 5.15 p.m.

The finest short walk from Baslow is up the hill behind the Hydropathic Establishment,* and then on to the moor, at the edge of which, from a *stone cross,* inscribed "Wellington. 1866," there is a glorious retrospect over Chatsworth, and along the line of the Derwent Valley—a vista-view of wonderful richness and variety. A few yards further, and from the plateau of the moor, rises the *Eagle Stone,* a huge rectangular block of gritstone. Those who are going on northwards should continue hence—by grace—along the private drive, which in less than a mile joins the Curbar Edge Road (p. 34) close to the old "pack-horse" Cross. Thence a sharp descent takes them to the Derwent Bridge at Calver.

There is nothing of note on the main road between Baslow and Calver (*Inns*) unless it be a new *Missionary College* built by Mr. Hulme of Manchester on the right of the road, a little short of the latter village.

To ascend **Froggatt Edge to Fox House,** without visiting Stoney Middleton or Eyam, leave the road here by the private drive (public footpath) which starts just short of the bridge, and after following the river-side for a short distance, ascends to the by-road from Curbar to Froggatt Edge. For distances and particulars as to this route see p. 35. To the *Chequers* on Froggatt Edge the distance is 1¼ miles; from the Chequers to Fox House, 3½ m. Fox House to Hathersage, 3 m.

---

* It was an evil moment for guide-book writers when the originators of these popular places of resort gave them such a terribly long name.

A quarter of a mile beyond the bridge over the Derwent at Calver, close to which is a huge mill made almost picturesque by its situation, there are cross-roads; that to Stoney Middleton and Eyam goes straight on; the direct one up the Derwent valley to Hathersage bends round to the right.

We reach **Stoney Middleton** through a straight avenue. Here are several inns, of which the least small is the "Moon." The church to the right of our route is a model of ugliness. It is octagonal in all its parts except the short square tower which in connection with the rest of the building looks rather like the head of a cat, the eight-sided sort of lantern which rises to a greater height from the body of the church behind representing the back of the same animal in an irritated frame of mind.

At the west end of the village we enter **Middleton Dale**, a limestone valley which has been rather over-praised. The rocks descend sheer and picturesquely, especially on the right hand, where is the orthodox "*Lover's Leap*" but the best part of the valley is utterly spoiled by hideous little black chimneys and lime-works. We do not breathe freely until, a long half-mile from the village, our road turns to the right and takes us up a picturesque dell to Eyam. The road straight onwards continues up the higher part of the dale, less striking but more pleasant, to the high ground separating the Derwent from the Wye valley, and in 5 miles reaches *Tideswell* (p. 80). There is a small inn at *Wardlow Mires* about 3 miles on the way, and a peep down the barren part of *Cressbrook Dale* (p. 94) just beyond it, but nothing else of any note. For Eyam and its many objects of interest see p. 81.

Returning into the Derwent valley from Eyam, whether making for Froggatt Edge or Grindleford Bridge, observe the directions on page 83.

Between *Grindleford Bridge* and Hathersage our road threads one of the most charming bits of the whole Derwent valley—a woody dingle, down which the stream flows with much more than its usual alternation of pool and rapid. Above it the road passes for a considerable distance through a wood. On approaching Hathersage the valley expands again, but the hill-girdle of it has a very picturesque appearance, Win Hill, with its perky little summit, appearing in front, and Bamford and Stanage Edges separated from it by the river, on the right.

To Castleton by Abney Moor 6½ m. Less than a mile short of Hathersage, and just before the bridge over the Derwent is reached, a by-road strikes up the woody valley on the left. This is certainly a much more taking route for the pedestrian than the regular route through Hathersage and Hope. It is described in detail the reverse way on page 91, so we shall only give a *précis* of it here. As far as Abney (3 m.) the road cannot be mistaken. Splendid views open out across the Derwent Valley during the ascent. Then we have nothing but moor, more or less cultivated, for a few miles. A short way past the little dip in the road at Abney, take a narrow cart-lane on the right. Follow this for a long half mile till it enters at right angles a rough old moorland route that looks as if it neither went to nor came from anywhere. Cross this at once, and bending somewhat to the left, follow a path through the heather, which brings you out on to the lane again by a stone step-stile, being careful to avoid a gradually deepening depression on your right. The step-stile is opposite a trespass board, and there is a gate across the lane a few yards further on. On the other side of the gate the path begins again, at once turning sharp to the left, and in two fields gaining the top of *Bradwell Edge*, whence a view, fine as it is sudden, breaks upon the eye. Below lie Bradwell and the wide green expanse of Hope Dale, rising to the slopes of Mam Tor and Back Tor, between and behind which is seen the long ridge of Kinder Scout. The village in the midst of the Dale is Hope.

There can be no doubt about the descent to *Bradwell*, whence first a road, then a footpath, then a road again, lead almost direct to *Castleton*, lessening by almost half the carriage route through Hope. (*See* p. 91.)

Our main road now enters Hathersage. For a full description of the village and the rest of the way to Castleton, see page 40.

Hardwick Hall.

From Matlock, 17 *m*; *Chesterfield,* 7 *m*; *Clay Cross, or Doe Hill Station, abt.* 5 *m.*

Open daily from 11 *to* 4.

This celebrated mansion, though it lies several miles away from any part of the Peak District, is often and deservedly visited by sojourners therein. From Matlock the journey there and back is easily made in a day. The charge for a carriage-and-pair is about two pounds, but during the season a public conveyance has latterly run twice a week. *Return fare,* 6*s.* Of the nearer places Chesterfield is the most convenient to hire from, and Clay Cross Station may be recommended as the best starting-place for pedestrians, who, if disposed to make a day of it on this side of the district, may with advantage continue northwards from Hardwick along the high ground to Bolsover, and return thence to Chesterfield Station. Clay Cross Station is a mile from the town. *Distances:* Clay Cross to Hardwick Hall, 5 *m*; Bolsover, 10 *m*; Chesterfield Station, 16½ *m.* *Comfortable Inn at the entrance to Hardwick Park.* *Country inns at Bolsover, &c.*

(1.) *Pedestrian route from Clay Cross Station.* This commences with a road which crosses the line by a bridge at the south end of the station, and bends southward to *North Wingfield Church,* whose chaste fifteenth century tower is a prominent object. In half-a-mile we double to the right round the church and rectory (*Inn on the north side of the churchyard*), and then turn left again at a sign-post directing to Pilsley. The road then entered upon crosses a brook in half-a-mile, and about the same distance further we diverge again to the left (the second turn beyond the brook) and enter a lane which, after passing an inn and going under a mineral branch of the Midland Railway, in 1¼ miles strikes into the Chesterfield and Tibshelf road. Follow this road southwards, towards Tibshelf, for half-a-mile, and then turn left again at the *Shoulder of Mutton Inn (Hardstoft)*. So far our route, though over a pleasantly undulating country, has been too much associated with coal mines to be thoroughly enjoyable.

The rest of it is along a grass-bordered lane with a fringe of trees on either side. As we proceed, the towers of Hardwick Hall, crowning a well-timbered eminence, appear in front. From the end of the lane we take the further of the two roads to the right, and in a few hundred yards reach the **Hardwick Inn**, at the entrance to the Park.

(2.) *Carriage-route from Matlock*, 17 m. This is the same as that described to Crich Stand and Wingfield Manor on p. 104. From South Wingfield it crosses the railway close to the station, and passes through the small town of *Alfreton* (Hotel: the *George*), leaving Alfreton Park on the left. Hence it drops to and crosses the main Midland (Erewash Valley) line, beyond which there is a pleasant prospect westwards during the rise to Tibshelf (*Inns*). A short two miles further the route from Clay Cross, above described, is joined at the *Shoulder of Mutton Inn*, and in yet another two miles we reach the *Hardwick Inn*, and the entrance to Hardwick Park.

From the entrance gate to the Hall it is about half-a-mile by a drive which makes a wide sweep in order to break the abruptness of the direct ascent. The first buildings passed are the *Stables*, on the right hand, a range so extensive and handsome as to suggest that the beast was as well looked after as its master in the palmy days of Hardwick hospitality. Then, on the left of the drive, we reach the remains of the **Old Hall**, dating from the first half of the sixteenth century. They consist of little more than one side of the shell, and that seems to be held together by the tenacity of the ivy which overgrows it in profusion, and which is the only relief to a gaunt and ungainly mass of masonry. A little further the present Hall rises on the right hand. It is entered through a square-walled court-yard now laid out as an ornamental flower-garden.

The Hall.

The general appearance of the exterior is far more regular and formal than that of most existing specimens of the picturesque period of architecture which it represents. The Hall was built in the last decade of the sixteenth century by the famous Bess of Hardwick, whose initals, E.S. (Elizabeth Shrewsbury), are part of the design of the stone fretwork which crowns the six towers. We have already in our description of Chatsworth commented on this remarkable woman's mania for building. As her rent-roll reached a sum which would now-a-days be fairly represented by £200,000 a year, amassed chiefly from the jointures of her four husbands, she was enabled to gratify it to her heart's content. She began to be married at 14, and the last of the dauntless four was the Earl of Shrewsbury, whence the initials.

In front of the main entrance there is a short colonnade, terminated at either end by the two towers which face this way. Then, entering the *Hall*, we have directly in front of us a statue of Mary, Queen of Scots, by Westmacott.

Underneath is an expressive inscription, of which the last half runs as follows :—

> " A suis in exilium acta, 1568
> Ab hospitâ neci data, 1587."

" Exiled by her own people, given to death by her hostess " suggests anything but an Elizabethan view of the treatment received alike from friend and foe by the unhappy Queen, in connection with whom we may further remark that it is an open question whether she ever visited Hardwick at all. The present mansion was probably not commenced until a few years after her execution, and there is no clear evidence of her ever having been an inmate of the old one. The several souvenirs now located here may have been removed from the old house at Chatsworth, in which she took a brief holiday on more than one occasion, during the long years of her captivity at Sheffield Castle under the espionage of the Earl of Shrewsbury. This nobleman was owner also of Tutbury Castle and Wingfield Manor, and by his marriage with the gallant " Bess " may be assumed to have acquired some interest, however small, in Hardwick, as well as in the old Chatsworth House, which his many-mansioned lady had received from a previous husband, Sir William Cavendish.

Other features of the Entrance Hall are the oak wainscoating and modern tapestry, the large fire-place and the antlers. Over the door by which we entered is the *Minstrels' Gallery*. Hence we proceed by the north staircase to

The **Chapel**, a small apartment hung with tapestry representing the life of St. Paul, and displaying some specimens of old needlework. Beyond it is

The **Dining Room**, which occupies the north-west angle of the building. It is a spacious apartment, with a deep recess which serves as a billiard-room. Over the chimney-piece are the everlasting initials, " E. S.," and the motto, " The conclusion of all things is to feare God and keep his commandements." The walls, wainscoted with oak, are hung with a multitude of portraits including Lord Walpole, and (one of many in various parts of the building) Georgiana, the " beautiful Duchess," who was the wife of the fifth Duke of Devonshire. We are also introduced to " Bess " herself, by a portrait which certainly fails to explain her magnetic attraction for the male sex.

From the Dining Room we pass through the *Minstrels' Gallery*, wherein is a fine specimen of the horns of the Irish elk, into

The **Drawing Room**, another spacious and comfortable-looking apartment. The effect of the large windows of Hardwick is much more pleasing from the inside than the outside. This room is also wainscoted to a considerable height with oak, but the space above is hung with portraits almost concealing the tapestry, which represents, we are told, the history of Esther. Amongst the portraits we may notice Sir William Cavendish, second husband of "Bess," Charles James Fox, Sir Joseph Paxton, Countess Spencer, mother of the "beautiful Duchess," and Jeffrey Hudson, the celebrated dwarf. A door opens out of this room into the **Duke's Bedroom**, which is hung with tapestry representing Abraham and Isaac, the Judgment of Solomon, &c. Hence we ascend another flight of steps to

The **State Room**, or **Presence Chamber**.—This extends along a great part of the west front, and measures about 65 by 30 feet, exclusive of a roomy recess. The tapestry, covering more than half the height of the walls, represents scenes from the Odyssey. Above it is parget work, or plaster, in high relief—subject: a stag hunt. The furniture is of the Late Stewart period, and includes a *Cabinet* dating from the reign of Charles II., and an old table brought from the ruins, and curiously inlaid so as to constitute a board for several games. At the north end of the room are a canopy-chair and a footstool of black velvet, richly embroidered; and in the recess stands the *State Bed*, adorned with crimson velvet and ostrich plumes. From this room we enter

The **Library**, which is hung with tapestry, and, amongst a number of portraits, contains one of the Duchess of Portsmouth, as well as another of "Bess." The *German Goblets* on the chimney-piece are worth notice. From the window of this room there is a charming view. Hence, passing through the **State Bedroom**, hung with old silk tapestry, we proceed to

Mary Queen of Scots' Room, as it is called from the circumstance that the furniture was used, and much of the needlework wrought by that ill-starred lady, the specimens including the silk embroidery of the bed, the quilt, and the covering of the chairs. Passing on through the *Blue Room* we notice, on our way, representations of the marriage of Tobias, Vulcan, Neptune, and the meeting of Jephtha and his daughter, and then we enter

The **Picture Gallery**. This, perhaps the most delightful room in the house, extends along the whole eastern side of it except the parts occupied by the towers. It is 166 feet long, and from 22 to 41 (in the recess) feet wide. Eighteen huge windows in this apartment are said to contain more than 25,000 panes of glass. Two fine chimney-pieces are surmounted by allegorical representations of Justice and Compassion. The walls are crowded with portraits, amongst which we may mention full-length ones of Queens Elizabeth and Mary at the south end, the latter, if we may trust history, as flattering a likeness as we may hope the one of the renowned "Bess," not far off, is the reverse; one of Arabella Stuart, who was granddaughter of "Bess" through the issue of the latter's second marriage; the celebrated full-length portrait of Mary Queen of Scots, taken before trouble and confinement had marred her good looks; two of the "beautiful Duchess," one as her 'ain sel,' and the other as Diana—floating about in a cloud; Hobbes, the philosopher, William Lord Russel, and one of the family of Charles I., which includes the most remarkable baby ever introduced to public notice. In various parts of the gallery most of the kings and queens since the Tudor period may be seen, and there is such an array of Dukes of Devonshire that their own descendants might be excused for "mixing" them.

From the Picture Gallery we descend by a *Staircase*, whose walls are hung with tapestry representing the love and fate of Hero and Leander.

From the leaden *Roof*, to which it is only worth while to ascend in perfectly clear weather, the view is rich and extensive. Crich Stand is a prominent object westward, and with a strong glass Lincoln Cathedral may be discerned in the opposite direction.

From the Hall to *Bolsover* it is nearly 5 miles; first, by the drive which strikes north-eastward through the Park, and then, due north for ¼ mile, into Hucknall Lane. Keep along this eastward for ¼ m., and you will enter a road which goes due north to Bolsover about ¼ m. east of the edge of the ridge all the way.

Bolsover Castle occupies a most commanding site, the view extending over a considerable breadth of undulating lowland westwards to the lofty moors which rise between Chesterfield, Sheffield, and the Derwent Valley. The present *Castle*, early in the 17th century, was built by Sir Charles Cavendish, younger son of "Bess of Hardwick," on the site of a Norman castle which owed its existence, like the famous "Castle of the Peak," to William Peveril, natural son of the Conqueror. There are traces of this Norman castle in the basement storey of the present one. Beyond its site, however, there is nothing specially noteworthy about it, but the remains of the **Palace**, which adjoin it, are interesting. This structure was also commenced by Sir Charles Cavendish, but not completed by him. It was remarkable for the size of its rooms, the dining-room measuring nearly 80 by 33 feet. It was visited several times by Charles I.; partially destroyed by the Commonwealth; repaired after the Restoration, and left to fall into its present condition in the next century.

The *Chesterfield* road starts down the hill on the north side of the Castle, and there is no risk of losing the way. Entering Chesterfield, it goes under the line, ¼ m. south of the station.

Wirksworth from Matlock.

Another interesting excursion may be made from Matlock Bath by taking train to Whatstandwell (3½ m.), and thence walking over the hill to Wirksworth (3¼ m.) and back over or under the Black Rocks and through Comford (*Wirksworth to Matlock Bath Stat.*, 3 m.). The "Bull's Head" at Whatstandwell, the "Lion" at Wirksworth, and the "Greyhound" at Cromford are comfortable resting-places. Wirksworth Church well repays examination, and the valley-views from the high ground on both sides of Wirksworth are very pretty.

From Whatstandwell Station cross the Derwent and take the road up-hill to the right. Soon you have a charming view over Lea Hurst and towards Matlock. The road passes on the right a clump, called the *Hag*, and then reaches its highest point (820 *ft.*) at cross-roads, Wirksworth with its huge limestone quarries appearing suddenly far down in front. Both road and path to it are obvious.

Wirksworth Church (*key at cottage S. side*) shows all manner of architecture, and was well but incompletely restored by Sir Gilbert Scott about 1872. The unfinished part is the nave, in which, as far as it goes, a high-pitched roof has been substituted for the old obtuse-angled one with battlements. The original style seems to have been E.E., and there are lancet windows in the chancel and the transepts. The East window, however, is Perpendicular, and others are Decorated. There are also plain round arches. The plan of the church is cruciform, and the most telling features inside are the Pointed arches with massive clustered shafts which support the tower. The chancel and transepts have lately been graced with many painted windows, and the general effect of these parts of this church is very pleasing. In the south wall of the chancel is a double piscina; on the north, sedilia. Several recumbent effigies are noteworthy—one of Antonye Lowe, Esqre., who served four sovereigns, Henry VII. and VIII., Edward VI., and Mary (*d.* 1555); others in marble, of the Gell family, to whom we owe the "Via Gellia"; the chief of these bears date 1583. Note also the two *Fonts*—the old one, disused, in the North transept, a capacious bowl *said* to be 900 years old, and the comparatively modern one in the South transept, which is dated 1662 and bears its years amazingly well. Most curious, however, of all the things to be seen are the fantastic mouldings which have been built into the walls of the South transept and the nave. The chief one, on the north side of the nave, was discovered under the chancel in 1821. It shows a variety of subjects—Christ washing the feet of the Disciples, the wise men, Roman soldiers, &c. These scrolls are remnants of an older church.

In the *churchyard*, close to the door at the south of the nave, is the tomb of Matthew Peat, who died in 1757, aged 109.

Except for a curiosity, called the *Miners' Standard Dish*, which was made in the same year as Flodden was fought, and is preserved in the Moot Hall, Wirksworth has nothing else to show the stranger. A branch line, 14 miles in length, connects it with Derby.

The road back to Matlock, over the hill, under the High Peak railway and to the left of the Black Rocks (p.103) needs no description.

INDEX.

N.B.—Where more than one page is referred to, that on which a locality is *particularly* described, is given first.

Telegraph stations are indicated by an asterisk.

The names enclosed in brackets indicate the postal town to which letters should be addressed.

Abbey Farm, 44, 30.
Abbey Grange, 44.
Abbeydale, 33.
Abney, 91, **133**.
Alderwasley, 9.
Alport, 126, **57**.
Alport Dale, 45.
Alsop-en-le-Dale, **56**.
Alstonefield, 79.
*Alton (Stoke-upon-Trent), **7**.
Alton Towers, 6.
*Ambergate (Derby), 106, 9.
Andle Stone, 125.
Arbelows (or Arbor Low), **56**.
***Ashbourne**, 46.
Ashford (Bakewell), 72.
Ashop Dale, 45, 28.
Ashopton (Sheffield), 43.
*Ashover (Chesterfield), 108, 107.
Ashwood Dale, 66.
Axe Edge, 63, 16.

Back Tor, 89, 75, 116.
Bagshaw Cavern, 91.
***Bakewell**, 128, 11, **71**.
Ballidon, 58.
Bamford, 43, 40.
Barber Booth, 26, 96.
***Baslow** (Chesterfield), **132**, 34.
Beauchieff Abbey, **33**.
Beeley, 110.

*Belper, 9.
Beresford Dale, 55, **48**.
Birchover, 124.
Black Brook, 41, 42.
Black Dyke, 29, 44.
Black Rocks, 103, 59.
Blackwell Dale, 75.
Blue John Mine, 88, 75.
Bolsover, 130.
Bonsall (Derby), 102, 122, **59**.
Bradford River, 57, 126.
Bradwell (Sheffield), 91, 134.
Bradwell Edge, 91.
Brassington (Derby), **59**.
Brassington Rocks, 58.
Bugsworth (Stockport), **21**.
Bull Clough, 29, 44.
Bunster, 49.
Burbage Bridge, 39.
***Buxton**, 60, &c.

Carl Wark, 39, 37, 40.
Calver (Sheffield), 36.
***Castleton** (Sheffield), 84, &c.
Castle Cliff Rocks, 67, 16.
Cat and Fiddle Inn (Buxton), 63, 18, 17.
Cave Dale, 85.
***Chapel-en-le-Frith** (Stockport), 21, 22, &c.
Chatsworth, 109–114.
Chee Dale, 64, 12, **70**.
Chee Tor, 64.

Chelmerton, 77.
Chequers Inn (Calver, Sheffield), 36.
*Chesterfield, 107.
Chinley Churn, 22.
Chrome Hill, 77, 56.
Corbar Wood Walks, 65.
Cranberry Clough, 29, 44.
Cratcliff Tor, 125.
Cressbrook Dale, 93, 11, 71.
Crich Hill, 105, 9.
Crich Stand, 104.
*Cromford (Derby), 103, 10.
Crowdecote Bridge, 78, 56.
Cumberland Cavern, 99.
Curbar Edge, 34.
Cut Gate, 44, 29.
Cut-throat Bridge, 42.

Darley Dale (Matlock Bath), 10, 71, 123, 127.
Demon's Dale, 130.
*Derby, 3.
Derwent Chapel, 44, 42.
— Edge, 42.
— Hall, 44.
— Valley, 39.
Devonshire Cavern, 99.
— Hospital, 62.
Diamond Hill, 65.
Dore, 33.
Dovedale (Ashbourne), 50, 79.
Doveridge (Derby), 5.
Dove Holes (Stockport), 74, 20.
Druid Inn, 124.
*Duffield (Derby), 9.
Duke's Drive, 65.
Duke of York Inn, 58.

Eagle Stone, 34, 132.
Earl Sterndale, 56.
Ebbing and Flowing Well, 74, 95.
Ecton Hill, 78.
Edale, 89, 22, 26, 96.
— Cross, 25, 96.
Edensor (Bakewell), 115.
Elden Hole, 75, 95.
*Ellastone (Ashbourne), 8.
Elton, 122.

Errwood House, 66, 20.
*Eyam, 81, etc.
Eyam Moor, 82, 91.

Fairbrook Naze, 28.
Featherbed Moss, 28.
Fishing House, Beresford Dale, 55.
Flash (Buxton), 67, 16.
Foolow, 81.
Fox House Inn (Sheffield), 38, 97, 132.
Froggatt Edge (Sheffield), 35, 132.

*Glossop (Manchester), 27, 45.
Glutton Dale, 77, 56.
Goyt Valley, 66, 18, 20.
Gradbach Mill, 67, 16.
Grange Mill, 59, 122.
Great Rocks Dale, 22.
Grindleford Bridge, 38, 27.

Haddon Hall (Bakewell), 117.
Hardwick Hall, 134.
*Hartington (Ashbourne), 55.
*Hassop (Bakewell), 36, 71, 73.
*Hathersage (Sheffield), 40, 37.
*Hayfield (Stockport), 23, 25, 45, 96.
Heights of Abraham, 101.
Hermit's Cell, 125.
Higgar Tor, 38, 39.
Highlow Hall, 92.
High Peak Railway, 85, 20, 9.
High Tor, 101.
High Wheeldon, 56.
Hollow Meadows, 42.
*Hope (Sheffield), 40, 27, 90.
—— Dale, 39, 40.
Howden Farm, 30, 44.
Hurking Stone, 42.

Ilam (Ashbourne), 49.
Izaak Walton Inn, 49.

Jacob's Ladder, 26, 96.

Kelstedge, 108.
Kinder Scout, 23, 45, 96.

INDEX.

Lady Bower Inn (Sheffield), **42,** 40.
Langsett, 29, 45.
Lathkil River, 129, **126, 78.**
Lea Hurst, 104, 9.
*Leek (Stoke-upon-Trent), **12.**
Lees, 96.
Little Hucklow, **93.**
Load Mill, 56.
*Longnor (Buxton), **77.**
Longstone, 11.
—— Tunnel, 71, 94.
Lose Hill, 89, 39, **43, 75.**
Lover's Walk, 101.
Lud's Church, 67, **16.**

*Macclesfield, **17.**
Mam Tor, 89, 22, **95.**
Manifold River, **49.**
Mappleton, **50.**
Masson, 101.
*Matlock **Bank** (Matlock Bath), **98.**
*—— **Bath**, 98, **10.**
*—— **Bridge** (Matlock Bath), 98, **10.**
*Mayfield (Ashbourne), **8.**
Middleton Dale, 133, 35.
—— by-Wirksworth, **104, 59.**
—— Youlgreave, 57.
Mill Brook, **44.**
—— Close, 124.
—— Dale, 54, 79.
*Millers Dale (Buxton), **12, 22, 70,** 80, **92, 131.**
Monsal Dale, 70, **11, 72, 93.**
Monyash, 78, **129.**
Moscar-Lodge, **42.**
Mytham Bridge, **40.**

Needle's Eye, 39, **97.**
New Bridge, 36.
Newhaven Inn, 56.
*New Mills (Stockport), **21, 19.**
Nine Stones, 123.
Norbury (*see* Ellastone), 8.

Oaker Hill, **126.**
Offerton Moor, **39.**
Old Roman Cave, **99.**

Ouzelden Bridge, 30, **43.**
Owler Bar, **34.**

Park Hill, **77,** 56.
Parwich (Ashbourne), **58.**
Peak Cavern, **85.**
—— Forest, 74, 22,
*Penistone, 28, **45.**
Peveril Castle, 81.
Pike Pool, **55.**
Poole's Hole, 68.
Porter Valley, 37.

Reynard's Cave, **53.**
Riber Castle, 103, **10.**
Riley Graves, **82.**
Ringinglow (Sheffield), **37.**
Rivelin Valley, 41.
Robin Hood's Stride, **125.**
*Rocester (Stafford), **5.**
Roches, the, 14, 68.
Rock-Hall, 14, 68.
Romantic Rocks, **100.**
Roosdych, 19.
*Rowsley (Bakewell), **127, 11, 110, 121.**
Rowtor Rocks, **124.**
Rushup Edge, **22.**
Rutland Cavern, **101.**

Salt Pan, **82.**
Seat Edge, **45.**
Sharplow Point, **52.**
Sheen (Ashbourne), **78.**
*Sheffield, **31.**
Sherbrook Dell, 65, **70, 72.**
Shutlings Low, **18.**
Sir William Road, **35.**
Slack Hall, **22.**
Slippery Stones, 29, **43, 44.**
Snake Inn, 45, **27, 25.**
Solomon's Temple, **65.**
South Head, **25.**
Sparrow Pit, **74.**
Speedwell Cavern, 86, **75.**
Stanage Pole, **41.**
Stancliff Hall, **11.**
Stanton, **125.**
Sterndale, **77.**
*Stockport, **19.**

Stoke Hall, 97.
Stoney Middleton, 133.
Sudbury Hall, 5.

Taddington (Buxton), 72, 130.
Tansley, 108.
Taxall, 20.
Thornhill, 43.
Thorpe (Ashbourne), 48.
Thor's Cave, 54, 79.
*Tideswell (Stockport), 80.
— Dell, 93, 70, 80.
— Lane Ends, 93.
Tissington (Ashbourne), 49.
Toad's Mouth, 39.
Totley, 34.
Tray Cliff, 95.
*Tutbury (Burton-on-Trent), 4.

Upper Haddon (Bakewell), 126, 78.
— Hulme, 13.
— Burbage Bridge, 37.
*Uttoxeter, 5.

Via Gellia, 122, 59.

Wardlow Hay Cop, 94.
Wardlow Mires, 94.
Waterfall, The, 81.
Waterloo Inn, 65, 72.
Weaver Hills, 7.
Wensley, 123.
Wetton (Ashbourne), 54, 79.
*Whaley bridge (Stockport), 19.
Whatstandwell (Derby), 9, 139.
Whirlow Bridge, 37.
Whirlow Brook, 37.
White Edge, 122, 123, 58.
Whiteley Wood, 41.
Willersley Castle, 103, 10.
Wingfield Manor, 105,
Wingerworth Hall, 107.
Win Hill, 43, 39, 75, 90.
Winnats, The, 87, 22, 75.
*Winster (Derby), 124.
*Wirksworth (Derby), 139.
Wootton Hall, 7.
Wyming Brook, 42.
Wye River, 127.

Yorkshire Bridge Inn (Sheffield), 40, 41.
Youlgreave (Bakewell), 57, 126.

London : J. S. LEVIN, Steam Printing Works, 75, Leadenhall Street, E.C.

www.ingramcontent.com/pod-product-compliance
Lightning Source LLC
Chambersburg PA
CBHW032157160426
43197CB00008B/958